Praise for the First Edition

"Drawing on his wide-ranging experience as one of the founders and leaders of our field, Mayer has given us a brilliant mosaic of conflict, its management, and resolution. This book is must reading for anyone who thinks deeply about the nature and origins of conflict and believes that a deeper appreciation for its complexity will enable us to transform our culture."

—Daniel Bowling, executive director,
Society of Professionals in Dispute Resolution

"Bernie Mayer is a natural teacher. His conceptual framework of conflict and resolution will challenge the most experienced professional to evaluate their own understandings. This is a must-read for both beginning and experienced professionals."

—Arnold Shienvold, president,
Academy of Family Mediators

"This is a great book. Mayer has delivered our field a gift—a reflective practitioner's handbook, complete with theoretical understandings and practical suggestions. Rooted in his marvelous intuition, shaped and authenticated from years of experience, and presented in a straightforward style true to his mediator and educator vocations, *The Dynamics of Conflict Resolution* should be on every conflict resolver's and trainer's bookshelf."

—John Paul Lederach, author,
Journey to Reconciliation and *Preparing for Peace*

"This book is high on my 'required reading' list! An outstanding contribution to the literature in the field."

—Katherine Hale, professor and chair,
Conflict Resolution Program, Antioch University

As an additional resource for this edition, suggested further readings on topics relevant to each chapter can be found at www.wiley.com/college/mayer. A sample syllabus based on the material in this book and an accompanying PowerPoint presentation are also posted there.

THE DYNAMICS OF CONFLICT

A Guide to Engagement and Intervention

Second Edition

Bernard Mayer

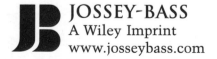

JOSSEY-BASS
A Wiley Imprint
www.josseybass.com

Published by Jossey-Bass
A Wiley Imprint
One Montgomery Street, Suite 1200, San Francisco, CA 94104-4594—www.josseybass.com

Jossey-Bass books and products are available through most bookstores. To contact Jossey-Bass directly
call our Customer Care Department within the U.S. at 800-956-7739, outside the U.S. at 317-572-3986,
or fax 317-572-4002.

Wiley also publishes its books in a variety of electronic formats and by print-on-demand. Some
material included with standard print versions of this book may not be included in e-books or in print-
on-demand. If the version of this book that you purchased references media such as CD or DVD that
was not included in your purchase, you may download this material at http://booksupport.wiley.com.
For more information about Wiley products, visit www.wiley.com.

Library of Congress Cataloging-in-Publication Data

Mayer, Bernard S.
    The dynamics of conflict : a guide to engagement and intervention /
Bernard Mayer.—2nd ed.
        p. cm.
    Includes bibliographical references and index.
    ISBN 978-0-470-61353-5 (cloth); ISBN 978-1-118-17822-5 (ebk);
    ISBN 978-1-118-17823-2 (ebk); ISBN 978-1-118-17824-9 (ebk)
        1. Conflict (Psychology)   2. Conflict management.   3. Negotiation.
    4. Problem solving.   I. Title.
    BF637.I48M39   2012
    303.6'9—dc23   2011044985

Printed in the United States of America
SECOND EDITION
HB Printing 10 9 8 7 6 5 4 3 2 1

Contents

In memory of Fritz and Carola Mayer
For their courage, love, and example

PREFACE TO THE SECOND EDITION
A Reflective Approach to Conflict

There is nothing so practical as a good theory.
LEWIN, 1952, P. 169

a way of thinking

Conflict intervention is a skill, a vocation, a profession, and a cause. We are all conflict participants and conflict interveners. We bring to this endeavor the totality of who we are—our life experience, our values, our natural talents and limitations, our personality, our training, and our professional background. How we handle conflict is central to how we handle life, whether or not we are conflict specialists, and so developing our capacity to deal with conflict is a lifelong challenge. As we seek to become more adept in conflict, we tend to focus on the central skills that conflict calls forth—for example, we want to increase our capacity to communicate, to negotiate, to use our power effectively, to respond to others' use of power, and to facilitate interactions among others. It's tempting to see these skills as residing in a series of techniques, a particular process, or a set of steps or stages. These are easy to learn, tangible, and often useful. But what makes us effective in how we engage in conflict is not a set of processes, methodologies, or tactics; it is a way of thinking, a set of values, an array of analytical and interpersonal skills, and a clear focus.

When I wrote the first edition of this book over ten years ago, I was convinced that being effective conflict specialists required

us to develop practical ways of thinking about conflict and conflict intervention. I believed that it was essential for us to identify
and embrace those concepts that help us make sense of our experience, that connect our efforts to the lessons learned by other
practitioners and researchers, and that help us find that elusive
but critical connection between theory and practice. I had come
to this conviction through my own experience as a mediator
and teacher, primarily through my work with CDR Associates of
Boulder, Colorado. As a practitioner, I knew that when I was in
the middle of dealing with a conflict what I most needed was a
set of clear and practical ideas about how to make sense of what
was going on and what my intervention choices might be. As a
teacher, I often noticed an interesting change that trainees experienced during the course of a class or workshop. Participants came
eager to be taught how to "do" things—how to open a mediation,
reframe a toxic comment, deal with a resistant party, or nail down
an agreement. But by the end of the training what seemed to have
had the biggest impact was their exposure to new ways of think-

ing about mediation, negotiation, conflict, and communication.
When they came away with a set of ideas and perceptions that
could guide their practice and help them integrate new skills and
techniques into their approach to conflict, something significant
had happened.

During the decade that has elapsed since the publication of
the first edition, many things have changed for me. I now live primarily in Canada. I am a faculty member at the Werner Institute
at Creighton University. I have written two books that seek to challenge some of the fundamental assumptions concerning the conflict field and move us toward a broader understanding of our
role and mission. I continue to work as a mediator, facilitator,
and consultant, but I am increasingly committed to developing
approaches that take us beyond a third-party, resolution-oriented
focus. What has not changed—what has in fact been reinforced—
is my view that developing our conceptual skills is the key to
becoming effective practitioners. This new edition, therefore,
continues to focus on the ways we can productively think about
conflict and conflict intervention, rather than on specific techniques and processes. Of course, all of these concepts must be
informed by our practical experiences and values. I believe that

our most creative moments as practical theorists come when we attempt to integrate the explanations of conflict and conflict intervention to which we are attracted with observations about what we actually do in real-life situations. I have always cherished those moments as a teacher when I have discovered a disconnect between what I am teaching and how I actually practice. The exploration of these inconsistencies always helps me refine my thinking and therefore my practice.

This new edition reflects the developments of my own thinking and approach to conflict during the past decade. Most significantly, I have come to believe that "conflict resolution" is a limiting description for the work we do and the challenges we face. I have written about this extensively in *Beyond Neutrality: Confronting the Crisis in Conflict Resolution* (Mayer, 2004a) and *Staying with Conflict: A Strategic Approach to Ongoing Disputes* (Mayer, 2009b), and I have incorporated this belief throughout the preparation of this edition (including adding a chapter that summarizes the ideas contained in these books). There is a creative tension that is pervasive throughout our field between the predominant view of our role as conflict resolvers and a broader definition of our purpose as conflict interveners whose fundamental task is to help people engage effectively and constructively in conflict. Even the title of this book reflects this tension. I have retitled this edition *The Dynamics of Conflict: A Guide to Engagement and Intervention* (the 2000 edition was titled *The Dynamics of Conflict Resolution: A Practitioner's Guide*) because I feel that the new title better reflects my current thinking. Although resolution is an important aspect of conflict intervention, it is only one element of the challenge conflict interveners face—and that perspective has informed this new edition.

I have also become increasingly committed to the view that an interactional and systems perspective is essential to understanding conflict. Analyzing individual motivations, conflict styles, communication approaches, and cultural beliefs can be an important tool for making sense of conflict, but at times this is also a limiting and potentially misleading focus. We cocreate conflict experiences with those we are in conflict with. Our approach to communication, negotiation, power, and conflict not only is influenced by the other people involved but also is essentially a product of the system of interaction that develops among disputants and

New Part [handwritten margin note]

interveners. For example, although an individual's most essential needs may not change from one situation to another, how that person experiences, expresses, and prioritizes them does. Our efforts to understand conflict, therefore, have to go beyond an analytical approach—that is, we have to do more than look at the parts that make up the whole. We can't just focus on the individuals, their interests, the alternatives each faces, or their particular histories. We have to look at system dynamics and interactional patterns. I have tried to infuse this book with a perspective that takes into account how individuals experience conflict and how people cocreate their experiences in conflict. In doing so I have been committed to making this viewpoint practical and operational.

In preparing the first edition I wrote primarily from the perspective of a third party, and I directed the book specifically at those who worked as third parties—mediators, facilitators, and system designers, as well as teachers and students of conflict. I have come to view the roles of allies and system interveners as essential to the work of conflict specialists, so in this edition, although I have retained a chapter on mediation, I am also addressing people who work as advocates, coaches, negotiators, and system interveners.

I am fortunate to have had the opportunity to work in a wide variety of settings and with many different kinds of conflict, and I have tried to use the range of these experiences to illustrate the concepts presented in this book. This does not mean that identical approaches should be taken to different types of conflict or that profound differences in the underlying structures of these conflicts do not exist. But I believe that if we discern a dynamic that is operative in, for example, both international conflict and family conflict, there is an important lesson to learn from the very breadth of that dynamic's relevance. The examples I use have therefore been drawn from my work with interpersonal, family, community, organizational, labor-management, environmental, public policy, and international disputes. I also discuss conflicts that have been in the news.

As I did with the first edition, I have included many case descriptions drawn from my experience as a conflict intervener, and sometimes as a disputant. Where these examples are a matter of public record, I have included identifying information. Where I felt it was essential to maintain confidentiality, I have withheld identifying information and changed some of the details to protect confidentiality. I have, however, maintained the key story line and interactional dynamics in each example.

Of course, the ideas in this book are not derived just from my own experience and observations. They are also influenced by the rich and broad tradition of conflict studies. This was certainly true of the first edition, and during my past several years at the Werner Institute at Creighton University I have had an even greater opportunity to immerse myself in this world. Throughout this book I reference the work of many others who have influenced my thinking. And as an additional resource for this edition, suggested further readings on topics relevant to each chapter can be found at www.wiley.com/college/mayer. A sample syllabus based on the material in this book and an accompanying PowerPoint presentation are also posted there.

When I was first introduced to the conflict field I felt that two important strands of my life were suddenly brought together. My first professional work was in child welfare and mental health. I worked as a psychotherapist and administrator in residential treatment centers for children, mental health centers, and drug abuse treatment programs, and in private practice. But I also came of age during the 1960s and was very active in a variety of movements for peace and social justice. The war in Vietnam, the antinuclear movement, and the civil rights movement were major forces in my development. Work in the conflict field seemed to pull these different parts of my life together, the part that was interested in providing services to people in various stages of crisis and the part that was committed to social change.

The conflict field still has these twin thrusts, as a service to people who need assistance and as a force for social change, but we can readily lose sight of this in the business of building a respected field of practice. In its earlier days it was easier to think of conflict intervention as a social movement because much of our focus was on demonstrating its relevance and effectiveness, creating new applications, and promoting a common set of practice principles and procedures. Now that the field is more accepted and institutionalized, its foundational values can easily be overlooked or taken for granted. I do not believe we can separate our actions, our theories, and our values. They are each essential to who we are and what we do. This book inevitably presents my particular integration of these elements. My commitment to helping people maintain control of their lives, especially when they are in crisis, and to creating more powerful and democratic ways of dealing with important questions of social justice and peace infuses the way I think about conflict and the way this book is written. It could not be otherwise.

But I have also tried to avoid being overly prescriptive about what conflict specialists should do or how we should think. I do not present the ideas in this book as *the* right conceptual frameworks but rather as ones that I have found useful and meaningful as I have worked as a conflict intervener and teacher. I hope that this will stimulate readers to deepen their own thinking or to put forward their own ideas—sometimes, perhaps, by way of disagreeing with mine.

I do not believe any of us can hold all these concepts in our head as we engage in the day-to-day, hour-to-hour work of helping those in conflict. But I hope that each of you will find at least some ideas in this book that resonate for you. Some of these ideas you may take with you into your practice. Some may help you reflect on the conflicts you deal with in your personal life. But no doubt some of these ideas will not resonate for you, in which case you will reject or more likely simply forget them. That is entirely as it should be. We each have to build our own theory of practice, and we do so by embracing and developing those ideas that speak to us and moving on from those that do not.

The ideas in this book are not presented as a unified theory of conflict, although they are meant to work together and to be internally consistent. I am suspicious of global theories that try to present a comprehensive understanding of the human experience, because I think they too easily become straightjackets or dogmas. We are simply too complex for one set of theories or one governing philosophy. Instead I present these ideas as a set of conceptual tools that build on each other and contribute to a multifaceted view of conflict and conflict intervention, but that also stand on their own.

My journey through the world of conflict has been exciting, challenging, at times extremely difficult, but in the end hopeful. I believe we can make a difference in people's lives and in how our communities and organizations approach conflict, but to do so we have to be modest about exactly what we can do. The essential strength and paradox of what we have to offer as conflict interveners is that we have the power to make a significant difference because we do not try to make things significantly different. From whatever perspective we take, our fundamental offer is to help guide people through a process that will essentially remain theirs.

The lessons I have learned from my years of practice and reflection have helped me embrace this opportunity and this paradox. But as I wrote ten years ago, what is in this book is only a snapshot of a particular time in an ongoing process of discovery that I am on and that we all are on. I hope that by sharing this snapshot with you, your journey will be enriched as mine has been.

AUDIENCE

I have written this book specifically for people involved in conflict intervention as a field of practice—including mediators, advocates, facilitators, coaches, human resource professionals, labor relations specialists, lawyers, organizational consultants, trainers, researchers, public involvement specialists, community organizers, diplomats, family therapists, and professional negotiators. But I have also tried to create a book that is accessible to others interested in conflict. I do not assume a broad familiarity with conflict literature or practice, and in setting the context for developing an expanded conceptual framework I take the time to describe some fairly basic principles. I try to focus on concepts that apply generically across different arenas of conflict. Although this book is specifically addressed to conflict interveners, I assume throughout that we are all participants in conflict as well. Therefore, when discussing how people engage in conflict, I am considering how all of us, not just our clients, handle the conflicts in our lives.

OVERVIEW OF THE CONTENTS

As with the first edition, this book is divided into two parts—the first, Chapters One through Four, focuses on the nature of conflict. In the second part, Chapters Five through Eleven focus on conflict engagement and intervention, and Chapter Twelve, a reflection on what motivates us as conflict specialists, serves as an epilogue. Chapter One describes the nature of conflict—in particular, the different dimensions along which conflict occurs, the sources of conflict, what motivates our participation in conflict, and the interaction between conflict as a means of expression and conflict as an attempt to achieve a particular outcome. Chapter Two focuses on our beliefs about conflict, how we engage in or avoid conflict, and the different ways we try to meet our needs in conflict. I also present a set of variables that can be used to understand the differences in how individuals approach conflict. Chapter Three discusses power—the beliefs we have about power, the types of power we bring to bear in conflict, the sources of our power, and the different ways in which power is applied in conflict. I discuss the relationship between an integrative and distributive approach to power and the nature and role of escalation in the conflict process. I conclude with a discussion of conflict and social justice. Chapter Four considers the role of culture in conflict—and in particular, the continuities and differences in how conflict is approached in different cultural contexts. I discuss culture as a dynamic and multifaceted process rather than a static set of behaviors and beliefs. Instead of focusing solely on the obstacles cultural differences present, I address how people from different backgrounds transcend cultural differences when engaging in conflict.

Chapter Five considers the nature of resolution and what constitutes a genuine resolution of conflict. In this chapter I present a model of the dimensions of resolution and examine a key challenge that conflict resolvers face—how to find the right level of depth at which to pursue the resolution of conflict. I also consider why conflict interveners tend to focus on outcomes and when these ought to be our primary focus. Chapter Six is an entirely new chapter that summarizes the ideas developed in *Beyond Neutrality* and *Staying with Conflict*. I look at how we can help people who are engaged in long-term conflicts that are not likely to end, the range of roles we can play as interveners, and the tension that exists between what we offer to disputants and what is at the heart of what they want. I also present the different "faces" of conflict that we might work on. Chapter Seven examines the heart of conflict intervention and human interaction—communication.

I consider the essential challenges we face when communicating in the midst of conflict, and I discuss what constitutes effective communication, including listening, speaking with power, and framing conflicts in constructive yet poignant ways. I also consider how communication tools can be used to help people change the fundamental way they understand a conflict.

Chapter Eight focuses on negotiation, which I see as an activity that we engage in virtually every day. I describe the contradictory pulls that most negotiators face and in particular the "negotiator's dilemma" that lies at the heart of all difficult negotiations. I also outline the strategic choices we face as negotiators and discuss the implications of how we handle these choices. Chapter Nine considers the nature of impasse in conflict and presents a way of understanding impasse as a necessary and often constructive aspect of healthy approaches to conflict. Chapter Ten focuses on mediation. I discuss the essence of what mediators bring to the table that helps alter the nature of a conflict interaction and what mediators actually do to affect the course of a conflict. I also look at some of the major differences of opinion within the mediation community concerning purpose and process.

Chapter Eleven presents a continuum of approaches to conflict intervention and considers what each element on that continuum offers. In particular, I discuss prevention, procedural assistance, substantive assistance, reconciliation, decision making, and design and linkage procedures. Chapter Twelve looks at the value base of conflict intervention. I discuss these values in terms of how conflict is handled; how conflict intervention efforts fit into more general values concerning peace, democracy, and social justice; and the personal impact that working on conflict has on conflict specialists.

ACKNOWLEDGMENTS

I am fortunate to have worked with incredibly dedicated, wise, and creative associates for over thirty years, all of whom have helped me develop, test, and refine the concepts in this book. Two groups of colleagues deserve special mention. The faculty, staff, and students at the Werner Institute at Creighton

University, where I have been a faculty member since 2006, have provided both support and feedback as I have prepared this new edition; they have been wonderful friends and colleagues as well. I acknowledge in particular Arthur Pearlstein, Jackie Font-Guzman, Noam Ebner, Debora Gerardi, Ran Kuttner, Bryan Hanson, Mary Lee Brock, Anat Cabili, Palma Strand, Robert Witheridge, and Theresa Thurin for their kindness and support. CDR Associates, my professional home since 1980, is the other collegial group that has supported me throughout my career as a conflict specialist. My colleagues at CDR have been my teachers, my friends, and my home team. I particularly thank Mary Margaret Golten, Christopher Moore, Louise Smart, Susan Wildau, Peter Woodrow, Jonathan Bartsch, Paula Taylor, Joan Sabott, Julie McKay, Suzanne Ghais, Mike Harty, Mike Hughes, and Judy Mares-Dixon.

My most important teachers throughout the past thirty years have been the many people who have accepted me into their conflicts and allowed me the privilege of working with them. The very large group of people whom I have taught in one forum or another, and particularly the students who used the first edition as a textbook, have also been critical to the development of this new edition. Thanks to all of you.

Thanks also to those who reviewed drafts of this revised edition (and also thanks to everyone who provided comments on the first edition). In particular, Joan Sabott, Christopher Honeyman, John Paul Lederach, Bill Warters, Jonathan Bartsch, Jackie Font-Guzman, Samantha Ho, Andrew Venrick, Elizabeth Troyer-Miller, Richard McGuigan, Don Selcer, Edy Horwood, Mark Mayer, and Julie Macfarlane provided candid, poignant, and useful comments as I worked on this edition.

My wonderful editor at Jossey-Bass, Seth Schwartz, patiently encouraged me to take on this revision (despite some initial resistance on my part) and then provided insightful, helpful, and very rapid feedback as I sent in drafts and redrafts of each of chapter. He has been a joy to work with. I also want to thank all his associates at Jossey-Bass for their help with the editing and production of this edition. Leslie Berriman was the editor for the first edition of this book, and without her there would be no book to revise. Francie Jones provided excellent services as the copyeditor for this edition, and I am very appreciative of the meticulous and thoughtful approach she took to this manuscript.

Finally, I thank my family for their ongoing love and support and for continually reminding me of what is most important in life. Thanks to my children, stepchildren, and grandchildren— Hopey, Ellie, Mark, Sibyl, Ethan, Elona, and Henry. My most special thanks go to my wonderful wife and brilliant colleague, Julie Macfarlane. Julie understands my approach to conflict, sometimes better than I do, and helped me immensely with this revision through dialogue, editing, and loving support. Julie has also been a model of courage in facing life and conflict with love and wisdom.

This book is dedicated to the memory of my parents, Fritz and Carola Mayer. They were survivors of the worst conflict of the twentieth century, and they drew from this a commitment to social justice and peace. Their strength and courage in the face of adversity were always matched by their kindness, humor, and love. My commitment to conflict work derives in no small measure from my life with them.

Kingsville, Ontario   BERNIE MAYER
January 2012

PART ONE

CONFLICT

CHAPTER ONE

THE NATURE OF CONFLICT

We are of two minds about conflict. We say that conflict is natural, inevitable, necessary, and normal, and that the problem is not the existence of conflict but how we handle it. But we are also loath to admit when we are in the midst of conflict. Parents assure their children that the ferocious argument the parents are having is not a conflict, just a "discussion." Organizations hire facilitators to guide them in strategic planning, goal setting, quality circles, team building, and all manner of training, but they shy away from asking for help with internal conflicts. Somehow, to say we are in conflict is to admit failure and to acknowledge the existence of a situation we consider hopeless.

This ambivalence about conflict is rooted in the same primary challenge conflict interveners face—coming to terms with the nature and function of conflict. How we view conflict affects our attitude toward it and our approach to dealing with it, and there are many ways of viewing it. For example, we may think of conflict as a feeling, a disagreement, a real or perceived incompatibility of interests, a product of inconsistent worldviews, or a set of behaviors. If we are to be effective in handling conflict, we must start with a way to make sense of it and to embrace both its complexity and its essence. We need tools that help us separate out the many complex interactions that make up a conflict, that help us understand the roots of conflict, and that give us a reasonable handle

---

Note: All of the examples from my own practice either are from public, nonconfidential forums or are heavily disguised to protect confidentiality.

on the forces that motivate the behavior and interaction of all participants, including ourselves.

Whether we are aware of them or not, we all enter conflict with assumptions about its nature. Sometimes these assumptions are helpful to us, but at other times they are blinders that limit our ability to understand what lies behind a conflict and what alternatives may exist for dealing with it. We need frameworks that expand our thinking, challenge our assumptions, and are practical and readily usable. As we develop our capacity to understand conflict in a deeper and more powerful way, we enhance our ability to handle it effectively and in accordance with our most important values about building peace. To simplify the task of handling complex conflicts, we need to complicate our thinking about conflict itself.

watch Blinders

A framework for understanding conflict should be an organizing lens that brings a conflict into better focus. There are many different lenses we can use, and each of us will find some more amenable to our own way of thinking than others. Moreover, the lenses presented in this chapter are not equally applicable to all conflicts. Seldom would we apply all of them at the same time to the same situation. Nevertheless, together they provide a set of concepts that can help us understand the nature of conflict and the dynamics of how conflict unfolds.

HOW WE EXPERIENCE CONFLICT

Conflict emerges and is experienced along cognitive (perception), emotional (feeling), and behavioral (action) dimensions. We usually describe conflict primarily in behavioral terms, but this can oversimplify the nature of the experience. Taking a three-dimensional perspective can help us understand the complexities of conflict and why a conflict sometimes seems to proceed in contradictory directions.

CONFLICT AS PERCEPTION

As a set of perceptions, conflict is our belief or understanding that our own needs, interests, wants, or values are incompatible

Cognitive / emotional / Behavioral

with someone else's. There are both objective and subjective elements to this dimension. If I want to develop a tract of land into a shopping center and you want to preserve it as open space, then there is an objective incompatibility in our goals. If I believe that the way you desire to guide our son's educational development is incompatible with my philosophy of parenting, there is a significant subjective component. If only one of us believes an incompatibility to exist, are we still in conflict? As a practical matter I find it useful to assume that a conflict exists if at least one person thinks that there is a conflict. If I believe that we have incompatible interests and proceed accordingly, I am engaging you in a conflict process whether you share this perception or not. The cognitive dimension is often expressed in the narrative structure that disputants use to describe or explain a conflict. If I put forward a story about an interaction that suggests that you are trying to undercut me or deny me what is rightfully mine, I am both expressing and reinforcing my view about the existence and nature of a conflict. The narratives people use provide both a window into the cognitive dimension and a means of working on the cognitive element of conflict.

CONFLICT AS FEELING

Conflict is also experienced as an emotional reaction to a situation or interaction. We often describe conflict in terms of how we are feeling—angry, upset, scared, hurt, bitter, hopeless, determined, or even excited. Sometimes a conflict does not manifest itself behaviorally but nevertheless generates considerable emotional intensity. As a mediator, I have sometimes seen people behave as if they were in bitter disagreement over profound issues, yet been unable to ascertain exactly where they disagreed. Nonetheless, they were in conflict because they felt they were. As with the cognitive dimension, conflict on the emotional dimension is not always experienced in an equal or analogous way by different parties. Often a conflict exists because one person feels upset, angry, or in some other way in emotional conflict with another, even though those feelings are not reciprocated by or even known to the other person. The behavioral component may be minimal, but the conflict is still very real to the person experiencing the feelings.

CONFLICT AS ACTION *Behavior related*

Conflict is also understood and experienced as the actions that people take to express their feelings, articulate their perceptions, and get their needs met, particularly when doing so has the potential for interfering with others' needs. Conflict behavior may involve a direct attempt to make something happen at someone else's expense. It may be an exercise of power. It may be violent. It may be destructive. Conversely, this behavior may be conciliatory, constructive, and friendly. Whatever its tone, the purpose of conflict behavior is either to express the conflict or to get one's needs met. Here, too, there is a question about when a conflict "really" exists. If you write letters to the editor, sign petitions, and consult lawyers to stop my shopping center and I don't even know you exist, are we in conflict? Can you be in conflict with me if I am not in conflict with you? Theory aside, I think the practical answer to both of these questions is yes.

In describing or understanding conflict, most of us gravitate first to the behavioral dimension. If you ask disputants what a conflict is about, they are most likely to talk about what happened or what they want to happen—that is, about behavior. Furthermore, any attempt to reach an agreement will naturally focus on behavior because that is the arena in which agreements operate. We can say we agree to try to feel differently or to think differently about something—and such statements are often built into agreements—but they are generally more aspirational than operational. What we can agree about is behavior: action or inaction. When we focus on arriving at outcomes it is natural for us to emphasize this dimension at the expense of the others, but in doing so we may easily overlook critical components of the conflict and the work necessary to address its cognitive and emotional elements.

Obviously the nature of a conflict on one dimension greatly affects how it plays out and is experienced on the other two dimensions. If I believe you are trying to hurt me in some way, I am likely to feel as though I am in conflict with you, and I am apt to engage in conflict behaviors. None of these dimensions is static. People move in and out of conflict, and the strength or character of conflict along each dimension can change rapidly and frequently. And even though each of the three dimensions affects the others, a change in the level of conflict on one dimension does not necessarily cause a similar change on the other dimensions. Sometimes an increase on one dimension is associated with a decrease on another. For example, the emotional component of conflict occasionally decreases as people increase their awareness of the existence of the dispute and their understanding of its nature. This is one reason why conflict can seem so confusing and unpredictable.

What about a situation in which no conflict perceptions, emotions, or behaviors are present but in which a tremendous potential for conflict exists? Perhaps you are unaware of my desire to build a shopping center, and I am unaware of your plans for open space. Are we in conflict? We may soon be, but I believe that until conflict is experienced on one of the three dimensions it is more productive to think in terms of potential conflict than actual conflict. The potential for conflict almost always exists among individuals or institutions that interact. Unless people want to think of themselves as constantly in conflict with everyone in their lives, it is more useful to view conflict as existing only when it clearly manifests itself along one of the three dimensions.

As well as individuals, can social systems—families, organizations, countries, and communities—be in conflict, particularly along the emotional or cognitive dimensions? Although there are some significant dangers to attributing personal characteristics or motivational structures to systems, practically speaking, systems often experience conflict along all three dimensions. We tend to use different terms, such as *culture, ethos, organizational values* or *family values, public opinion,* or *popular beliefs,* to characterize the greater complexity and different nature of the emotional and cognitive dimensions in social systems, but we intuitively recognize that group conflict has cognitive and emotional as well as behavioral dimensions. Is there an emotional and a perceptual aspect to the conflict between Iran and the United States or between Israel and Palestine? Of course, and we cannot understand the nature of these conflicts if we do not deal with these aspects. This does not mean that every individual member of each country shares the same feelings or perceptions, or even that a majority do. It means instead that the conflict evokes certain reactions and attitudes from a significant number of people in each society. Similarly, when we look at conflicts between union and management, environmental groups and industry associations, progressives and conservatives, it is important to understand the attitudes, feelings, values, and beliefs that these groups have concerning each other if we are to understand what is occurring.

How we describe a conflict usually reflects how we are experiencing it. The same conflict or concerns can be described using the language of feeling ("I feel angry and hurt"), perception ("I believe you are completely missing the point and do not have a clue about this"), or action ("I want you to do this or I will have to take further action"). Frequently, in observing people in conflict, we can see that one party may be using the language of feeling and the other the language of perception, and this alone can exacerbate a conflict. There are in fact several inventories of conflict styles that focus on this (for example, the Strength Deployment Inventory on the Personal Strengths, USA Web site, "SDI," n.d.).

How conflict is experienced by one party is closely intertwined with how others experience it. Although one party may be more likely to express and react to the emotional dimension, for example, and another party may be more attuned to the behavioral dimension, their approaches affect each other. For example, if one party describes and experiences a conflict in emotional terms, other parties may gravitate toward this dimension, thereby reinforcing the way the first party experiences the conflict. Or they may be encouraged to take a more cognitive approach by way of reaction. How parties cocreate their experiences of a conflict is an essential part of the conflict story.

By considering conflict along the cognitive, emotional, and behavioral dimensions, we can begin to see that it does not proceed along one simple, linear path. When individuals or groups are in conflict, they are dealing with complex and sometimes contradictory dynamics in these different dimensions, and they behave and react accordingly. This accounts for much of what appears to be irrational behavior in conflict. Consider this typical workplace dispute:

> Two employees assigned to work together on a project soon find themselves in conflict over whether they are both pulling their

weight and passing along important information to each other. The situation escalates to the point where they engage in a public shouting match, and as a result their supervisor intervenes and brings them together to talk. At this meeting they agree on a workload division and certain behavioral standards, to which they then seem to adhere. Has the conflict been resolved? It may have been alleviated along the behavioral dimension. But each goes away from this meeting feeling victimized by the other and unappreciated by the boss. One of the employees decides that these feelings just result from the nature of the job and believes that the immediate conflict is over, but the other continues to see the conflict being acted out every time the other person comes late for a meeting or sends a terse e-mail. Thus progress has been made on the behavioral dimension; the emotional dimension is, if anything, worse; and there are contradictory developments along the cognitive dimension.

This kind of result is not unusual in conflict, and it can cause people to behave in apparently inconsistent ways because on one dimension the conflict has been dealt with, but on another dimension it may actually have gotten worse. Thus the employees in this example may cease their overtly conflictual behavior, but the tension between them may actually increase.

WHAT CAUSES CONFLICT?

Conflict has multiple sources, and theories of conflict can be distinguished from one another by which origin they emphasize. Conflict is seen as arising from basic human instincts, from competition for resources and power, from the structure of the societies and institutions people create, from flawed communication, and from the inevitable struggle between classes. Although most of these theories offer valuable insights and perspectives on conflict, they can easily point us in different directions as we seek a constructive means of actually dealing with conflict. What we need is a practical framework that helps us use some of the best insights of different conflict theories.

If we can understand and locate the sources of conflict, we can create a map to guide us through the conflict process. When we

FIGURE 1.1 WHEEL OF CONFLICT

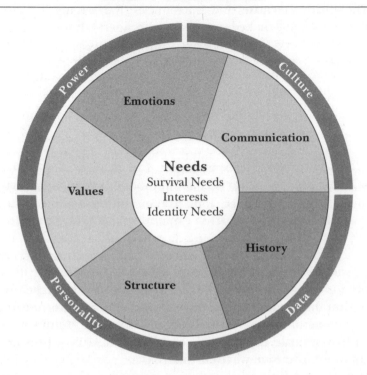

understand the different forces that motivate conflict behavior, we are better able to create a more nuanced and selective approach to handling conflict. Different sources of conflict produce different challenges for conflict engagement. The wheel of conflict, illustrated in Figure 1.1, is one way of understanding the forces that are at the root of most conflicts. This conceptualization of the sources of conflict arose out of my work as a conflict practitioner and conversations with colleagues at CDR Associates and elsewhere, and it is derivative of the circle of conflict developed by Christopher Moore (2003). Moore's circle consists of five components: relationship problems, data problems, value differences, structural problems, and interests. This has proven a valuable tool for analyzing the sources of conflict, but I have chosen to rework it to reflect a broader view of human needs and the issues that make it hard for us to directly address these needs.

Human needs are at the core of all conflicts. People engage in conflict either because they have needs that are met by the conflict process itself or because they have needs that they can only attain (or believe they can only attain) by engaging in conflict. I discuss the system of human needs in detail later in this chapter. My point here is that people engage in conflict because of their needs, and conflict cannot be transformed or resolved unless these needs are addressed in some way. We should not understand needs as static and unchanging. We all have a range of needs, but how we experience these is influenced by the context and the unfolding interaction. For example, I might start negotiating to sell a house mostly concerned about money, timing, and certainty, but if the hard work I have done to remodel my home is dismissed as sloppy or in poor taste, then I might suddenly find myself more concerned with issues of identity, pride, and self-image. In this way, the needs we experience are constantly evolving and changing as we interact with others.

Needs are embedded in a constellation of contextual factors that generate and define conflict. To effectively address needs, it is usually necessary to work through some of these elements, which affect how people experience their needs and how they choose to pursue them. Five of these factors are particularly critical to understanding how conflict unfolds: the ways in which people communicate, their emotions, their values, the structures in which they interact, and history (see Figure 1.1). Let's examine each of these sources further.

COMMUNICATION

We are very imperfect communicators. Sometimes this imperfection generates conflict, whether or not there is a significant incompatibility of interests, and it almost always makes conflict harder to deal with effectively. Sometimes, however, imperfect communication is what allows us to work together in the face of serious differences (Honeyman, 2006). Unclear communication allows us to move forward despite our differences by obscuring disagreements or different interpretations of agreements. Although this can eventually cause worse conflict, sometimes it allows us to get through a particularly problematic interaction successfully.

Human communication has inspired a large literature and multiple fields of study, and I will discuss the role of communication in conflict and conflict intervention in Chapter Seven. The main thing to consider here is how hard it is for individuals to communicate about complex matters, particularly under emotionally difficult circumstances. We should keep reminding ourselves just how easy it is for communication to go awry. Conflict frequently escalates because we act on the assumption that we have communicated or understood someone else's communication accurately when we have not. When we learn that others are acting on the basis of different information and assumptions, we often attribute this to bad faith or deviousness and not to the imperfections of human communication.

Many factors may contribute to communication problems. Culture, gender, age, class, cognitive capacity, and environment have a large impact on communication. We frequently rely on inaccurate or incomplete perceptions, form stereotypes, and carry into our communication conclusions drawn from former interactions or experiences. Often we are inclined to try to solve problems before we understand them. The greater the duress we are under, the harder it is for us to communicate effectively (and often the more important it is as well). Sometimes communication takes more energy and focus than we are able or willing to give at a critical point, and it is easy to become discouraged or hopeless about communicating effectively in serious conflicts.

Successful communication requires that people enter into a de facto partnership with each other in which informal but powerful norms and strategies are developed to allow communication to occur. This involves a reciprocal process of sending and receiving messages about how to communicate, what is working in an interchange, and how to adjust communication to make it work better. This process of metacommunication (communicating about communicating) is seldom intentional or conscious, but it is nonetheless critical—and takes place in all types of communication, ranging from formal business interactions to parent-child interchanges (Tannen, 1986). When this process works, very effective interactions can occur, even in the midst of conflict, but when communication is dysfunctional even the simplest of interactions can become extremely difficult and conflictual. This is one example of why conflict has to be understood in terms of the nature of the interaction that is created, and not simply the tools or approach of each of the individual parties involved.

Despite all these problems, we can and do find a way to communicate, and we can work on improving our communication, even in very intense conflicts. Communication is one of the greatest sources of both difficulty and hope in dealing with serious conflicts.

EMOTIONS

Emotions are the energy that fuels conflict. If we could always stay perfectly rational and focused on how best to meet our needs and accommodate those of others, and if we could calmly work to establish effective communication, then many conflicts either would never arise or would quickly de-escalate. But of course that is not human nature. At times emotions seem to be in control of behavior. Sometimes they are also a source of power. They contribute to the energy, strength, courage, and perseverance that allow us to participate forcefully in conflict.

Emotions are generated both by particular interactions or circumstances and by previous experiences. When someone points a finger in our face in a conflict, we have a reaction based on the immediate context and meaning of that behavior, but we may also be reacting to all the times in the past when that gesture has been made at us in anger.

Disputants often find it necessary to work on the emotional content of their experience to make progress. Conflict may provide a valuable opportunity to engage with the emotions that are otherwise suppressed or ignored. Dealing with the intense emotions often associated with conflict usually requires finding some opportunity to express and release emotions and to experience someone else's understanding and empathy. We often talk about the need to ventilate, to let an emotion out through a direct and cathartic expression of it. Frequently, however, ventilation is neither possible nor desirable. A direct display of feelings can escalate a conflict. Instead it can be more constructive for disputants to discuss feelings without demonstrating them, to work toward establishing a safe environment for the expression of emotions, to let emotions out in safe increments, or to express them to a third party rather than directly to the other person. Sometimes (although this may go against some popular beliefs of our culture), the wisest course is to contain our feelings until a more appropriate opportunity for dealing with them presents itself. But of course sometimes this is not at all the wisest course. We often try to shut down an emotional interchange because we are afraid that a situation will spin out of control or because we feel unable to deal with the intensity of the feelings being expressed. Sometimes, however, such an exchange is exactly what is needed, and one of the best services interveners can offer is to provide a safe container for the expression of intense feelings. Judging when an expression, description, or exchange of feelings is called for, and when a more circumscribed approach to the emotional content of a dispute is the wiser approach, may be one of the most difficult but important decisions we make in dealing with conflict.

Emotions fuel conflict, but they are also a key to de-escalating it. Many emotions can <u>prevent</u>, <u>moderate</u>, or <u>control conflict</u>. Part of everyone's emotional makeup is the <u>desire to seek connection</u>, <u>affirmation</u>, and <u>acceptance</u>. The genuine expression of sadness or concern by a party to a dispute can be essential to addressing the conflict effectively. A challenge for interveners in many conflicts is finding an adequate way to deal with the feelings of all participants so that these are neither ignored nor allowed to escalate out of control. Sometimes it may be necessary to let a conflict escalate somewhat, enough to deal with emotions but not so much as to impair people's ability to eventually address the situation constructively. The art of dealing with conflict often lies in finding the narrow path between the useful expression of emotions and destructive polarization. This is one reason why it is often helpful to employ the services of a third party.

VALUES

Values are the beliefs we have about what is important, what distinguishes right from wrong and good from evil, and what principles should govern how we lead our lives. When a conflict is defined or experienced as a struggle about values, it becomes more charged and intractable. Because we define ourselves in part through our core beliefs, when we believe these values are under attack, we feel that *we* are being attacked. Similarly, it is hard for us to compromise when our core beliefs are in play because we feel we are compromising our sense of integrity and self.

Although some conflicts are inescapably about fundamental value differences, more often disputants have a choice about whether they will define a conflict in this way. When we feel unsure of ourselves, confused about what to do, or under attack, it is tempting to define an issue as a matter of right or wrong. This empowers and fortifies us, allowing us to "take the moral high road," even as it rigidifies our thinking and narrows acceptable options. Often it is easier to carry on a conflict if we can view ourselves as honorable and virtuous, and opponents as evil, malicious, and dangerous. This stance, comforting though it may be, tends to escalate and perpetuate conflict. Complicated public conflicts (for example, debates about health care policy, climate change, or the economy) are often characterized by extreme, almost fantastical appeals to values, as if the issue involved were a choice of good versus evil or democracy versus dictatorship rather than a debate about the merits of different approaches to dealing with complicated problems. This appeal to values builds support for a position and energizes people, but it also makes a constructive debate much more difficult.

When value differences are genuinely and inescapably a core element of a conflict, we are unlikely to easily find our way through the conflict by employing a rational problem-solving process. We can often determine if this is the case by articulating the relevant values and beliefs that we think are in play, and doing so in affirmative terms (what people believe in rather than what they don't believe in). If the most significant values of those involved are clearly in opposition (and this is the case far less often than we might think), then we are not likely to end the conflict through a process of compromise or creative problem solving. We may be able to arrive at some understanding about how to move forward, despite value differences, but the core conflict will probably remain until circumstances change, larger values intervene, or those involved modify their core beliefs in some way.

Although values are often a source of conflict and an impediment to its resolution, they can also be a source of commonality and a constraint on conflict escalation. Disputants usually can find some level on which they share values. And often they have values about interpersonal relations that support collaborative efforts. Recognizing when values are in play in conflict is critical to moving the conflict in a constructive direction. When individuals address values directly and express their beliefs affirmatively, they can address conflict more constructively.

STRUCTURE

The structure or framework within which an interaction takes place or an issue develops is another source of conflict. Structural components of conflict include available resources, decision-making procedures, time constraints, legal requirements, communication mechanisms, and physical settings. Even when compatible interests might move people toward a more cooperative stance, the structure in which they are working may promote conflict. An example of this is the litigation process. Litigation is well designed for achieving a decisive outcome when other, less adversarial procedures have not worked. However, it is also a structure that exacerbates conflict, makes compromise difficult, and casts issues as win-lose, right-wrong struggles. Voting is another interesting example. When voting is used to resolve serious differences about an issue, the issue tends to become polarized, and constructive communication can become difficult. Candidates for office often try to seize the center of the political spectrum on important issues, but at the same time they look for so-called wedge issues that can differentiate them from their rivals and build support, they hope, among a large segment of voters. This approach to campaigns increases divisiveness about such complex issues as affirmative action, abortion, gun control, economic policy, climate change, national security, or health care in a way that makes a constructive and nuanced approach to policymaking difficult.

Sometimes these structural realities can be changed through a conflict resolution process. Often, however, part of what that process must accomplish is to help disputants identify and accept those structural elements that are unlikely to be altered. It is also important to consider system dynamics. Structure is one important element of a conflict system, and it is often profitable to consider how system dynamics are expressed in conflict. Conflict can be understood as an inevitable and necessary expression of human systems and an important means by which systems maintain their adaptability and adjust to change. Of course, conflict can also be very dysfunctional for systems if not dealt with effectively. Understanding how complex adaptive systems operate—and in particular how energy flows through systems; how systems emerge, adapt, adjust, and reorganize; and how conflict in one part of a system may be an expression of system dynamics or conflicts in another part of the same system—can be critical to how we intervene in a conflict (Innes and Booher, 1999; Jones and Hughes, 2003). The wheel of conflict can be viewed as one approach to understanding the components of a conflict system.

History   *Past ~ Context ~ Parties*

Conflict cannot be understood independent of its historical context. The history of participants in a conflict, of the system in which the conflict is occurring, and of the issues themselves has a powerful influence on the course of that conflict. When we try to understand a conflict in isolation from its historical roots, we are sometimes baffled by the stubbornness of the players or the intractability of the issues. History provides the momentum for the development of conflict.

But history is not a determinant of conflict, although sometimes it can seem that way. The long history of conflict in the Middle East, Kashmir, or Iraq, for example, does not mean that present conflicts in these regions will never be settled. That form of historical determinism is dangerous and misleading. However, such conflicts cannot easily be addressed without an understanding of the complicated systems of interaction that have developed over time and the degree to which the conflict has become part of the disputants' identity.

These different sources of conflict—communication, emotions, values, structure, and history—interact with each other. For example, people's historical experiences and their understanding of history influence their values, communication style, and emotional reactions, and the structure in which they operate. Furthermore, history is constantly being made, and the ways in which the other sources of conflict change and develop over time are an important part of that history.

GENERAL CONTEXTUAL FACTORS

Four variables seem particularly important to understand as contextual factors that cut across all the sources of conflict. These are culture, power, personality, and data. Culture affects conflict because it is embedded in individuals' communication styles, their history, their ways of dealing with emotions, their values, and the structure within which conflict occurs. Power is a very elusive concept, one that can obscure the roots of a conflict but can also help us understand the nature of an interaction. Power is partly embedded in the structure within which the conflict is occurring, but it has to be understood as a product of personal styles and interpersonal interactions. A great deal has been written about how personality affects conflict, but this too is a very broad concept, perhaps best understood in terms of styles of conflict engagement and avoidance. I deal with personality, power, and culture more extensively in Chapters Two, Three, and Four, respectively.

I do not view information or data themselves as a major source of conflict, but how data are handled and communicated can exacerbate conflict. Disputants often engage in a battle about information (for example, about how real global warming is), but data are usually not the essential source of conflict, and it is often misleading to see data in this way. I believe it is more profitable to view data, or information, as an issue within both communication and structure.

There are of course many other forces affecting conflict that I have not included in the wheel but that could be added if this would enhance the value of this model for a particular dispute (for example, group dynamics, cognitive styles, or external events). There is nothing sacrosanct about this or any other model of conflict. The wheel of conflict is a construct, and its ultimate test is how useful it is in providing insights into a given conflict and how to constructively engage in disputing. The sources of conflict I have identified are the ones that I find particularly important to consider as we seek to unpack the nature of a conflict. In particular, the wheel of conflict is a tool for considering where people are stuck, where insights are needed, and where opportunities to improve a situation can be found. (For an overview of the major theories of conflict and its origins, see Wehr, 1979; also see Deutsch, Coleman, and Marcus, 2006; Frost and Wilmot, 1978; Kriesberg, 1982; Macfarlane, 2010; Schellenburg, 1982; Schelling, 1960.)

The value of an analytical tool such as the wheel, and the model of the three dimensions of conflict described earlier, is illustrated by the case of the ten cousins.

> Ten cousins who lived in various locations in the United States and Canada jointly inherited a valuable piece of oceanfront property in New England. This property had belonged to their grandfather, who had decided to leave it directly to them in large part because of his distress about the poor relationships among his three children, the cousins' parents. The property had been the site of many of the happiest moments in the cousins' childhood, but now it was in disrepair, and the existing house and road needed replacing. The cousins ranged in age from twenty to forty-five, and their financial circumstances ranged from quite poor to very wealthy. For the property to be usable a considerable investment would have to be made, which not all the cousins were in a position to provide. They had very different views about what should be done with the property. Some wanted to sell it and divide up the equity. Others wanted to preserve it as a family center. And a couple of them proposed dividing it up so that each cousin could have a parcel to do with as he or she wished.
>
> Complicating the picture were tense relations within at least two of the three sibling groups. Furthermore, the cousins and their parents in one group had been out of contact with the rest of the family for most of the past fifteen years, largely because these cousins' mother did not get along with her siblings. Not knowing how to proceed, the cousins contacted me and, together with a colleague, I met with nine of them in a retreat setting.
>
> How could we get a handle on the nature of this conflict? It was clear that all three dimensions of conflict were in play. There were behavioral issues that needed to be attended to (what to do with the disputed property); cognitive issues involving entrenched perceptions about the situation and each other (how they thought about one another and the conflict); and a great deal of emotionality. Although work had to be done on the behavioral, or

action, issues, the long-term success of the cousins' co-ownership depended more on their ability to work on the attitudes about and emotions concerning each other that had been part of their family dynamics for so long.

It was not at first obvious where to focus our attention given the complexity of this situation. There were conflicting needs to be addressed. Some cousins wanted to maintain this property in the family and to "honor grandfather's legacy and wishes." Others were worried about the time and resources this might demand. Most hoped to promote better family relations but were concerned that the opposite might occur. These needs were firmly embedded in the elements found in the wheel of conflict. There had been poor communication (and in some cases no communication) among the cousins for years. The property represented the complex emotions that all had about their family relations. It was a symbol of both the problems in the family and the best the family had to offer. The cousins had different values regarding sharing the property, developing it, equalizing contributions, and taking into account different resources—and about how families ought to interact. The structural problems were enormous. The cousins had no easy way of communicating, making decisions, or overseeing work on the property, and the disparity in their resources greatly complicated the picture. Furthermore, numerous local land use regulations limited their options for subdividing the property or building additional structures. Finally, history was a heavy presence. In many ways the cousins were continuing a multigenerational family saga. The conflicts among the parents were in danger of being replicated. There was also a positive history as well—the childhood memories that they had of their time at the property were almost all positive and were a motivation to seek a constructive resolution.

Because this situation was so complex and our time to deal with it was relatively limited (three days), we decided that we could not deal with issues internal to sibling groups and that we should instead focus on the relatively positive attitudes they were expressing across sibling groups. We felt that the history needed to be addressed and that the major immediate focus had to be on the structural barriers to moving forward. We therefore started by asking each cousin to share his or her memories of time spent on the property and his or her hopes and fears for its future. As an outcome of this discussion they all decided they really wanted to keep the property if at all possible. They agreed to work on a

Needs Based approach + Positivity

plan for keeping the property, and they also agreed that everyone should have some access to it, regardless of his or her contribution.

Once these general agreements were made, we then focused on the structural issues of how to communicate, make decisions, work with local authorities, and get information about different options. The cousins left with some general decisions made and an interesting communication and decision-making structure. They set up a steering committee with one representative from each sibling group.

Our intervention flowed from our analysis of the structure and causes of this particular conflict. Without some way of organizing our thinking about this complex situation, we would not have been able to develop a coherent strategy for how to proceed. Was our analysis correct? Was the strategy we chose optimal? Probably not in all respects, but it nonetheless provided us with a road map for how to help them take the next step in their relationships with the property and, more important, each other.

Human Needs

At the center of the wheel of conflict model are the human needs that drive people's actions, including their engagement in conflict. Many theorists, from Sigmund Freud to Abraham Maslow, have characterized fundamental human needs (Freud, [1930] 2005; Maslow, 1954). Several of them describe the different levels of needs that people experience. In the literature on conflict, a distinction is often made between interests and needs. Interests are viewed as more transitory and superficial, needs as more basic and enduring. Sometimes it is argued that resolutions that address interests but not needs are less meaningful, more Band-Aids than real solutions (Burton and Dukes, 1990).

Rather than conceiving of interests and needs as fundamentally different, I find it more useful to think of a system of human needs, roughly paralleling Maslow's hierarchy (1954). Maslow suggested a hierarchy of human needs and argued that before we can focus our efforts or awareness on attaining higher-level needs, more basic needs must be met. His concepts are often portrayed as a triangle of needs, with the most fundamental needs at the base and higher-level needs at the apex. Most basic, according to Maslow, are our physiological needs for food, clothing, and shelter.

Next are security needs, then social needs, then needs for esteem and self-esteem, and at the top level in his most common formulation is self-actualization. I am less convinced of the hierarchical element of Maslow's formulation because I have often worked with people whose fundamental needs for security and even survival were threatened but who nonetheless were very motivated by relational, moral, or aesthetic needs. Furthermore, I think that there is a great deal of overlap between how these needs are experienced in conflict situations. I propose we consider three overlapping types of needs that operate in conflict and that can assist us in understanding the core of what motivates people in conflict. Interests then become a category of human needs that exists along with basic survival and identity concerns (see Figure 1.2).

A challenge we face in the practical understanding of conflict is to determine what level of needs best explains a conflict. When we have too superficial a view of the sources of a conflict, we cannot address it meaningfully. If a community is concerned about a proposal to place a chemical plant nearby, there are many levels at which we can understand the nature of the problem. For example, the needs of the community to minimize odors, noise, traffic, and toxic exposure may be contrasted with the needs of

FIGURE 1.2   HUMAN NEEDS IN CONFLICT

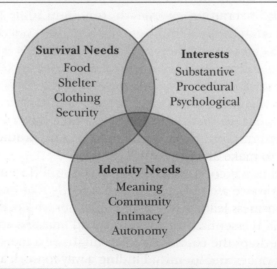

the plant operators for a practical, cheap, and convenient location. This may be a satisfactory level for analyzing the conflict, but if the motivational system for either the community or the plant operates at a more basic level, we may need to delve deeper to get a handle on what is really driving the conflict. The community may have fundamental concerns about the image this plant will create, and its impact on the community's overall desirability and therefore on the attractiveness of the community to investors, upwardly mobile families, and adult children of residents. Similarly, the plant may be concerned about its public reputation and the ease of attracting and retaining a workforce. If we fail to look at the deeper levels of interests, we are likely to end up working on the wrong issues and overlooking some important areas of mutual concern.

But we could go overboard on this and focus too deeply. When we address the sources of conflict at a level that is too deep, we make the conflict much harder to resolve and we may also fail to match the reality experienced by the disputants. For example, in this situation we could concentrate on such fundamental concerns as business versus the environment, the nature of community, and the sense of self that both business leaders and community leaders have and how this is tied into their views concerning the chemical plant proposal. But although these might be real factors in the conflict, they might neither be its practical source nor provide a useful basis for crafting an intervention, and some participants may feel that delving into these issues is inappropriate or intrusive. If we focused at this deeper level, we would not be addressing the conflict on the level that it is experienced by these participants, and we would be concentrating on a set of concerns probably not conducive to a practical intervention process. However, if participants did see these deeper questions as important to resolving the conflict, then at some point these issues would have to be addressed to make any progress.

An additional complicating factor is that different disputants often experience a conflict at different levels. For one party, perhaps the business leaders in the preceding example, this may be a conflict that is essentially about profits and business efficiency. For another, perhaps the community, this might be a more fundamental issue of values and identity. Finding a way to work at both levels may be essential if progress is to be made. To do this each party has to be willing to address the conflict at the level at which it is experienced by others, but disputants are often resistant to doing this.

Finding the most useful level of depth is not an abstract consideration, and it does not take place in a vacuum. Only through interacting over time with key players can we understand the roots of a conflict in a practical and usable way. The art of conflict intervention is highly dependent on the ability to get to the right depth of understanding and communication in each conflict.

Interests

Interests are the most easily accessible or observable type of need and lie at the heart of most negotiations. Interests can be viewed simply and superficially, or in great depth. If we think of interests as the practical concerns that drive participants in most conflicts, then most frequently it is on interests that we first need to focus when we try to understand a conflict. It is also in the realm of interests that most specific agreements can be attained. If people can present their concerns to each other in a constructive way and are receptive to understanding each other's interests, they are most likely to make progress in working their way through a conflict.

The concept of interests (and interest-based negotiation) was popularized by Fisher and Ury in *Getting to Yes* (1981) and has become a basic element in the negotiator and conflict intervener's lexicon. But to people outside our field, this is often a confusing term (and one not easily translatable into other languages), seeming to refer more to our areas of interest (hobbies, sports, politics, and the like) or to our self-interest. As a mediator, I find myself talking more about "concerns," "what is important," or "needs" than about interests to avoid confusion or jargon.

It is helpful to consider different types of interests: short-term and long-term interests, individual and group interests, outcome-based interests and process interests, and conscious and unconscious interests. Moore (2003) suggests three types of interests: substantive (concerns about tangible benefits), procedural (concerns about a process for interacting, communicating, or decision making), and psychological (concerns about how one is treated, respected, or acknowledged). Often people are most vocal about one kind of interest but most genuinely motivated by another. For example, if we have not received a job promotion that we expected, we may assert that the process for considering us for that promotion was unfair, when our real concern is that we did not receive the salary raise and additional status that the promotion would have provided. We can often achieve progress in a conflict, even when disputants have incompatible interests of one kind, if we are careful to address other types of interests.

The democratic philosophy of government provides an interesting example of how procedural and substantive interests interact. At the root of democracy is a commitment to addressing procedural interests, even when substantive interests cannot always be met. Citizens continue to feel loyalty to their government, even when they disagree with its policies and have not voted for its leaders, if they fundamentally support the process by which these leaders are selected. The basic deal in a democracy is that we may not always get our way, but we will always have our say, and in return we will remain loyal citizens.

As conflict specialists, we need to analyze the different types of interests that people bring to a conflict and endeavor to understand everyone's interests (including our own) broadly enough and at the right level of depth to gain a practical handle on what is occurring in that conflict.

Identity Needs

Fundamental to our sense of ourselves are what we can call identity needs (Rothman, 1997). These are the needs we all have to preserve a sense of who we are and our place in the world. I find it useful to think of four particular elements of identity: the needs for meaning, community, intimacy, and autonomy.

The need for _meaning_ has to do with establishing a purpose for one's life, existence, actions, and struggles. Sometimes pursuing a conflict is a great source of meaning for people. In that case the resolution of the conflict entails a significant loss of meaning. Unless they can find a new source of meaning, this loss may be devastating and may cause them to hold on to a conflict regardless of how well the proposed solution addresses their interests. I once acted as a mediator in an age discrimination case involving someone who was about to retire. When I asked him about his retirement plans, he told me that he was going to pursue his case until he was fully vindicated. Despite the fact that he could have obtained much in a settlement with the company and that his prospects for a successful legal challenge were poor, I knew this mediation was going nowhere. For many who have been involved in long-term struggles, whether about issues of nationalism, such as in Iran, Ireland, or the Middle East, or other causes, such as environmentalism, animal rights, or small government, the specific issues involved do not tell the whole story. The meaning that the struggle itself has given to people's lives is itself a key motivating factor. This is one reason why many of these disputes seem so intractable.

Community refers to that aspect of people's identity that derives from feeling connected with groups with which they can identify and in which they feel recognized. A sense of community can arise from an actual physical neighborhood or geographical area. The nostalgic yearning of some urban dwellers for small-town life is in part an expression of this need. Similarly, the desire many people have to participate in the communal life of their neighborhood is connected to establishing identity. But community can come from other group affiliations as well, with a company, for example, or with a social action organization; a church, synagogue, or mosque; an athletic or artistic subculture; a profession; or an ethnic group. Community can be experienced in both positive and negative ways. Individuals may identify with others on the basis of what they all share or what they are all against. As an identity need, community is not simply about feeling part of a group; it is about having a social home in an impersonal world—a home in which people feel connected, safe, recognized as individuals, and appreciated. When people pursue a conflict to solidify a sense of community or to protect their community against the forces of disintegration, they are in part struggling to preserve their identity.

Intimacy is the need for a different kind of connectivity. It goes beyond needing to be recognized and involves wanting to be special, unique, and important to other people. Most intimacy needs are met in family and friendship structures. Intimacy implies some form of reciprocity. Often people cling to the symbols of intimacy or to a pretense of intimacy but actually feel quite alone. In divorces, it is often the loss of intimacy (or sometimes the fact that a façade of intimacy has been shattered) that causes so much pain and challenges people's sense of themselves—their identity. Divorcing spouses frequently experience needs at this level that are usually impossible (and often not desirable) to deal with in the context of divorce mediation or negotiation. This means that people may feel unfulfilled by the outcome, even when a fundamentally sound agreement has been reached. A longer healing process is often necessary to deal with the loss of intimacy.

If intimacy and community are aspects of individuals' fundamental need for connection, *autonomy* is the flip side of the coin. At the same time as we need connection, we also need a sense of independence, freedom, and individuality. In relationships we often struggle with how to find a deep sense of both connection and autonomy at the same time. This struggle to establish needed ties and their boundaries is a source of much of our internal conflict, and it is also at the heart of many interpersonal conflicts. Parents and adolescents frequently experience conflict that is ostensibly about immediate issues, such as chores, curfews, or school, but that is more often about dependency and autonomy. We can also see this need expressed in the struggles of many ethnic groups to be recognized as autonomous political entities. When people or groups feel that they do not have meaningful autonomy, independence, or freedom, this fundamental identity need is not being met and serious conflict is likely.

Identity Needs

Some conflicts cannot be effectively dealt with unless identity needs are addressed. These disputes are often not amenable to a negotiation process. They usually require an incremental process of change in which people, groups, or organizations gradually achieve a different level of understanding and acceptance. They often call for a social change effort or a personal growth experience of some kind. Conflict intervention efforts in which the focus is more on the relationship and system of communication among disputants and less on achieving a specific outcome are often more valuable in dealing with identity-based conflicts than efforts to arrive at tangible agreements.

Survival Needs

Survival needs include fundamental concerns about safety and security, but also about food, shelter, and clothing. Sometimes in the conflicts we deal with survival is at stake, such as when we work on conflicts involving domestic violence, gang warfare, or ethnic conflicts in war torn areas. But at other times we may be dealing with people who feel that their survival is at stake even if that does not appear to be the case from our external viewpoint. For example, in cases of divorce it is not uncommon for one or the other spouse to express a fear of complete ruin—of being homeless, without work and without any means of support. We sometimes hear this from people who have a good education, family support, and access to financial resources.

Even if this fear is not based on a genuine threat, we still face the challenge of understanding how it affects people's approach to conflict. What may be irrational behavior if one's survival is not at stake may seem fully appropriate if it is. When people (or animals) are genuinely endangered, the fight or flight response, for example, may be very functional—but if no genuine danger is present this stance can exacerbate a conflict considerably. When we face an immediate and severe threat (such as an impending accident in an automobile), all of our attention and focus ought to be on the immediate consequences of our actions; but at other times a consideration of longer-term consequences or opportunities may be more important. And when someone feels severely at risk, reassurances that all will be well in the end are usually ineffective. What is needed is immediate assistance or attention to the threats that the individual is experiencing.

In the case of the cousins described earlier, a major consideration was which needs to focus on and how deeply to go into them. For some of the cousins the oceanfront property seemed to represent their need for community and even meaning. For others it was more valuable as a potential resource and a beautiful vacation home. My colleague and I decided to touch briefly on the identity-based concerns because they needed to be acknowledged, but given the immediate needs and availability of the group we focused on their interests, feeling that an agreement about how to proceed on these more tangible concerns was likely to provide the most beneficial next step for them.

TENSION BETWEEN EXPRESSION AND OUTCOME

Disputants often act in ways that seem to go against their best interests. Sometimes they seem more interested in having their day in court than in arriving at a solution that gives them what they need. They are sometimes more interested in expressing their feelings than in getting results. Conversely, people sometimes dismiss attempts to explore what they are experiencing as inappropriate or touchy-feely.

Lewis Coser proposes two components of conflict in his classic work, *The Functions of Social Conflict* (1956). One, which he labels "unrealistic," involves people's need for some form of energy release. The other component, which he labels "realistic," relates to people's desire for a result that will meet their needs. The unrealistic component will not be satisfied by a good solution, but instead requires listening, ventilation, acknowledgment, validation, a "day in court," or some other means of expressing or releasing the feelings and energy associated with a conflict. The realistic component requires a satisfactory outcome or solution, one that addresses people's essential interests.

Coser's labels are sometimes confusing to people because both components are in some sense realistic—that is, they are real to those people who are experiencing them. We might think of them instead as the expressive and the outcome-oriented aspects of conflict. The first component involves the need to deal with the anger, hurt, tension, frustration, sadness, and fear that disputants may be feeling. The second element relates to their concerns about arriving at a satisfactory outcome that addresses their more tangible concerns. Efforts to deal with a conflict with significant expressive elements by focusing on potential solutions or agreements—that is, by skipping over the expressive elements—will not succeed. Similarly, efforts to address the outcome-oriented component by focusing on the expression of feelings may also fail. We all have experienced a time when our emotions were too intense for us to focus on a rational solution to a problem. But most of us have also experienced a time in a conflict when what we really wanted was a good solution, not more exploration of feelings or clarification of values.

Often (although not always) people must find a means of dealing with the expressive aspects of conflict—sometimes directly in the conflict interaction, sometimes elsewhere—before they can effectively focus on an outcome that will adequately address their needs. But we see the reverse as well. Sometimes before people can deal with their feelings or release their tension they need to see that some of the most important outcomes they are seeking will be addressed. For example, they need to see that an issue that is important to them is on the agenda for discussion. Or they seek a tangible sign of good faith from the other party, such as providing critical information or agreeing to meet face-to-face, before they can deal with their feelings of mistrust and anger and take the next steps forward.

accordion

The movement between the expressive and outcome-oriented aspects of conflict is not a linear process in which people always start in one place and work their way to another. They go back and forth; events throw them from a focus on their emotions to a focus on results, and both are frequently mixed together in ways that are hard to discern. Yet, as complex as the interactions between these two elements of conflict are, the distinction between them is often obvious, and people instinctively respond to them with different strategies.

At times a symbolic act indicates that people are ready to let go of some of the expressive aspects of a conflict and become more outcome focused. The very moving picture of Ian Paisley, the longtime leader of the Democratic Union in Ulster, and Martin McGuiness, a one-time leader of the Provisional IRA, smiling side by side after they had just been sworn in as First Minister and Deputy First Minister of Northern Ireland, respectively, was such a moment. These bitter enemies were now to be the coleaders of Northern Ireland. That picture, seen around the world, represented the movement from the outer rim of the wheel of conflict to its inner core, saying, as it were, "We can put our feelings and our past behind us and together try to focus on how best to meet the needs of all the people in our country." Of course, this single photo opportunity did not end the conflict or dissipate all of the feelings of mistrust and anger that had developed over many generations. The search for a stable and durable peace in Northern Ireland is by no means over. But that act nonetheless had tremendous symbolic and practical importance and helped move the conflict to a new and ideally more constructive phase.

WHY THINK ABOUT CONFLICT?

The premise of this book and the field of conflict studies in general is that understanding conflict is critical to reaching a better understanding of human behavior and when and how to intervene to assist disputing parties. There are many alternative models of analysis. Professionals concerned with how people handle their differences can focus on decision making, negotiation, communication, stimulus response, power exchanges, peace studies, system dynamics, and so forth. So why should those of us who have identified ourselves as conflict professionals focus on conflict? Does this not direct our attention to the negative aspects of the interchange, to the part that has people at odds rather than the part that addresses the mutual concerns people share? Of course, focusing on conflict does not exclude a focus on peace building or communication or social change. But it does suggest that a focus on conflict can be a powerful tool in dealing with important issues and social dynamics. Why?

Conflict is not in itself a bad thing. It is in fact a necessary ingredient in the growth and development of individuals, families, communities, and societies. Conflict can help build community, define and balance people's needs as individuals with their needs as participants in larger systems, and help them face and address in a clear and conscious way the many difficult choices that life brings to them. Working through a conflict can be an important bonding experience and an opportunity for personal growth. The strength of social systems lies not only in how they prevent serious conflicts but also in how, when conflicts do arise, they address them to maintain system integrity and preserve the well-being of their members. Also critical is the capacity of systems to encourage and allow for the expression of genuine differences that exist. By facing major conflicts, addressing them, and reorganizing as needed to deal with them, and staying engaged with them as long as necessary and productive, social organizations learn to adapt to changes in their environment. Understanding the dynamics of conflict therefore provides conflict resolvers and related professionals with a basic tool for addressing the essential forces that shape the development of individuals and social entities.

It is easy enough to say that conflict is inevitable and is not in itself good or bad, but for many people accepting this simple premise is an uphill battle. There may be an important lesson for us in the resistance that people have to acknowledging conflict in their lives. This may be something other than dysfunctional conflict avoidance. Perhaps there is an inevitable shift in the way people interact with each other once they acknowledge the presence of conflict, giving them good reason to approach that admission with caution. If this shift in focus, energy, attitude, or behavior is a natural consequence of the emergence of conflict, and if conflict is itself necessary, inevitable, and often healthy, this poses a fundamental dilemma for all of us. We had therefore better strive to comprehend the nature of conflict in all its complexities. Understanding conflict becomes the vehicle for understanding the many contradictions that are necessarily present in our efforts to be social beings. Understanding these contradictions is also essential to comprehending how we evolved as a species (Nowak, with Highfield, 2011).

Furthermore, something can almost always be done about conflict. This does not mean that it always can or should be resolved, but a productive response can usually move conflict in a more constructive direction. Sometimes this response may be to escalate a conflict so that it emerges into people's consciousness or takes on a higher priority for action. Sometimes the response may be to do nothing and let events develop, allowing the conflict to mature. Sometimes it may be to help people understand their needs and express their feelings at a deeper, more meaningful level. Sometimes it may be to find some Band-Aid to stop the bleeding. Sometimes it may be to look for creative solutions that all parties can accept. There is no single correct response to conflict, but that does not mean there are not wise and unwise responses to any particular conflict. Our success as individuals, communities, organizations, and societies is in no small measure related to our developing wisdom concerning how we can respond to the many conflicts we face.

CHAPTER TWO

HOW PEOPLE APPROACH CONFLICT

No two people approach conflict in exactly the same way. Furthermore, each of us handles conflict differently at different times, and our approach to conflict evolves over our lifetime. This seems obvious. What is less obvious, however, is how to characterize the complex and changing ways in which we respond to conflict and how each pair of people, or each group, develop their own style or pattern of conflict interaction—how they learn their conflict dance.

How we handle conflict is basic to our sense of ourselves, to how we try to make our way in life, and to how we relate to others. Our approach to conflict derives from what we have been taught about conflict, our experiences in conflict, our personality, culture, the nature of the conflicts we find ourselves in, and the roles we are playing. At any given time we tend to have very different approaches to how we handle conflict in our family, social life, and work life. We handle conflict differently when we are under stress, tired, anxious, or scared. Certain people evoke particular kinds of conflict responses from us, and we from them. Characterizing conflict styles is not so simple, and it is important to remember that system dynamics can be even more powerful than individual traits in determining how people respond to conflict.

We can also see patterns in how each of us approaches conflict, and it is often very helpful to try to understand these as we approach our own conflicts or work with other people in conflict. In trying to understand a conflict, we need to look at both the individual patterns of behavior in conflict and the different styles of interaction that particular disputants establish with one another.

Many frameworks can be useful in understanding the differences in how individuals approach conflict. For example, it is often useful to look at individuals' past experiences with conflict, the way conflict was handled and their typical role in conflict in their family of origin, disputants' cultural norms and practices pertaining to conflict, a range of personality variables, and the particular skills they bring to the conflict. There are in fact so many potential variables to consider that we can easily be overwhelmed. The desire to focus on a simple categorization of conflict styles is understandable, but ultimately misleading. If we want to take a more dynamic and nuanced approach to understanding how people handle conflict, there are a number of factors we should consider. These are values and beliefs about conflict, how people explain conflict, approaches to avoiding and engaging in conflict, styles of conflict engagement, the roles people are drawn to play in conflict, and patterns of conflict interaction.

VALUES AND BELIEFS

When we are involved in a conflict, we are often more focused on the values or beliefs that surround the issues involved in the conflict than on our values about conflict itself. But our approach to conflict may be heavily influenced and at times even determined by these core values concerning conflict, even though we are often unaware of them. Some of these beliefs are rooted in the culture in which we have been brought up and the era in which we have come of age. For example, challenging authority was relatively normative for those of us who grew up in the 1960s but less so for people who came of age in the 1950s. But even within a particular culture, or family for that matter, we find tremendous variation in individuals' specific beliefs about conflict. Our most important beliefs deal with our basic attitudes about conflict, how people should behave in conflict, and what kinds of outcomes are possible or acceptable. Let's consider these three areas.

What Are Our Basic Attitudes About Conflict?

One way to get at the range of attitudes that people hold about conflict is to consider some of the most common aphorisms about conflict. For example:

- "If you can't say something nice, don't say anything at all."
- "If it isn't broken, don't fix it."
- "Don't look for trouble, it will find you by itself."
- "People in glass houses shouldn't throw stones." ("Let he who is without sin cast the first stone.")
- "Let sleeping dogs lie."

These and other similar expressions warn us against engaging in conflict or raising divisive issues. They even suggest that preventive action is unwise. The underlying message is that conflict is dangerous, usually a sign of dysfunction, and to be avoided. A more nuanced interpretation might be that we think twice before entering into conflict. The underlying tone of all these sayings, however, is that conflict should, if possible, be simply ignored, suppressed, or avoided. The prevalence of this kind of folk wisdom about communication and conflict reflects a widespread belief that conflict is dangerous and perhaps even immoral.

Conversely, consider these sayings:

- "An ounce of prevention is worth a pound of cure."
- "A journey of a thousand miles begins with a single step."
- "Barking dogs seldom bite."
- "You can't make an omelet without breaking eggs."
- "Conflict is inevitable. Combat is optional."

Each of these expressions suggests that it is better to act preventatively, to have the courage to engage in a difficult process, and to deal with feelings or concerns proactively. They also suggest that although conflict is inevitable, we have a role in determining whether it is destructive or constructive, and that it is not conflict itself that we need to fear but how it is handled.

Our attitudes toward conflict are in part the result of how we balance our belief that conflict ought to be avoided with the recognition that avoidance is itself a major problem. How we achieve this balance depends, in part, on our ideas about the role that conflict plays in our lives. Many people believe that conflict is a natural part of their lives and that it is perfectly acceptable to be in conflict. In fact, some believe that if they are not engaged in some conflict they are not dealing with life's challenges and opportunities. For others, conflict is a sign of failure—of personal, organizational, or societal malfunction. How people go about raising potentially difficult issues with each other is often a direct manifestation of their attitudes toward conflict.

A related issue is whether we believe that there can be a conflict in which no one is wrong. ("It takes two to tango." "You're either part of the problem or part of the solution.") On the one hand, if we think that two individuals (or two societies) can have a major difference of opinion about an issue without either party's being wrong or bad, then it is easier for us to see conflict as acceptable and less threatening. If, on the other hand, we think that at least one party in any conflict must be wrong, then the existence of conflict is more likely to threaten our relationships. This belief also makes it difficult for disputants to think of anything short of complete victory as an acceptable outcome.

HOW SHOULD PEOPLE BEHAVE IN CONFLICT?

We also operate from a set of norms about how to behave in conflict. These are sometimes related to values about respect, violence, honesty, and transparency. Poker metaphors are very prevalent in the language people use to talk about conflict and negotiation ("up the ante," "bluff," "put your cards on the table," "go all in"). I see two important beliefs about conflict embedded in these metaphors. One is that conflict is a win-lose (zero sum) game. The other is that it takes cunning, deception, and even lying to be effective in conflict. I often ask students whether they consider it to be a lie when in a negotiation one party indicates that a certain price is a bottom line offer beyond which they cannot go, when in reality it is not. Responses to this range from "It's not lying, it's bargaining" to "It's lying, but it's OK" to "That's why I hate to negotiate—because you have to lie." A related set of beliefs suggests that "the ends justify the means" or that "winning isn't everything—it's the only thing." Clearly one set of values urges us to be tough, decisive, even ruthless if we find ourselves in conflict.

But there is a different set of values that call for us to be open-minded, to acknowledge other points of view, to be fair, to see both sides of an issue, and to respect the humanity of those with whom we are in conflict. ("Turn the other cheek." "There is more than one way to skin a cat." "The truth shall set you free." "Don't judge a man until you have walked a mile in his shoes." "You catch more flies with honey than with vinegar." "It's better to give than to receive.") The implication here is that it is better to be nonreactive, nonjudgmental, polite, and open-minded.

How we bring to bear these often contradictory values in different conflict situations reflects our personal beliefs, but it is also influenced by the values of those with whom we are in conflict. It is a lot easier to buy into collaborative values and approaches when the other side shares them. But of course, this is frequently not the case. And there is something about the way conflict unfolds, even when we share collaborative values, that can bring out our most adversarial selves. Sometimes we have one set of beliefs about how we should behave and another set of beliefs about how others should act.

We also have values about many specific elements of conflict behavior—about forgiveness, apologies, direct dealing, how to use power, taking personal responsibility, assertiveness, disclosure and openness, and the appropriate balance between strength and kindness, to name a few. These and many other values that people have about how to behave in conflict are a complex and often contradictory mix. Everyone struggles at times with contending values. For example, many people value being fair-minded, trusting, sensitive, and accommodating, but at the same time most do not want to be naïve or weak. People want to be firm and flexible, optimistic and realistic, accommodating and tough. Sometimes these contradictory pulls are resolved as people work their way through a conflict, but often they constitute a major problem that interferes with disputants' ability to handle conflict in a measured, consistent, and powerful way. This is an expression of the negotia-tor's dilemma, discussed further in Chapter Eight.

IS CONFLICT SOLVABLE?

People have widely variable views about whether conflict can be solved and people can change. (For example, "You can't teach an old dog new tricks" and "A leopard cannot change its spots" versus "Everyone makes mistakes," "Pessimism is a self-fulfilling prophesy," and "Yes we can.") The more that we believe conflict is solvable, the more likely we are to aim for a full resolution of our differences, a genuine transformation of the conflict, and the restoration of a positive relationship. If we do not believe that sig-nificant conflict can be resolved or even made less toxic or that people can genuinely change as a result of experience, we are more likely to look for quick fixes, superficial solutions, or ways to circumvent the conflict.

FLEXIBILITY OF VALUES

Some people have set and inflexible beliefs about conflict. Others have values that vary according to the particular conflict and its context. For example, many people have one set of values about conflict in their personal lives and another about social or organi-zational conflict. As a result, they often have completely different approaches to conflict in these different arenas. I may, for exam-ple, be very accommodating and easygoing in my approach to dis-agreements with my spouse but very confrontational and positional in how I approach disagreements about workplace conflicts.

People are often unaware of their own values about conflict, much less the values of others. Probably far more often than we realize, conflict behavior is as much motivated by disputants' val-ues about conflict as by their desire to achieve a particular goal, as in the following case.

Perhaps I did not want to make a decision in this arbitration, but I found myself particularly frustrated by what appeared to be the self-destructive intransigence of one of the disputants. I was the chair of a panel that was hearing a case about a public housing resident's potential eviction. Before the final decision was delivered, the housing authority made a settlement offer that appeared to meet the needs of the resident, but he declined it. I asked the resident what he did not like about the proposal. "My father lent me the money to go through this hearing," he told me, "and he would kill me if I wimped out now." He valued "hanging tough" in this conflict, particularly in front of his father, and that was his primary motivation for turning down an offer that he acknowledged was a good one, far better than the eventual (and fairly obvious) outcome of arbitration.

How People Explain Conflict

One revealing window into how people approach conflict is the narratives they construct to explain their disputes. For example, sometimes individuals explain a conflict in very personal terms, emphasizing the characters or personalities of the disputants. Other times they focus on the dispute's structural or systemic roots. Still other times some external force or entity (divine will, a malevolent manipulator, karma, the universe) is brought into the picture.

One interesting take on this examines how people explain why someone has acted in a way that they experience as harmful. Called attribution theory (Allred, 2000; Heider, 1958), the fundamental insight is that how we explain the causes of behavior has a major impact on how we respond to it. For example, if we are sitting in a restaurant waiting to meet someone who is late, we might believe that we are being stood up, that the other person is irresponsible, that she thinks her time is more important than ours, or that she does not particularly value our friendship. These are variations on what are referred to as dispositional (or internal) attributions, based on the personality or character of the other person. Alternatively, we might think that the person never got our message confirming the meeting, that she is stuck in a traffic jam, or that she has been in an accident. These are referred to as situational (or external) attributions. That is, the situation dictated the behavior that was harmful to us. Of course, our historical experience with the other person influences this assessment. If she is always late, we may assume this is dispositional, but if she is rarely or never late, we are more likely to blame it on circumstances.

Attribution theorists describe three kinds of bias: fundamental, actor-observer, and intergroup (Allred, 2000). Fundamental bias refers to the likelihood that our first assumption of why someone has behaved in a way we experience as harmful is that the behavior is attributable to that person's nature or disposition. The more significant the injury or harm that we experience, the more fiercely we hold on to dispositional attributions, even in the face of competing evidence. Actor-observer bias suggests that we tend to ascribe our own harmful behavior to circumstances, but that of others to disposition. If it turns out, for example, that our friend is sitting in another restaurant, acting on information from a recent e-mail, rather than face our own failure in this communication we are likely to blame this on the rash of last-minute messages, the pressures on us, and so on. In other words, we are likely to excuse our own behavior because of the circumstances. Intergroup bias means that we are more likely to give the benefit of the doubt to those within our own group (club, family, friendship circle, race, political affiliation, and so on) than to outsiders.

Understanding the attributions that people make to explain conflict is critical to unpacking their conflict narrative. We often default to a dispositional attribution in conflict because it is easier and perhaps emotionally more gratifying than taking personal responsibility or looking for systemic or structural explanations. The more severe the conflict, the more likely we are to fall back on one of three dispositional explanations, each of which avoids a genuine effort to understand the conflict. These explanatory "crutches" are to attribute conflict to evil, stupidity, or craziness.

We often resort to these when the events are too horrible (for example, the Holocaust), our anger too intense, or the structural causes too complex or obscure (for example, the financial meltdown of 2008) to understand or to face. So we explain events by describing the perpetrator as evil (Saddam Hussein), crazy (Muammar Gaddafi), stupid (pick your least favorite politician), or all three (Adolf Hitler or Idi Amin). Certainly people's approach to conflict is affected by their moral values, their wisdom, and their cognitive functioning, but these attributions are crutches because they don't really explain why particular conflicts have arisen or developed in the way they have—or what is really going on for the individuals involved and how they might make sense of their own actions, however irrational or repugnant they appear to us. These explanatory crutches allow us to bypass the hard work of understanding the structural or systemic roots of conflict. Moreover, they interfere with our ability to understand a conflict from the perspective of those engaged in it.

Understanding just how people are making sense of a conflict and the stories, histories, or narratives they create to give voice to this is a very important part of understanding the conflict—and of intervening in it (Goldberg, 2009; Winslade and Monk, 2000). The following are some of the specific variables to consider when looking at how people explain a conflict.

- Are the explanations personal (dispositional) or systemic (situational)?
- How rigid and narrow are the explanations (as opposed to multifaceted and open to change)?
- Can disputants understand what is motivating the people they are in conflict with from those people's perspective, or can disputants only see it from their own point of view?
- Are they aware of others' narratives—or of their own, for that matter?
- Have disputants incorporated other points of view into their own explanation?
- What are the dimensions of disputants' narratives (how far back do they go, how deeply do they delve, how broad a set of issues and players do they incorporate)?
- Have the explanations changed? Recently? Frequently? Never?
- Do the explanations focus on behavior, feelings, or attitudes?
- Are the narratives hopeless (tragic)—suggesting that nothing can improve—or hopeful (comedic)?
- What are the metaphors used to explain the conflict, and what are their implications?
- Are the explanations specific to the conflict, or do disputants tend to explain all conflicts in the same way?
- What are the cultural contexts of the narratives?
- How widely held—versus how idiosyncratic—are disputants' views of the conflict?

Paying attention to how disputants explain a conflict—and how we ourselves explain it, whether we are parties or interveners—can open important windows into why a conflict develops in the way it does and into the assumptions and values of each of the parties, including our own.

AVOIDING AND ENGAGING IN CONFLICT

We all choose sometimes to avoid and at other times to engage in conflict. Rather than thinking of avoidance or engagement as conflict styles per se, I think the more useful and interesting question is to consider how and when we choose avoidance or engagement. These are two very different processes. The emotional and behavioral jump from avoiding conflict to engaging in it is often enormous. As a result, we sometimes observe what appear to be significant discontinuities in behavior, attitude, and interactional style when a conflict becomes manifest. We have all seen people who appear calm, easygoing, or accommodating until suddenly some switch seems to be thrown that unleashes a much more confrontational, emotional, or rigid approach. It may be that some personal value or deep emotion has been touched, but for many this change is largely a result of the different styles they exhibit when they are avoiding a conflict and when they are engaging in one. Of course, for some the jump from avoidance to engagement is not so dramatic, and they are less likely to change their behavior or approach as they engage a conflict. But for most of us there is some emotional and behavioral shift that occurs when crossing the subtle barrier that separates avoidance and engagement.

Both avoidance and engagement are key parts of the conflict process, but they involve very different stances toward it. When we are avoiding conflict, our efforts are focused on preventing a conflict from surfacing, denying a conflict's existence, or staying out of an ongoing conflict. In general we are limiting our investment of emotion and energy in a conflict. When engaging, our energy is directed toward participating in a conflict, asserting our needs, expressing our feelings, putting forward our ideas, and promoting particular outcomes. We sometimes go back and forth between avoidance and engagement many times during the course of a conflict, particularly when long-term relationships are involved.

Often the switch between avoidance and engagement produces a change in energy level. Some people resist engaging in a conflict with all the tools at their disposal, but once engaged they do not want to give it up. They are like the person who resists joining a dance or diving into a swimming pool—but once in, that is where he or she wants to stay. Sometimes when people withdraw from engagement and go back to avoidance they feel a loss of meaning. The energy and vitality that engagement in conflict often generates can be as hard to give up as the relative comfort and security of avoidance.

Some people are much more comfortable engaging in conflict quickly and if necessary repeatedly. Others will go to great lengths to avoid conflict, to disengage as quickly as possible, and to prevent its recurrence. The specifics of the conflict of course have a lot to do with the pulls people experience toward avoidance and engagement. Most of us can think of conflicts that we would prefer to avoid at almost all costs, and others that we are very willing to engage in, that seem almost fun.

Kenneth Thomas (1983; also see Thomas and Kilmann, 1974), a management researcher and teacher, has suggested five general strategies people use to approach conflict. These strategies reflect a varying relationship between satisfying one's own interests and addressing the interests of others. *Collaboration* involves an effort to solve both sets of interests; *accommodation* focuses more on satisfying others' interests; *competition* emphasizes one's own interests; *avoidance* involves a low commitment to addressing either set of interests; and *compromise* is directed toward sharing losses and gains jointly. Thomas and Ralph Kilmann (an organizational development specialist) have created the Thomas-Kilmann Conflict Mode Instrument, which is based on these concepts, to assess how people approach conflict. This instrument and the model upon which it is founded have been very useful to conflict resolution practitioners because they provide a simple way of analyzing the different approaches that people take to conflict. They also offer a way for all of us to assess our own natural tendencies in conflict.

But the Thomas-Kilmann model has some distinct shortcomings. It does not take fully into account just how variable approaches to conflict can be under different circumstances. In many conflicts people move among all of these strategies, and, as

I have discussed, I believe avoidance strategies and engagement strategies are fundamentally different in nature. There is also an implication that collaboration is the best style and that others are distinctly inferior. If you take the Thomas-Kilmann inventory and determine that your essential style is that of an avoider, compromiser, or accommodator, for example, it can feel as if you have somehow failed the test. But there is no one style that is always preferable, and the cultural meaning of these approaches varies tremendously. We are probably most effective in conflict if we can develop the capacity to use a variety of different approaches depending on the circumstances we find ourselves in and the approaches of other disputants.

How People Avoid Conflict

Eight distinct methods of avoidance seem prevalent in conflict. These are as follows:

Aggressive Avoidance ("Don't Start with Me or You'll Regret It")

Aggressive behavior is sometimes an effort to avoid conflict. Even though it often seems to escalate conflict (and, as with all avoidance strategies, aggressive avoidance often exacerbates conflict), for many people aggressive behavior is best understood as an effort to intimidate others and thus keep them from engaging in a conflict. Escalation can be fight as a means to flight.

Passive Avoidance ("I Refuse to Tango")

Staying removed from and nonreactive to a situation is the approach we most often associate with avoidance. There are many passive ways of avoiding a conflict, such as withdrawing from a relationship, avoiding contact, remaining silent at crucial times, creating distractions, changing the subject, or disappearing from the scene. Passive approaches are efforts to avoid conflict through inaction of some kind.

Passive Aggressive Avoidance ("If You Are Angry at Me, That's Your Problem")

We have all encountered people who are masters at provoking others without owning up to their own actions in any way. By getting others to react as they remain above the fray, they often try to have it both ways, both to have a conflict and to avoid it. Sometimes they will use hit-and-run tactics: for example, they will make an emotionally charged statement without allowing for a direct response, thereby relieving some of their own tension but preventing genuine conflict engagement. Sometimes people indicate their anger or disapproval of something nonverbally (an expressive roll of the eyes, for example) while verbally denying any dispute or disagreement.

Avoidance Through Hopelessness ("What's the Use?")

One of the easiest ways to avoid a conflict is to view the situation as beyond repair or to deny that one has any power to affect a problem. If there is no hope, then what is the point of engaging in conflict?

Avoidance Through Surrogates ("Let's You and Them Fight")

Some people are masters at setting up or at least allowing others to fight their battles while they remain on the sidelines. Sometimes people avoid a conflict about a sensitive issue by engaging over a less sensitive one. Likewise, sometimes people will engage in a conflict with a person who functions as a surrogate for a more intimidating adversary.

Avoidance Through Denial ("If I Close My Eyes, It Will Go Away")

The simplest (and most primitive) approach is frequently the most prevalent. Often people deny that a conflict exists, hoping that in some way the denial will become the reality. Sometimes the existence of a conflict is acknowledged, but its scope or magnitude is minimized.

Avoidance Through Premature Problem Solving ("There's No Conflict; I Have Fixed Everything")

Trying to solve a problem before the timing is right, the conflict is understood, feelings have been expressed, values have been articulated, and people have been heard and acknowledged can be a very powerful way of avoiding conflict. Sometimes all someone wants is a solution, but to the extent that the conflict possesses a significant expressive element or more deeply entrenched issues, problem solving can be equivalent to conflict avoidance. Many conflicts are long term or enduring (Mayer, 2009b). By focusing on short-term solutions to long-term conflicts, people often avoid the most significant and difficult elements of those conflicts.

Avoidance by Folding ("OK, We'll Do It Your Way; Now Can We Talk About Something Else?")

People sometimes avoid engaging by caving in—by accepting more responsibility than they really feel or by conceding on all the issues. Sometimes disputants will sacrifice very important needs to avoid engaging in a conflict or even seeing whether a conflict really exists. People may also make premature or insincere apologies at least in part to avoid engaging in a conflict. An apology under such circumstances can be very close to saying, "What more do you want? I have apologized. Do I really have to listen to you go on and on?"

These eight approaches to avoiding conflict are used in a variety of combinations. Someone may first try a passive aggressive approach, and then, when this does not work, have a go at an aggressive outburst to forestall further engagement. In the end he or she may resort to folding or premature problem solving as the avoidance approach of last resort. It is not unusual to see both parties in a conflict participate in a sort of collusion of avoidance, as in the case of the two accountants.

Doug and Alex seemed happily mired in their conflict. Both were accountants, with adjoining offices in a midsize corporation. They could not stand each other, and they made this very clear to their supervisors, colleagues, friends, and anyone else who would listen. They once had a screaming match, heard by their whole department. But they never raised their genuine issues directly with each other. They exchanged curt e-mails and communicated their feelings in many nonverbal ways, and their talk with each other was often dripping with sarcasm and innuendo, but they always danced around their actual differences. Their supervisor asked me to look into the possibility of mediation. Both were more than happy to share their tales of woe with me separately, but they adamantly refused to sit in the same room with each other. They said it was hopeless, that talk was cheap, and that they would be better off just ignoring each other. It was amazing how similarly they viewed the situation in that regard. Their discussions with me did help to defuse the situation temporarily, and they did agree to try to minimize involving others in their conflict. But they were allies in avoidance. Eventually they were both transferred to different departments.

These two individuals employed many different avoidance strategies, including hopelessness, the use of surrogates, aggressive avoidance, and at times folding. But both of them were especially adept at the passive aggressive approach—making their feelings clear through innuendo and gestures but refusing to take on the conflict directly. Given the eventual outcome, avoidance may have been their best strategy. For me, it was an example of how constructive engagement efforts cannot proceed when people are deeply committed to avoidance.

There are times when avoidance is appropriate and necessary. Sometimes timing or priorities make this desirable. Avoidance may also be the best alternative when someone does not have the power or the emotional resources to get his or her needs met through a conflict. And sometimes conflict should be avoided because it is physically or emotionally dangerous. At other times, however, avoidance is a significant problem that can result in later escalation or the sacrifice of important needs and relationships.

If we want to comprehend the many different ways in which people approach conflict, we need to have a nuanced understanding of the many faces of avoidance. We can look at avoidance as a style, a decision, a tactic, or a personality trait, but however we categorize it we should not underestimate its prevalence in people's approach to conflict. Avoidance, although sometimes necessary and even constructive, is more often a major obstacle to dealing with conflicts in a constructive manner.

How People Engage in Conflict

There are those who never give up trying to avoid conflict. But most people, when faced with ongoing conflict, will eventually engage. When disputants engage in conflict, they do so with an attitude or approach to meeting their needs that is based on both their general assumptions about conflict and the particular circumstances they are facing. We can observe five basic ways in which people try to meet their needs when engaged in conflict. As Ury, Brett, and Goldberg (1988) have suggested, they may work through the exercise of power, an assertion of rights, or an interest-based negotiation process. But there are at least two other significant approaches that do not easily fall within this tri-part framework. One is normative, essentially involving an appeal to fairness, morality, ethics, or values. The other approach involves the use of manipulation or indirection (not directly dealing with the issue or conflict but addressing it through surrogate issues or actions).

Power-Based Approaches

Power-based approaches to conflict are often destructive, are sometimes violent, and seldom lead directly to improved relations. However, they are not always harmful. Strikes, public protests, letter-writing campaigns, boycotts, and efforts to obtain political power may all be thought of as the legitimate exercise of power that can produce positive results.

Sometimes individuals or groups must develop their potential to exercise power and demonstrate their willingness to use it before less confrontational approaches can be effective. Most social movements in our country have begun by promoting their cause through the (sometimes violent) exercise of power. The labor movement organized a series of worker actions. The civil rights movement employed nonviolent direct action campaigns, as did the women's suffrage and environmental movements. Sometimes these led to direct reforms, but often their main result was to create a framework for a different approach to conflict. Until environmentalists demonstrated that they could effectively assert their power through direct action, political campaigns, boycotts, and legal actions, they were not significant players in policy formation. Once they began to show that they were a force to be reckoned with, laws were passed and policies were established that created a framework for a rights-based approach, and environmentalists were increasingly invited into policy development and problem-solving processes. Today it is hard to imagine a major environmental conflict being resolved without some involvement of environmental activists.

Rights-Based Approaches

Because power-based approaches are often disruptive, costly, and hard on relationships, social structures usually try to implement alternative mechanisms for dealing with conflict. This is particularly the case once it becomes clear that power is sufficiently distributed among the contending parties to make power-based approaches costly and the outcome doubtful. The usual response when this happens is the creation of a rights-based framework, through which disputants can attempt to get their needs met by asserting their privilege or claim under some established structure of law, policy, regulation, or procedure. Rights-based approaches require some codification of entitlements and responsibilities, as well as mechanisms for deciding how these should be brought to bear in any particular situation. The court system is, of course, a primary example of this, but so are disciplinary procedures in schools, organizational policies and procedures, and grievance systems. In fact, almost any formal system is characterized by at least some rights-based decision-making structures. Families informally establish such structures as well. For example, any time we tell our children that they can watch TV for one hour per day and that they must alternate who gets to choose the program, we have created a rights-based framework.

Rights-based structures are a necessary counterforce to power-based approaches. When it was clear that the environmental movement was a force to contend with (and that environmental issues could not be ignored), a number of federal, state, and local laws and implementing regulations were passed (such as the National Environmental Policy Act, the Clean Water and Clean Air Acts, and the Endangered Species Act). Supplemented with implementing regulations and court decisions, this legislation became the foundation for a rights-based framework for conducting environmental conflicts. As a result many environmental conflicts now take place through debates and struggles over legal rights, requirements, and prerogatives. Similar developments have occurred in the areas of labor relations, family policy, civil rights, and special education.

Rights-based conflicts are fundamentally different from power-based conflicts. In a power-based struggle, the essential message is, "Do what I want because I have the power to reward you or punish you." In a rights-based struggle, the message is, "The law (or organizational bylaws, or our contract) requires you to do what I want." The structure of rights-based conflicts tends to focus us less on what we need and more on what we have the right to get. This is both a strength and weakness. On the one hand, it discourages destructive power struggles and sets parameters around both the process and the potential outcome of the conflict. On the other hand, it tends to distract people from considering what their needs really are or what the wisest approach to the conflict might be, and it can emphasize form over substance, justification over motivation. Rights-based approaches can be costly, time consuming, and unpredictable as well. Much of the current cynicism about lawyers and courts arises from a sense that an alienating and somewhat out-of-control rights-based approach has taken over and complicated too many areas of conflict intervention and decision making in our society. At the same time, however, a major strength of any democracy is the existence of a popularly accepted rights-based approach to resolving conflicts. When people refer to the rule of law, this is essentially what they mean.

Although power- and rights-based approaches are very different, they are not mutually exclusive. For example, there are many rights-based frameworks for conducting power struggles. There are laws that govern strikes, boycotts, and the exercise of parental authority. Developing one's ability to engage in rights-based efforts, or threatening to do so, can in fact be a power play. ("I'll sue if you don't do what I want.")

Interest-Based Approaches

Interest-based problem solving involves asserting one's needs or concerns and working toward a resolution that adequately addresses them. This also entails trying to understand and address the interests of others. (I discuss this approach in more depth in Chapter Eight when I consider the negotiation process.) Interest-based approaches, though often collaborative, are certainly not always so. For example, I have seen many divorcing couples engaged in furious fights over who should have the children at a particular time, and these fights have focused on what was in the children's best interests. Instead of resorting to overt power tactics or arguing about the divorce agreement, the disputants have focused on why it is important that the children be with them at that time and how they think their proposal would best meet the children's needs. Nonetheless, some of these interchanges have been destructive, angry, and hurtful.

Furthermore, not all interests are constructive or reasonable. The desire for revenge, to hurt someone, to exclude someone from a certain racial or ethnic background from a leadership role, to make a great deal of money at someone else's expense, or to be able to exploit natural resources for a profit are all interests that could be motivating someone in a conflict. Just because someone is focusing on interests does not mean that he or she is being ethical, fair, or collaborative. However, to the extent that disputants are focusing on their genuine interests or needs, they are addressing the most essential elements of a conflict, and these form the basis on which progress is most likely to be made.

The essence of the interest-based approach is not that the disputants are necessarily collaborative or nice but that they try to deal with the conflict by discussing the various needs they have as opposed to trying to impose a solution through the application of power or the assertion of rights. The goal of many collaborative problem-solving efforts is to transform a power- or rights-based approach into an interest-based one. This was, for example, the purpose of the Child Protection Mediation Project.

> When a day care provider reported a number of bruises on the back of a five-year-old, the local child protection agency was called. Its representatives placed the child in protective custody; notified the parent, Mrs. J.; and told her to come to the agency's offices the next morning. After gathering background information, the caseworker explained the child protection laws to the parent and discussed with her what options she had.
>
> The caseworker said that if the mother agreed to attend parenting classes and regular meetings with a counselor, the child could be returned home. Mrs. J. said she would do whatever she had to, but then she missed her first two appointments. The caseworker referred the case to the Child Protection Mediation Project (Golten and Mayer, 1987; Mayer, 1985, 2009a), a CDR Associates project that I codirected.
>
> In the ensuing mediation Mrs. J.'s concerns about attending classes and counseling while trying to hold down a job and take

care of two children were discussed. She also shared her belief that everyone in the classes and counseling sessions would treat her as if she were a "bad person." The caseworker discussed her need for assurances from Mrs. J. that she was learning better ways to discipline her children and that the child was not in danger. Mrs. J. agreed that she could use support in figuring out how to deal with her sometimes aggressive young child. The two worked out an agreed-upon schedule for attending a parent support group, and the mother also agreed to meet with the caseworker once a week, after her shift as a supermarket cashier ended.

By engaging in a mediated discussion that focused on the concerns and needs of the parent, the caseworker, and the child, the parties reached an agreement based on their interests rather than on what Mrs. J. thought she had to do. Although this solution was fairly similar to the one originally negotiated, it proved more durable.

Normative Approaches (Appeals to Fairness)

We often try to get our way in a conflict by asserting a moral right to a certain outcome or course of action. In doing this we are trying to meet our needs through an appeal to what is fair, ethical, moral, or just. We can call this a normative or principled approach. It is similar to the interest-based approach because principles are related to interests. However, instead of focusing on interests (what our needs are), we are focusing on what is the "right" thing to do, and we are invoking an external standard of fairness or justice. In appealing to this external set of standards, a principle-based approach is similar to a rights-based approach, but the nature of the standards are different and there is rarely an adjudicative mechanism. Furthermore, normative standards are not appealable to a formal and legally sanctioned oversight body (at least not in secular societies). They are instead based on a mix of a cultural consensus and individual beliefs.

The essence of a normative approach is the invocation of some specified or implied standard of conduct. If I say that it is only fair that I get to have something, I am implying that there is some standard of fairness that says it is mine. The heart of my approach in this case is not to assert what my needs are or to argue that I have a right to something because of some established rule; instead I am asserting a value, which may or may not be formally codified.

Manipulation-Based Approaches (Indirection)

A final approach is through indirection or manipulation. There are of course countless ways of doing this. At times this approach may be a form of conflict avoidance, but it can also characterize a conflict engagement strategy. As with all of these approaches, manipulation can be destructive or constructive. If I lie, cheat, mislead, and in general behave in an untrustworthy way, the potential for conflict escalation and long-term destructive consequences is great. But manipulation is not always destructive, especially when compared to the alternatives. Consider, for example, the challenge of dealing with an elderly parent about his increasingly unreliable driving. The parent may be very resistant to openly giving up the "right" to drive. Suppose, however, that alternative arrangements are always made for transportation, the car license is not renewed, and the parent goes along with this, without ever actually agreeing not to drive. Can we really say that this is a destructive approach to handling that particular conflict? Or consider how frequently less powerful people in organizations get their needs met through manipulations of their managers or of the rules of the organization. Exploited and disempowered people often have no alternative for addressing their needs in a conflict except to use indirection or manipulation. Manipulation is a very common way in which people handle conflict, and to some extent it is probably present in most conflicts. The essence of manipulation is to try to get others to meet one's needs without directly confronting the issue or putting one's needs or desires clearly on the table. This may be motivated by a sense of powerlessness or vulnerability.

People blend and mix these different approaches in many ways, but there are fundamental differences among them. At any given time, one of these is likely to be the dominant way in which an individual engages in a particular conflict. We often go through a succession of approaches—when one does not seem to work, we go to another. We commonly start with a more normative or interest-based approach but then move to a rights- or power-based approach when we find our needs are not getting met. We also may change our approach in response to how others are approaching us. Consider, for example, the different ways in which a parent might try to enforce a bedtime on a child and how the child might try to resist.

Interest Based

Parent: Go to bed; you need your sleep.
Child: But I want to watch the end of this program.

Rights Based

Parent: We agreed that you could watch one late program a week, and you did that Monday.
Child: You said that if I cleaned up my room I could stay up late.

Principle Based (Normative)

Parent: I should not have to argue with you about bedtime.
Child: You're being unfair—all my friends get to watch this show.

Power Based

Parent: Go to bed or I will take you to bed.
Child: If I can't watch this program, I'm going to hold my breath.

Manipulation Based

Parent: Let's have some ice cream while I read you a bedtime story.
Child: OK, I'll be right there. [Keeps watching the TV]

There are consequences for any approach that is taken, and there is a problem if a social structure does not achieve a good balance among approaches. It is easy for those of us in the business of collaborative conflict engagement to promote an interest-based approach, but at times it is in fact the application of power, rights, fairness, or even manipulation that is needed. Overreliance on power, rights, fairness, or manipulation can escalate conflict and damage relationships. However, when disempowered disputants engage in an interest-based conflict process without having taken steps to develop their power or assert their rights, they are often very vulnerable.

Problems frequently arise when disputing parties use incompatible approaches to conflict. If an employee raises personal job scheduling needs with a manager who responds by citing the provisions of the employment contract, a communication breakdown may easily ensue. Each might well feel unheard and believe the other to be unreasonable. Or if the parent in the earlier example continues to rely on the agreement made, and the child continues to agree to turn off the TV in a minute—but doesn't, an escalation is likely.

STYLES OF CONFLICT ENGAGEMENT

If we know someone fairly well, we can often predict, without even knowing what the issues are, how that person will handle a conflict with someone else. Most of us have a characteristic approach to dealing with conflict. But we also have the capacity to vary our responses to fit the situation. One of the most important differences among disputants is in the flexibility of their response to conflict. Some have a fairly rigid or limited response, whereas others can vary their style from situation to situation. Flexibility of response is one important predictor of how well people will handle conflict in their lives.

There are several basic variables that I find helpful in defining the styles that people use in conflict. Each variable may be thought of as a continuum, and people tend to occupy different segments of that continuum in different types of conflicts. For example, one conflict style variable is how direct or indirect an approach one takes to communication. Some people are very blunt, outspoken, and clear about their feelings and their desires. Others are more circumspect and abstract. Most of us can probably employ at least a little of both tendencies if the context requires, even though we may prefer being closer to one end or the other of this spectrum. Our styles vary, so understanding how someone approaches conflict is a matter not simply of categorizing him or her in accordance with these variables but of recognizing the range of styles a person is apt to use and the circumstances (and people) that evoke different styles.

The following variables may be divided into three groups: those relating to individuals' cognitive style (their way of understanding conflict), to their emotional style (how they express and relate to emotionality in conflict), and to their behavior in conflict. These groups are analogous to the three dimensions of conflict (cognitive, emotional, and behavioral) discussed in Chapter One. Each variable can be thought of as defining a continuum between two polar extremes.

COGNITIVE VARIABLES

Cognitive variables describe differences in how people make sense of conflict, how they present their ideas and needs, and how they approach the problem-solving process. Myers - Briggs

Analytical Versus Intuitive

The analytical style is characterized by the use of logical reasoning and data analysis. Individuals attempt to weigh costs, benefits, and choices and to consider issues one at a time. Individuals using the intuitive approach rely more on perceptions, insights, and feelings as guides to how to proceed.

Linear Versus Holistic

A linear style is characterized by taking issues one at a time and considering facts, options, costs, and benefits sequentially. In the linear style of communication, one person speaks at a time and one subject is considered at a time. People employing a holistic style consider many issues simultaneously and move around easily among a focus on interests, an expression of feelings, a consideration of solutions, and a discussion of issues. In holistic communication, people may speak about several different things at once.

Integrative Versus Distributive

The integrative style promotes a focus on common interests and opportunities for joint gain. People exhibiting this style have a tendency to think in terms of maximizing everyone's satisfaction. Disputants with a distributive style focus more on how to divide existing benefits among disputants and are usually particularly oriented to determining how to maximize their own gain or minimize their loss.

Outcome Focused Versus Process Focused

Many people focus primarily on outcomes in conflict. They want to figure out what is going to be done and when. Others are more concerned about the process of the interaction.

Emotional Variables

Emotional variables describe people's attitudes and feelings concerning conflict and how they handle these in conflict.

Enthusiastic Versus Reluctant

People have widely different tolerances for being in conflict. Some are "conflict junkies" who feel most alive and engaged in the middle of a conflict. I can recall many meetings in which someone (sometimes me) has decided to liven things up by starting a conflict. Some individuals seem to feel that any current or potential conflict must be raised at every opportunity, and that if they are not in conflict they are not fully alive. Most of us, however, are at least somewhat reluctant or fearful about being in conflict, and as a result occasionally use several of the avoidance strategies described earlier. Sometimes people will go to great extremes to maintain their distance or minimize their participation in a conflict and to avoid having any direct interaction with anyone with whom they are in conflict.

Risk Taking Versus Risk Averse

The major goal for some in conflict is to minimize risk or potential harm. For others the primary goal is to maximize the possible benefits that might be accrued. The former's approach to conflict is characterized by caution, the latter's by risk taking.

Emotional Versus Rational

The emotional and the rational are not necessarily opposite as personality traits. In conflict, however, some people are more likely to be emotionally expressive and to focus on their feelings, whereas others are more likely to concentrate on employing an ostensibly logical process to work through the conflict.

Volatile Versus Unprovocable

Some people seem to remain consistently calm, even, and not easily provoked in conflict, whereas others seem always on the edge of a temper tantrum or emotional meltdown. Individuals often become less volatile as they mature or develop their interpersonal skills.

BEHAVIORAL VARIABLES

An enormous number of variables could be identified to describe our different behavioral tendencies in conflict, ranging from our overall demeanor to our particular responses to specific situations. The following seem to be particularly pertinent to the different individual approaches we see in conflict:

Direct Versus Indirect

Some people assert their needs, issues, or feelings directly and openly, and others express them indirectly through surrogate issues, metaphors, or third parties. There are people who feel that openly sharing their concerns or feelings is a personal violation and profoundly embarrassing. Others look to conflict as an opportunity to unburden themselves and value directness and transparency in their communication.

Relational Versus Substantive   — *workaholic*

Team Build

A relational style focuses on building, repairing, or maintaining a relationship, whereas a substantive style is oriented toward addressing the issues in dispute. Sometimes these differences of style are manifested in the amount of time that each person wishes to devote to visiting, getting to know one another, or informally interacting before turning to a discussion of difficult issues (see Moore and Woodrow, 2010).

Submissive Versus Dominant

Submissive and dominant behaviors have less to do with whether people get their needs met than with the roles these individuals play in a conflict. At one end of this continuum are those who are always content to let others take the lead in a conflict interaction, even when they are in extreme disagreement with them. At the other end are those who must be the driving force of the process. Sometimes the submissive style is actually the most powerful in controlling the course and outcome of a conflict—meekness and humility can be a morally effective strategy and can induce others to work very hard to obtain the submissive disputants' agreement.

Threatening Versus Conciliatory

Some people try to get their way by intimidating others, threatening consequences, and using whatever sources of coercive power they have. Others try to placate, repair relationships, and avoid the direct application of coercive power at all costs.

For a behavior, emotional stance, or cognitive method to be an individual's conflict style, it has to be a characteristic approach, preference, or marked tendency for that person and not simply a product of the particular circumstances. That does not mean that circumstances do not elicit certain styles or approaches, however. We may observe individuals who seem to vary their styles to fit the circumstances to the point where we wonder whether they have any continuity of style at all. Often they have more consistency than we may initially observe, but it is a consistency that can be understood only in context. For example, I have worked with people who appear to be calm, submissive, and even meek when there is no pressure to make an immediate decision. But when circumstances require a decision, they become emotional, dominating, and demanding. They do have a consistency of style, but understanding it requires attention to different contexts.

The stylistic variables I have outlined here are not independent of one another. They are also not by any means an exhaustive inventory of styles, but they are significant descriptors of the different tendencies people exhibit in handling conflict.

In considering conflict styles, conflict interveners confront two further important questions. First, do groups, organizations, communities, and societies have conflict styles? For example, does the United States have a conflict style? Does the United Auto Workers? Google? New York City? A particular class in a school? Your family? As parties to conflict these entities do exhibit styles of conflicting, but this does not mean that all the individuals who make up each entity themselves share these approaches. Although the descriptions of the variables given here might have to be slightly altered to apply to groups or organizations, the variables themselves are very relevant. As a general rule, the larger a group, the harder it is to identify a style without stereotyping or making unsupportable generalizations. But that does not mean we cannot find some predominant characteristics or themes in how any particular group, organization, community, or system handles conflict. Just consider the differences you might expect to encounter in how conflict is dealt with in New York City versus in Omaha, Nebraska. In New York, direct confrontation about differences is more normative, and "politeness" is a less encompassing interactional value than it is in Omaha.

The second question is more complicated. Are there good and bad conflict styles? An extreme or rigid approach in any style may be harmful to the individuals or groups exhibiting it and to those with whom they interact. But I believe it is less productive to think about whether conflict styles are good or bad than to consider whether they are effective or nonproductive in any given circumstance. Extremes of style aside, most of these approaches have been effective at different times. The most important question here is how adaptable and flexible people can be in the style they bring to any given conflict. When people can alter their style to adapt to a particular situation, they are likely to be more effective than when their approach is extremely limited.

ROLES PEOPLE PLAY IN CONFLICT

Another way of understanding how people approach conflict is to consider the roles that they are most inclined to take on when in conflict. The roles that we as individuals are ordinarily most comfortable with are no doubt related to the professional or formal roles we may choose to assume as conflict interveners, but these formal roles are not identical to the roles that conflict may demand of us, which we usually assume informally and often unconsciously. Although people play many de facto roles in conflict, the following six seem the most prevalent.

- *Advocate (negotiator):* Arguing or pushing for a particular outcome or set of interests

- *Decision maker (arbitrator):* Deciding among competing positions or claims
- *Facilitator (mediator):* Helping others communicate and negotiate
- *Conciliator (empathizer):* Tuning into and addressing the emotional elements of a conflict
- *Information provider (expert):* Providing information or opinions to decision makers or negotiators.
- *Observer (witness, audience):* Watching, reporting, and reacting to others in conflict

There are certainly other roles people can play in conflict (for example, coach, record keeper, cheerleader, publicizer, convener, gatekeeper). But these six are the key roles in the structure of most conflicts. Each can be played in many different ways, and each can contribute to conflict escalation or de-escalation. Elements of several different roles are often present in how people participate in any given conflict, and no matter what a person's role is, he or she always has personal needs in play (for example, to do a good job, to be seen to be competent or in control, to be empathetic and supportive).

Often disputants enter a conflict primarily in one role but then change roles, sometimes repeatedly and rapidly. Conflict can easily escalate when people present themselves as playing one role (for example, facilitator or information provider) but actually take on a different role (arbitrator or advocate). Maintaining clarity about the role we are playing and how it might be altered as circumstances change is a significant challenge we all face when we enter into conflicts as disputants or interveners.

PATTERNS OF ENGAGEMENT: THE CONFLICT DANCE

Focusing on the approaches and motivations of the individuals involved in a conflict is an important start to understanding the nature of a conflict, but we are only focusing on one part of the picture if we don't also consider the interactional patterns among disputants. Disputants cocreate a system of interaction. We can call this process the "conflict dance." Much like two people doing a tango, people embroiled in a dispute play off each other's conflict approaches, shifting back and forth between complementary and opposing tactics. For example, whether I take an interest-based approach to conflict depends on whether the person I am in conflict with cooperates, in a sense, with my use of my preferred approach. If my efforts to discuss our concerns are continually responded to with threats to take me to court or to impose consequences on me, I may be forced (or at least strongly induced) to adopt a different style in response. And even if someone I am in conflict with wants to adopt a more collaborative approach, if by doing so that person feels pushed or manipulated into a position he or she is not comfortable with, that individual may end up resorting to power-based responses, thereby eliciting those responses from me. As we continue to modify and change our approaches, this conflict dance continues.

In this and many other ways, the approach we take to conflict, the role we end up playing, and our style of engagement or avoidance are determined not solely by our individual conflict preferences or tendencies but also by the interactional system among all conflict participants. We can see this in almost any conflict interaction, and sometimes we experience this very dramatically. Some people "push our buttons" or "bring out our worst selves" as opposed to encouraging our "better angels." And of course we do the same for others. Sometimes understanding how this conflict dance operates can provide an important clue as to how to move a conflict in a better direction:

> Gillian was an assistant to the CEO of Foodspace USA, a grocery chain. Serena was the leader of a community group protesting what they considered to be Foodspace USA's price-gouging policies in poor neighborhoods. After several weeks of increasingly angry protests, Foodspace USA agreed to enter into mediation with me and a colleague. Gillian was the major negotiator for Foodspace USA, and Serena led the community group's team.
>
> Both sides had many reasons to come to an agreement. The protest was beginning to run out of steam, and Foodspace USA was trying to open a new store in a neighborhood nearby and was facing resistance from the city planners due to the unrest they were currently facing. Furthermore, both Gillian and Serena seemed

committed to and fairly skilled at collaborative approaches to negotiation. But their approaches to conflict did not mesh very well. Gillian was relationally oriented and holistic. Serena was very issue focused and linear. And of course both were suspicious of each other. Meetings would begin with Gillian, quite sincerely, wanting to find out a bit more about Serena, her family, her interests, and her life in the community. Serena would experience this as intrusive, manipulative, and evasive. She wanted to move quickly to a discussion about pricing, quality, and service. Gillian would discuss these as well, but in a context of trying to talk about the overall experience of customers, managers, and workers.

Every time Serena tried to push a specific discussion about prices, Gillian felt that she was being attacked and would respond with a fairly personal discussion of how difficult it had been trying to make this business work. In the course of this, she would often try to connect with Serena as a working mother. This in turn felt like more evasiveness to Serena, who in response would get more specific about prices. It felt like they were in a repetitive pattern of interaction that they did not know how to end. Interestingly, taken alone, Gillian was not an extreme example of a relationally focused person, nor was Serena completely committed to a substantive style. But their interaction was exacerbating the differences in their respective styles rather than bringing them together.

My colleague and I were able to assist by pointing out this pattern and by being "stylistic interpreters" for both Gillian and Serena. We would engage Gillian in a personal discussion and redirect her to substantive concerns; we would engage Serena in a substantive discussion but check in with her about how she thought she and her group were doing and how they were feeling about the development of a bargaining relationship with Gillian.

Obviously this conflict dance can play out in many different ways, even with just two disputants. With a group, the possibilities proliferate as the conflict system becomes more complex. A few of the patterns we might look for include the following:

- *Opposites attract.* Styles that are very different can sometimes work well together. Submissive can work with dominant, linear with holistic, analytical with intuitive. These approaches can sometimes effectively balance each other out, each disputant allowing the other to stay in his or her comfort zone and still move the process forward. Similarly, if one person prefers a facilitator role and another the advocate role, each can enable the other.

- *Opposites repel.* As in the Foodspace USA mediation just described, sometimes one style provokes the opposite style in another, and this encourages the first party to move further toward the extreme of his or her natural style. This can increase the heat and make constructive interaction more difficult.

- *Similarities attract.* We are sometimes much more comfortable working with people with a similar engagement style. If we are most comfortable taking a rights-based approach to conflict, for example, we may gravitate toward others more apt to use that style (for example, when two lawyers converse informally about a case). Also, by responding with rights-based arguments, we may elicit that style from others as well. This is an important element in how conflict is handled in the legal community.

- *Similarities repel.* Sometimes it is very hard for both parties in a conflict to adopt the same style because certain approaches require the energy or input of other approaches to be effective. For example, if both want to be the facilitator, if both want to take up the emotional space in a group, or if both take a very assertive approach to promoting their point of view, the conflict can stagnate or escalate.

- *Styles converge.* Sometimes disputants with very different styles prompt each other to move toward a common or at least overlapping style, more toward the middle of the spectrum of approaches. For example, I start out very rational, you emotional, but gradually you focus on a more linear, substance-oriented approach and I become more expressive and holistic. I have witnessed parties who completely switch approaches over the course of a conflict.

- *Multiple styles coexist.* Sometimes we find that multiple styles can evolve, and groups in particular find ways to accommodate quite a few different approaches. People may move rapidly among different styles in response to others who are moving rapidly among different styles. This can seem volatile and confusing, but sometimes it works remarkably well, for example when participants in an interaction seem to rotate through the roles of facilitator, analyzer, emoter, and decision maker. We can sometimes observe this phenomenon among peer groups of young children whose members seem to know instinctively when it is all right to take up emotional space and when, instead, they need to leave that space for others to occupy or even provide the nurturing to enable others to go there.

- *Conflictants adopt a new style.* Disputants sometimes find a third way—one that is completely different from either of their natural tendencies but allows them to interact. In this circumstance, each participant moves into a relatively new approach—one that can move the conflict forward in a productive or nonproductive way. Two people in a conflict might both naturally be fairly nonlinear in their approach, but to move a process forward they might both adopt, with varying degrees of comfort, a more linear approach (for example, when trying to come up with an agenda of issues to discuss). Or because they are both caught up in an emotionally intense conflict, two people who are naturally more integrative in their approach might become much more aggressive and positional.

Over the course of a conflict we might observe parties adopting and maintaining a relatively stable approach, or we might see that the approach they take with each other changes quickly and often. Sometimes a stable approach to conflict is perfectly functional, but sometimes people get locked into nonproductive patterns of interaction. Sometimes changing approaches are a sign of individuals' adapting to each other, but rapid changes in approach may also be a source or symptom of conflict escalation or communication breakdown.

When we are trying to change the nature of a conflict process, it is important to pay attention to both the pattern of interaction and the individual approach of each participant. When it comes to conflict, we never dance alone.

As with so many other efforts to understand human behavior, in conflict we face the structural versus individual dilemma: To what extent is behavior in conflict primarily a result of the structure within which the conflict takes place, and to what extent does it reflect what individuals bring to that structure? Does the situation call forth the behavior, or do individuals' values, styles, and role preferences determine their approach? It is obvious that both the nature of the conflict and the nature of the disputants are important. We err if we think we can understand a conflict without examining the values, styles, and preferences of the individuals involved. But we also make a mistake if we fail to pay adequate attention to the structural elements of the conflict. Understanding any conflict requires simultaneously paying attention to both the individuals in the conflict and the system or structure from which the conflict arose. In the next chapter I discuss one defining feature of the structure of conflict—the nature and role of power.

CHAPTER THREE

POWER AND CONFLICT

Power is the currency of conflict. Whether its exercise is intentional or not, when we are engaged in conflict our power is in play. The choice in conflict is not whether to use power but how to use it and how to respond to the inevitable use of power by others. Power can be used intentionally or unconsciously, collaboratively or coercively, obviously or implicitly, constructively or destructively. When we try to meet our needs in the face of resistance or opposition, we are exercising power. When we try to persuade others to change their behavior or approach to a conflict, we are exercising power. In fact, almost every move we make to further our goals in a conflict situation involves the exercise of some kind of power, no matter what our role is. Whether we will succeed in accomplishing our aims depends in part on how much power we are able to muster and how wise we are in using it. The exercise of power is not necessarily coercive, antagonistic, escalatory, or combative, although it certainly can be any of these. All of us exercise power continually, and we often do so in a way that promotes rapport or reconciliation. If we do not understand the nature of power and how power affects conflict, we cannot understand conflict itself.

Note: Parts of this chapter are adapted from B. Mayer, "The Dynamics of Power in Mediation and Conflict Resolution," *Mediation Quarterly,* Summer 1987 (16), pp. 75–86.

REALITIES AND MYTHS ABOUT POWER

People have many different images about what power is, some of which are quite misleading. Power is variously defined as the ability to act, to influence an outcome, to get something to happen, or to overcome resistance. In physics, power is defined as the amount of work performed per unit of time. For the purpose of understanding the dynamics of conflict, power may be defined as the ability to get one's needs met and to further one's goals. (For other definitions of power, see Coleman, 2000; Deutsch, 1973; Moore, 2003.) Power of this type (as opposed to the power of an engine or the power of the sun, for example) can be understood only in context. Even when we are talking about willpower or the power of concentration, which seemingly reside entirely within us, we must understand the environment in which we are exerting this power and the forces with which we are interacting. When we discuss power in conflict, therefore, we are speaking of power within an interaction. With one group of friends I may have great influence on what movie we will choose to see or on how we will settle a disagreement about where to go skiing, but with another group (or the same group under different circumstances) I may have very little influence. One key variable that defines our power is our intention and focus. If there is something I want very badly, and if I focus all my energy on getting it, for that moment my power will be greater than it will be when I care only mildly about an issue or decision.

Parent-child interactions provide a clear example of how complicated power dynamics can be. Imagine yourself as the parent of a four-year-old child who is accompanying you on what you hope will be a quick trip to the grocery store. Your child wants you to buy a candy bar, but for a variety of reasons you do not want to give in to this request. Now think about the different ways this interaction can play out and how likely it is that on some occasions the child will prevail and on others you will. If under all circumstances one or the other person gets his or her way, it is very likely that there are some serious problems in this relationship. Furthermore, the use of power in such an interaction is clearly embedded in the context, the parent-child relationship, and the complex of motivations, skills, and energy that each brings to the interchange.

For a conflict to develop, all involved must have some power that they can bring to bear, even if it is slight. In situations in which one group completely dominates another, conflict is unlikely to exist, at least along the behavioral dimension. There is instead a *potential* for conflict, which may be realized as the dominated group develops power.

We have many misleading images of power that cloud our ability to understand the way power is expressed in conflict. Perhaps the most prevalent is the idea that power can be balanced. This is a derivation of the view many have that power is a measurable quantity. I believe that *balance of power* is a confusing and possibly meaningless concept. We can look at differences in power, at whether someone has the power to make something happen, at sources of power, and at people's vulnerabilities to the power of others. But the idea that power can be balanced to produce some equality or even equivalence of power is very misleading. Such a way of viewing power fails to account for the dynamics of power and the interactional context in which power must be understood. Instead of thinking that people need an equivalence or equality of power, we might more usefully think that people need an adequate basis of power to participate effectively in conflict. They require enough power that others must at least consider their concerns and enough power to resist any solution that fundamentally violates their interests. This does not mean that disputants with an adequate base of power can always "win" or attain a particularly desirable outcome or process, but they can at least engage in conflict with some hope of being influential and effective. Without this power, their participation in a conflict engagement process may end up being the means for their needs to be ignored and their interests overrun, but with a sheen of participation or consultation.

We also use the image of a level playing field when we consider power relationships. As mediators, for example, we often believe it is our responsibility to create a level field for negotiations. The advantage of this image is that it does not suppose that we can balance the parties' power, but instead challenges us to create and conduct a process that does not unfairly advantage one party or another. But of course, all processes or interventions have an impact that is not always the same for all parties. For example, if we slow down a process, we benefit those who stand to gain by delay or maintaining the status quo for as long as possible. If we promote a rational, information-based exchange, we may inadvertently undercut those whose power is located in their ability to make a strongly emotional appeal.

The truth in these images may be more aspirational than achievable. Particularly when acting as third parties, our goal ought to be to promote the ability of all disputants to advocate for their legitimate interests in an effective and constructive way. I have often said to disputants that my intention is not to promote any one person or party's interests at the expense of another's. As political philosopher Jane Mansbridge put it in commenting on an effort to build consensus in community-planning efforts:

> The goal . . . is a deliberation in which power, in the sense of the threat of sanctions and the use of force, is absent. Such a goal is unachievable, because power permeates the world in which we live. We cannot even speak without using language that encodes power imbalances of all kinds.
>
> But the fact that we cannot achieve the goal should not keep us from trying to approach it. The ideal, like lots of ideals . . . should be thought of as what political theorists call a regulative idea: a goal at which to aim, without expecting that one will achieve the ideal in all its fullness. [Mansbridge, 1999, pp. 979–980]

Another misleading image is that of power as a fixed quantity in a relationship. That is, people often think of power as being in limited supply. If I don't develop and use my power in a relationship or conflict, according to this view, I will lose it. And the more power others have, the less I have. In human relations, power is more complex than that. Depending on how we use our power and the types of strength we draw from, our power can increase as our adversaries' power also increases.

Often the potential power that individuals or groups have can be realized only when it is joined to the power of the others in the conflict. Sometimes the best way for a group to enhance its own power is to use it to empower a potential adversary with whom the group has some mutual and some conflicting interests. Similarly, the attempt to exercise power separately from or in opposition to others frequently leads to a loss of power. This

dynamic may often be observed in negotiations between unions
and management:

> One of the most poisonous labor relations atmospheres I have
> worked with existed between the union and the management of a
> state hospital. There were as many outstanding grievances as there
> were represented employees, and these grievances were not getting
> resolved. The overall adversarial atmosphere was mirrored in many
> acrimonious interchanges between individual managers and union
> representatives. Despite numerous efforts by the parent union and
> the overall agency leadership to intervene, the situation was dete-
> riorating and morale was sinking. A colleague and I were asked to
> work with the union and the management to help improve their
> relationship. There were many thrusts to our effort. We provided
> training, mediated interpersonal disputes, assisted in designing
> new grievance mechanisms, and facilitated discussions between the
> union and management teams in which they could talk about their
> relationship.
>
> A key step in the process occurred when we decided the time
> was ripe to mediate about sixty of the grievances collectively. All of
> these related to how overtime was assigned and calculated, and we
> felt it would be more productive to negotiate them as a class than
> one at a time. It was a bold move on the part of the management,
> the union, and us to try to do this. We were taking a big bite.
> Success would remove one major obstacle to improved relations
> and would allow people to look at some of the more fundamental
> issues of communication, trust, and decision making. Failure
> could discourage everyone and set the whole effort back (or
> maybe scuttle the whole process). We felt, however, that everyone
> would become suspicious of all the nice words the process was
> generating if no significant and tangible progress were made on
> important issues.
>
> Once the negotiations got under way, a potential solution was
> not that difficult to figure out, but each side was terribly worried
> about giving in to the other and appearing to weaken its own
> position while enhancing the other's. However, everyone was also
> tired of the conflict and knew that some risks had to be taken to
> change things. With great trepidation the two sides reached an
> agreement, despite each side's fear that it had been manipulated.
> But the upshot was that relations did start to improve significantly.
> After this the union was able to talk over its particular concerns
> more openly and effectively with the management, and managers

were able to deal with some difficult personnel issues that they had been avoiding.

Later, when the state agency overseeing the hospital criticized some decisions the hospital management and union had made on other issues, they were able to work as a team to protect the hospital's interests. They were also invited to share their new approach to handling grievances with other facilities, which increased the prestige of both the union and the facility leadership. The decision to use their power jointly rather than in opposition to each other was very difficult. By taking a chance that might have empowered the other side to the risk taker's own disadvantage, the management and the union increased their individual and collective power.

TYPES AND SOURCES OF POWER

Power is an elusive concept because it has so many manifestations. We all have multiple potential sources of power, many of which we are frequently unaware of. Some of these sources are fairly independent from a conflict, but others can be enhanced or diminished by the conflict process. In fact, increasing power is often one of the goals people have in conflict. Some types of power are best used sparingly, if at all; some are negative or escalatory. However, others are more constructive and amenable to repeated direct application.

STRUCTURAL (SYSTEMIC) AND PERSONAL POWER

We can identify two general categories of power: structural and personal. Structural or systemic power is lodged in the situation, the objective resources people bring to a conflict, the legal and political realities within which the conflict occurs, the formal authority disputants have, and the objective choices that exist. Personal power has to do with individual characteristics, such as determination, knowledge, charisma, wit, courage, energy, and communication skills.

Going back to the grocery store example, we can ask why you, as the parent, do not always get your way. You have the formal authority, financial resources, physical strength, and ability to reward or punish the child. But we know how often a child may prevail in such a situation. Why? The child has energy, focus, desire, the willingness to use whatever power he or she may have (including the power to embarrass), and usually a great deal of creativity. Often it is the variations in personal power that explain the widely different outcomes to conflicts that appear structurally similar.

A more serious example is one I have encountered in many divorce negotiations. One party seems to have the financial resources and the legal rights to successfully pursue his or her interests, but because that person does not have the determination, emotional resilience, or clarity of purpose of the other party, he or she ends up in a weaker position. This is one reason why victims of domestic violence, whose sense of personal power has often been systematically undermined, are often vulnerable in divorce negotiations.

As a general rule, conflict intervention systems and practitioners are more able to affect differentials rooted in personal power than they are those rooted in structure. For example, mediators can set up procedures to discourage intimidation, browbeating, unequal access to information, and so forth, but they can do little to change the fundamental resources available to each side or the legal framework that defines the alternatives the different parties have should negotiations fail. Changes in structural power usually require systemic change, which may be an outcome of a conflict interaction but is not something mediators themselves are generally able to bring about.

In considering how to deal with differentials in personal power, we should never underestimate the degree to which people enhance their own power by engaging in a constructive conflict process. Although we often discuss how to empower people, it is easy to overlook the potential that people have to empower themselves. They do this by naming a conflict, by confronting their own avoidant tendencies, by finding a voice and constructing an effective conflict narrative, by getting clear about their own genuine needs and those of others, by developing effective alternatives, by informing themselves about the issues involved, by gaining experience in raising issues effectively, and in many other ways. Our desire to protect others (or ourselves) from direct participation in painful conflict interactions may derive from very humane instincts but it can actually prevent people (and ourselves) from developing their personal power to engage in conflict effectively.

SPECIFIC SOURCES OF POWER

People can be enormously creative in finding different ways to bring power to bear in conflict, and there are several key sources of power that disputants repeatedly mobilize. Although some of these sources of power overlap, and although there are certainly others, these are the ones I believe to be most useful for understanding the potential power that individuals or organizations can bring to a conflict interaction.

Formal Authority

Formal authority is the authority given by an institution, by a set of laws or policies, or by virtue of one's position in a formal structure. Principals, judges, police officers, executives, elected officials, parents, and military officers all have some degree of formal authority. Most people in leadership positions have some power based on their formal authority and some based on their personal influence. Formal authority is a form of structural power. How effective people are in using it is often related to their personal power.

Social Legitimacy

The cultural or social belief that someone's authority is legitimate, that he or she has the right to make decisions or enforce consequences, is as important as formal authority in most settings. Parents may have the formal right to exercise power over their children, and police officers might have the right to enforce the law, but their power derives as well from the community's belief that they have this right, and their power diminishes when this belief does not exist or is undermined.

Legal Prerogative

Everyone has rights and choices defined by law or policy. Disputants' legal rights and obligations often define their alternatives to consensual agreements. An important related source of power is the resources (financial and emotional) a person has to pursue a legal case.

Information

Data and knowledge are important sources of power. In many situations the actions people take to share, discover, or conceal information are key to how a conflict develops. A variation on the power of information is expert power. This is the power that derives from having expertise relevant to a conflict or access to such expertise.

Association

People derive power from their connection with other powerful individuals or organizations. Political power is an interesting variant of this. Most political power stems from people's ability to bring the power of others to bear in a political context. The power of neutrals partly derives from their ability to maintain an association with all conflicting parties, thus making themselves valuable to each of them.

Resources

Access to resources, such as money, time, or labor, is a major source of power. A related source is the ability to provide or deny resources to others. Resources may be either tangible or intangible. Tangible resources, such as money, personnel, or property, are extremely important, but often the intangible resources, such as reputation, the ability to handle stress, and physical endurance, are as critical to people in conflict.

Rewards and Sanctions

The ability to provide or withhold meaningful rewards and the ability to impose negative consequences on others or to prevent those consequences are twin sources of power. All power can be defined to some extent in terms of the ability to reward or sanction. People generally think of rewards as more constructive than sanctions, but there is sometimes very little difference between the two as sources of power. Withholding a reward is essentially a sanction, and withdrawing a sanction is a reward. The power of a reward or sanction is often defined less by the action's severity than by its immediacy. The long-term threat of a lawsuit, for example, although serious, may be less influential on a corporate decision maker than the immediate prospect of increased sales revenues.

Nuisance

Related to sanctions as a source of power, this is the ability to irritate, bother, interfere, or harass, but it falls short of the ability to impose significant consequences or penalties. It is sometimes referred to as the "power of the flea over the dog." This may be the most significant source of power the child in the supermarket can bring to bear.

Procedural Power

Procedural power arises from the ability to control or influence a decision-making process. This is separate from control over the outcome. The power of a judge in a criminal trial or a mediator in a negotiation is in large part procedural but certainly not insignificant.

Habitual Power

Habitual power derives from being in the position of trying to prevent change as opposed to fomenting it. Sometimes this is referred to as the power of inertia. It is usually easier to keep things the way they are than to change things. This power partially explains why community groups opposed to development have often been able to cause large corporations with considerable resources and political connections to stand down.

Moral Power

Power can flow from an appeal to the values, beliefs, and ethical systems of others or from an attack on the values of those with whom someone is in conflict. Also, people's belief that they are acting in accordance with important values is a significant source of personal power. Mahatma Gandhi referred to this as the force of truth (*satyagraha*). When individuals are advocating what they believe to be a worthy cause, such as the rights of an oppressed group, that belief helps them be steadfast and energetic in their advocacy. Also, people are more likely to be swayed by a person perceived as doing good work than by a person viewed as interested mainly in personal gain. Of course an assertion of worthiness may also lead to a perception of self-righteousness, or it may bring into conflict people who do not share the same evaluation of the worthiness of the cause. When people portray themselves as the victim or the underdog, they are usually trying to invoke this type of power.

Personal Characteristics

People may derive power from a broad set of personal characteristics that they bring to bear in conflict. Their intelligence, communication skills, physical stamina and strength, concentration, wit, perceptiveness, determination, empathy, and courage are key factors in determining how well their needs will be met in any conflict. Another factor is endurance. How long individuals can tolerate being in a conflict and how well they are able to withstand others' power are key aspects of their own power. As discussed above, these characteristics are not immutable, and we all can develop our personal capacity to participate in conflict in an effective way.

Perception of Power

The beliefs people have about their power and that of others are often as important as the power itself. For example, if disputants believe that a court is likely to rule favorably or that they have the resources to go to court if necessary, the belief itself, regardless of its accuracy, can be a source of power, especially if others share it. Similarly, if others believe that a person has considerable resources or significant connections with powerful people, that belief alone can enhance the person's power. People's ability to modify the perceptions that others have about power is therefore itself a source of power.

Definitional Power

The ability to define the issues and the potential outcomes in a conflict is a crucial source of power. It makes a big difference whether workers see themselves negotiating for better wages, for their jobs, or for ownership of a plant. The framing of a conflict is often the key to how it is resolved.

Some of these types of power are more naturally constructive than others, but any of them can be used to escalate or de-escalate a conflict. Some are more amenable to change during the course of a conflict. For example, disputants can often increase their power by improving their access to information and by developing effective associations with others. However, changing one's authority, legal position, or ability to impose sanctions may be more difficult.

Certain types of power are compatible with each other, but others are not, and frequently conflict develops when a person tries to use incompatible types of power. If I try to get someone to do what I want by using my moral authority and by threatening sanctions, I am very likely to be working at cross-purposes with myself. The reaction of those who are threatened is likely to be defensive and hostile, diminishing their openness to an appeal to principles and fairness. However, there are also times when one type of power can be employed effectively only when it is supplemented by another. For example, legal power is often ineffective if a person does not have the resources or emotional stamina to use it. Sometimes a person with formal authority in an organization has very little personal, social, moral, or association power. This can lead to serious organizational conflict. I have worked with a number of conflicted teams that were experiencing significant struggles between an individual with formal authority and an individual who was the natural leader of the group. This was clearly the situation in a dispute I observed several years ago.

It did not take Louis long to dig a big hole for himself after being hired as the director of a human services agency. Sid, one of his team leaders, had been the acting director while the search process for a new director was being conducted, and he had announced his intention to retire from the organization several months after the new director arrived. Sid now felt slighted and unappreciated for his contribution as acting director. Louis felt that Sid was undercutting him in many subtle ways, and thought that Sid needed to be put in his place. Both found plenty of ways to irritate each other and complicate their jobs. Sid made his views about the new director known to his colleagues but never attacked Louis directly. Louis openly criticized decisions Sid had made as acting director. Whenever Louis had an opportunity to use his formal authority over Sid, he did.

All this came to a head several weeks before Sid's departure, when Louis ordered Sid to place one of his staff members on probation under very stringent terms. Sid refused, and Louis threatened to fire him. Sid replied to this threat by saying, in effect, "Go ahead, make my day." Of course Louis could not carry this threat out effectively in the time that remained before Sid's scheduled departure. As a result of this conflict, Louis's authority, leadership, and influence declined considerably, and this continued to be the case long after Sid had departed.

Louis had a considerable amount of power. He squandered it by relying almost exclusively on his formal authority and his ability to sanction. In the end he retained little real power to affect the climate in the organization. He had publicly taken on a popular employee in a relatively meaningless conflict that he could not win, and he never developed his personal power with his staff. The more Louis used his formal authority and threatened sanctions, the more Sid used his power of association and his ability to be a nuisance. In a sense they reinforced each other in the power choices they made. As a result, instead of using their respective power together, Louis and Sid turned it against each other, doing considerable damage to the agency's program and to their personal standing.

An essential question in conflict, in addition to how much power the different individuals have, is how they choose to use it. As the example of Louis and Sid illustrates, power can be used effectively or ineffectively. The types of power people choose to apply, their timing, and their sense of how they can use their power to meet their needs—and the responses that their use of power will engender from other disputants—are all critical to their effectiveness. The more intelligently disputants use their power, the more sustainable it will be. People often make decisions about using power with a very short-term view of their goals and the consequences of their decisions. Most significant disputes take place over time, and a wise expenditure of power is one that is sustainable (Mayer, 2009b). Power that is expended ineffectively tends to diminish.

We cannot understand any person's potential power independent of how that power interacts with the power of others in conflict. In many circumstances the effectiveness of one disputant's use of power is best understood by how that person's power affects others in their use of power, and vice versa. When one party to a conflict employs reward power, the goal may be to encourage others to do the same, but whether that effort is successful depends on the reactions of others and more particularly on their decisions about what power to bring to bear in return. The use of power involves a system of interaction, and to some extent our goals in conflict involve finding a constructive and coherent system of power exchange.

IMPLIED AND APPLIED POWER

One of the greatest challenges in using power is knowing how direct one should be in its application. Implied power is often far more effective than power brought directly to bear on a situation. For example, developing the capacity to sue and building a strong legal case are often much more effective than actually suing or threatening to sue. Arming oneself with relevant information is usually more empowering than demonstrating how well informed one is. Developing alternatives to a collaborative solution is generally more important than threatening to use those alternatives. Understanding how to develop power quietly and to use it sparingly is one of the arts of effective conflict engagement. This was the essential message behind the famous aphorism of Teddy Roosevelt: "Speak softly and carry a big stick" (an approach that was not very characteristic of his presidency).

Of course, this does not mean that disputants should never bring their power directly and overtly to bear. Sometimes it is important to use power explicitly and unambiguously to change a situation, and sometimes it is necessary to show a willingness to use power. But this is a very tricky proposition, and using power in too obvious or blatant a manner can easily lock disputants into a nonproductive approach to conflict. Unions, for example, to be effective negotiators, often need to develop a creditable threat of engaging in job actions or strikes. Sometimes, however, the ability to strike cannot be developed, let alone projected, without creating a momentum that makes a job action inevitable or at least difficult to avoid. It is tempting to believe that strikes are generally a sign of the shortcomings of either the negotiation process or the negotiators. But if a union never strikes or a company never shows its willingness to endure a strike, then the possibility of a strike or a lockout becomes a much less potent force in negotiations. Yet we have all witnessed strikes or other job actions that were clearly harmful to all involved and that occurred because a momentum was created by the overly direct application of this type of power. In the various international discussions about how to induce North Korea and Iran to change their policy on nuclear weapons development, we have seen this dilemma as well. How directly should sanctions be threatened or applied, given that they would almost certainly create a backlash? However, if there are no consequences for proceeding with a nuclear weapons program, why should these countries change their approach? One possible answer, of course, is to offer rewards for pursuing a different policy—an approach that has met with some success— but if these rewards are not very powerful they are not likely to be effective.

This raises the question of whether we can prepare for war and peace at the same time, so to speak. There are contradictions between putting our energy into collaborative conflict engagement efforts and at the same time preparing for an adversarial contest. For example, the more reticent negotiators are to share information, the more difficult it is for them to find creative solutions to contentious problems. But if negotiators readily share too much information, they can compromise their ability to prevail later in a legal forum. (I return to this issue when I discuss negotiation in Chapter Eight.) Nevertheless, people in conflict can and often must prepare to cooperate and to contest at the same time. If disputants do not develop their ability to be effective in an adversarial context, they often fail to give others a reason to work collaboratively with them. But if they are too preoccupied with preparing for an adversarial encounter, they will create a momentum that is hard to escape, and they will complicate the process of developing the rapport and establishing the communication necessary to work collaboratively. The art of engaging in a constructive conflict process depends in part on knowing how to balance these two needs. Although the idea that we cannot prepare for war and peace at the same time carries an important sentiment and value, it is a flawed concept if we are trying to understand how to engage in conflict effectively.

HOW POWER IS USED

Our sources of power are not the same as our uses of power. Regardless of from where our power derives, we have a choice about how to apply it. It is useful to consider three primary ways we can use power to try to influence others' behavior (and they ours). First, we can appeal to other people's values, beliefs, and best selves. By framing our persuasive efforts in terms of values and by making use of normative symbols, we can attempt to get others to comply with our wishes by convincing them that what we propose is the right and wise thing to do. This is often called the normative approach to the application of power. A second approach is to appeal to people's self-interest or to indicate that they will obtain certain tangible benefits if they do what we wish. This is sometimes referred to as the utilitarian approach. A third method is to try to force people to agree to something by threatening significant sanctions or by manipulating the external environment to take away their freedom of choice. This may be thought of as the coercive approach. Sometimes these three approaches are categorized as persuasion, reward, and punishment. Regardless of the terminology, these are key ways power is applied in conflict. (In this section I draw on the work of sociologist Amitai Etzioni, 1975, particularly his discussion of organizational compliance theory. For other somewhat similar descriptions of the ways people exercise power, see Deutsch, 1973; Gamson, 1968; Kriesberg, 1982.)

I want my son to mow the lawn, but he keeps putting it off. First, I talk about how he agreed to do this, how little he really has to do around the house, and how important it is for the health of the lawn. Next, I say that I will pay him an extra five dollars if he will get it done within twenty-four hours. Finally, I say that if he does not get it done by the end of the weekend, I will hire someone else to do the mowing, the fee will come out of his allowance, and I will also ground him for the following weekend. In this everyday example, we see the quick and to some extent consciously sequenced use of these different applications of power. We can see these same approaches in almost any conflict. Any time we talk about the "carrot and stick," we are referring to two of these approaches. If we add the option of personal affirmation or some other social reinforcement (sort of a scratch behind the ear, a carrot, and a stick), then we have all three applications of power.

How do environmentalists try to influence policymakers? First, they argue that what they advocate is the right thing to do for the planet and thus appeal to people's desire to do what is right. Second, they offer their political support and contributions. Third, they threaten lawsuits, direct action campaigns, or political retribution. We can look at almost any significant conflict and see the use of these three different ways of applying power.

Sometimes we can join these different approaches together, in effect saying, "Let's work together on this, it's the wisest approach; otherwise we will end up wasting all sorts of resources suing each other." Often, however, these approaches contradict or undercut each other. Should the United States try to promote democracy in Iran by offering Iran greater acceptance into the international community and a higher level of trade, or by threatening sanctions? A version of this issue has been debated for years (in regard to the USSR, China, South Africa [during Apartheid], Iraq, Libya, North Korea, and so on). To try to take normative, utilitarian, and coercive approaches at once is complicated (but sometimes unavoidable). Containment and constructive engagement are not very comfortable bedfellows. If a divorcing parent wants to discuss how to share parenting in the interests of the children, she or he is more likely to succeed using a normative, or persuasive, approach, emphasizing what is best for the children. To try to influence the other parent with financial incentives or threats of court action is likely to undercut the impact of the normative focus on the children's best interests. One of the most frequent dilemmas divorce mediators face arises when one parent tries to force the other to enter into a cooperative parenting agreement. Using coercion to set up a decision-making process that requires the use of normative forms of influence is seldom appropriate. I was once caught squarely in the middle of such a contradictory approach when I was trying, of all things, to provide training in collaborative decision making.

> The intention of the new school superintendent seemed admirable, even visionary. He wanted to introduce a more cooperative

management style to his district, so he asked a colleague and me to provide all his administrators and principals with training in conflict resolution and collaborative decision making. But he did not practice what he preached. When we arrived, we found that the administrators had been ordered by the superintendent to attend and that he had further directed each one to develop a plan for initiating a team management approach in his or her division or school. All this occurred without any discussion among the managers, the principals, and the superintendent. Furthermore, the seminar had been scheduled for the week before school began, a very challenging time for principals in particular.

Needless to say, we found ourselves in the middle of a significant contradiction, which we should have discovered before we arrived. Somehow we had to find a way to give participants an opportunity to consider the team management philosophy for themselves, independently of the pressure placed on them by their boss. We did this by using real issues that concerned the whole district as case studies and as material for simulations. Using the procedures and skills we presented, the administrators discussed how to allocate financial resources to different programs, how to come up with unified disciplinary policies, and how to take a coordinated approach to responding to parent complaints and staff grievances.

By conducting these problem-solving discussions around topics that engaged the administrators, we created a situation in which they were able to begin to think about the collaborative process on their own terms. This also required the superintendent, rather reluctantly, to reconsider his own management style, now obviously at odds with what he was promoting for his administrators. Despite trying to make the best of the situation, neither my colleague nor I felt confident that there was much immediate chance for real change in the district's approach to management and decision making.

I have seldom seen a coercive approach to instituting a cooperative management process work. Unless the primary motivation of most employees for engaging in new types of team structures is a commitment to these structures' underlying values and philosophy, these initiatives almost always fail.

Coercive approaches are sometimes necessary. People in positions of privilege seldom give away their advantages unless they are to some extent forced to do so. There are also times when normative or utilitarian approaches are inappropriate and disempowering. Stopping domestic violence, for example, usually requires, at least initially, some form of coercive intervention. The attempt to stop violence through rewarding people for changing their ways or through appealing to their values about human relations not only is ineffective but also can play into the cycle of violence.

INTEGRATIVE AND DISTRIBUTIVE POWER

When a sales tax was set to expire in Boulder, Colorado, a number of years ago, two groups saw a golden opportunity to fund important programs, and each one organized a petition campaign to extend the sales tax. One group wanted the money designated for park and recreational facilities, the other for human services programs. Each group at first tried very hard to organize support for its own proposal, from both elected officials and the public. But the more the groups organized, the more obvious it became that they were well on the way to defeating both initiatives. They therefore decided to work on a joint initiative, but given their history this was not easy. They asked me to mediate a joint proposal, and we succeeded in working out the terms of a joint initiative, which did get on the ballot.

Now, however, other groups, including the city council, felt that they were being left out; they organized against the measure, and it went down to a narrow defeat. This led to a wider dialogue that included business leaders, city officials, open space advocates, and others. For this dialogue to succeed, each group had to work hard to get beyond its tendency to advocate solely for its own cause, and to look at the wider picture—to "wear a very broad hat," as one participant put it. As they did this, the whole power dynamic completely changed. Instead of applying power against each other, they were now applying power to assist each other. In the end, as an outcome of further mediation, this expanded group agreed on a joint proposal that was overwhelmingly passed in an election at a time when many other tax proposals were soundly defeated.

These onetime disputants made an important transition in how they viewed and used their power. They started to apply power with each other rather than against each other, and they focused on using their power to augment each other's influence rather than to get their way at each other's expense. When people use their power to increase the overall influence of all the parties involved in a dispute or negotiation, they are applying their power in an *integrative* way. When they try to get their way by directing enough power at others to force a compromise or concession of some kind, then power is being applied in a *distributive* way.

Distributive applications of power are sometimes necessary. At times the only way to attain a satisfactory outcome is to do so at someone else's expense. There may be no more joint gains realistically available, and therefore, in order for one party to achieve greater benefits, another party needs to be induced to sacrifice something. But people in conflict tend to assume this is the situation; they do not fully explore the possibility of an integrative outcome. Thus disputants are often quick to apply distributive power, and this tends to escalate conflict. The challenge in many situations is to find ways to redirect disputants from thinking about distributive power and to focus them on their potential integrative power. In her seminal work on conflict, Mary Parker Follett (1940, p. 72) eloquently expressed this challenge: "It seems to me that whereas power usually means power-over, the power of some person or group over some other person or group, it is possible to develop the conception of power-with, a jointly developed power, a co-active, not a coercive power."

ESCALATION AND DE-ESCALATION

Conflict professionals tend to think that escalation is a dirty word. Our job is to help de-escalate conflict, to calm things down, to bring people to the negotiating table, and to encourage mutual understanding. Escalation tends to reduce communication, encourage negative attributions, and make cooperation more difficult to achieve. But as with the challenge of preparing for peace and war at the same time, we have to understand that escalation is sometimes necessary. If we are reflexively against escalation we will not be credible to people engaged in serious conflicts, and we won't be able to make wise decisions about handling our own conflicts either. Sometimes escalation is necessary—to make it in someone else's interest to take our concerns seriously, to bring an issue to the forefront of people's attention (see the discussion of Rosa Parks later in this chapter), or to respond effectively to others' destructive use of power.

The challenge is knowing when to escalate and how to escalate in a way that does not make future cooperation impossible. Sometimes it seems that when people decide to escalate a conflict they give up all thought or hope of ultimately bringing about a more constructive relationship. If we follow the maxim that we should treat adversaries as potential allies, we can consider what it means to escalate constructively. For one thing, we should always question whether escalation is wise. But if we think that it may be, we should consider how to escalate incrementally, proportionately, in a time-limited way, and in keeping with our own values. (For a fuller discussion of this, see Mayer, 2009b, pp.172–178.) One of the most valuable functions we can serve in working with others in conflict as either third parties or allies is to help them consider whether, when, and how to escalate. Sometimes our most valuable intervention occurs when we help people escalate strategically and with restraint.

The Power of Alternatives

To a large extent people's choices in conflict are determined by their power. The more resources, information, authority, or endurance an individual has, the more choices he or she has. But it is also true that power is defined by choices. Often the best way to enhance one's power is to develop better choices. (For an argument that this is the fundamental basis of all power in negotiations, see Korobkin, 2006; also see Fisher and Ury, 1981.) It is generally useful to develop alternatives to negotiated agreements and alternatives for negotiated agreements. That is, it is important for people to maximize the choices they have should the negotiation not result in a satisfactory agreement, and it is also important for people to create alternatives that can be brought to bear within the negotiation itself. Developing alternatives is not simply about having a way to opt out of a collaborative process; it is about making it more likely that collaboration will be successful.

Like the exercise of power, the development of choices can occur in a distributive or integrative manner. I can develop alternatives that give me leverage over others, or I can develop alternatives that make it more appealing for other people to work with me. Similarly, I can develop my alternatives independently of others or in concert with them.

Sometimes, by spending the time to both identify alternatives and put out the effort necessary to make them feasible, disputants can completely change the power relationship. That notion is behind this practical advice from a consumer service organization: "If you know how much markup is in a car's asking price, you're in a better position to ask for a discount. And if you know what you want, you needn't depend on advice from a salesperson who may be trying to push a high-profit or slow-selling model. . . . The surest way to get the best price is to shop for the same model at several dealerships. If you're armed with the invoice price, you should command more respect from the sales staff" ("New Cars," 1999, pp. 16–17).

POWER AND SOCIAL JUSTICE

Developing collaborative approaches to conflict and promoting social justice are not the same thing. One of the major criticisms of mediation and related cooperative approaches to conflict is that they do not necessarily promote social justice or protect the disempowered. Unless all the involved players have sufficient power to represent themselves effectively, a collaborative process can easily result in an unjust conclusion. This concern has been raised in many different contexts. Advocates for victims of domestic violence have been concerned that mediation may lead to further victimization. Community activists have worried that negotiation with developers may become a means of co-optation. Environmentalists have been afraid that policy dialogues may ease the pressure on industries to improve their performance and may also undercut the rigor of regulatory enforcement. Whether and how to negotiate with dictators have been major points of political debate.

There is no doubt that many of these concerns are well taken and that cooperative efforts can lead to unfair results, just like any other decision-making process. Certain circumstances call more for political or community organizing than for participation in collaborative processes. One version of a mediator's nightmare, I have long thought, would be getting plunked down in Montgomery, Alabama, in 1956 to resolve the dispute between Rosa Parks and the Montgomery bus company. What was important about the Montgomery bus boycott was that it became a rallying point for the nascent civil rights movement. Only after the advocates of integration had organized themselves, obtained widespread demonstrations of public support, and raised the issue to the national stage did it make sense to try seriously to resolve the dispute. After a year of a successful boycott of the bus services, massive publicity and public support for Montgomery's African American community, and clear proof that African Americans could challenge the white power structure, the power dynamics had undergone a monumental change. When the leaders of the boycott had developed enough support and power to obtain the kind of outcome they wanted, they, the bus company officials, and the city leaders did participate in discussions, which were organized by the churches of Montgomery. A negotiated agreement was then reached that ended the discriminatory policies of the bus system. This was a crucial step in building the civil rights movement and furthering the cause of social justice.

Collaborative efforts are not the enemy of struggles for social justice, but neither are they movements for social change in themselves. An important consideration is whether such efforts are in some way impeding unempowered individuals' or groups' access to sources of power that they might otherwise have. There are two ways in which they may do this. First, they may deter people from choosing approaches that might give them access to more power. For example, if a victim of domestic violence chooses to negotiate an agreement rather than seek the protection of a court order, she or he might end up in a less powerful and more dangerous position. Second, they may lead people to seek a solution before they have developed their own power to a fuller level, as could have occurred in Montgomery.

It is important to view these possibilities in context, however. Movements for social justice and individual empowerment unfold in many different ways. Progress is intermittent and characterized by frequent setbacks. Unions have often had to settle for minor gains after hard struggles to maintain support from members or simply to survive. Environmentalists have sometimes decided to participate in lopsided processes because the alternative was to have no voice at all. Victims of domestic violence have often chosen to sacrifice many things to which they might have a legal right because what they needed most was a quick and relatively safe way out of the relationship. There are times when movements grow by collaborating in the short run to consolidate some gains and encourage people to continue a longer-term struggle.

These decisions may have been far from ideal, but they may also have been the best that could be achieved given the political, personal, and financial resources of the less powerful party. This is not to justify the social situation that created this choice. But sometimes a collaborative process is the optimal way for individuals or groups to choose among the limited options they realistically have, even if all of these options are poor. However, there are also times when it is better to sacrifice modest immediate gains to better enable a longer-term organizing effort than to cooperate prematurely for token gains.

The national debate about health care policy that occurred in the United States in 2009 exemplified both strategies. For the most part, members of the Republican Party decided not to participate in a cooperative approach to policy development, believing that this stance would better set them up for longer-term political gain, whereas the Democratic Party opted to accept a plan that was far from ideal in the eyes of many of its activists but that provided some significant gains and perhaps set a new platform for the next level of struggle around health care policy.

None of this means that the conflict intervention field is ethically neutral about social change. Built into the underlying philosophy and approach of most practitioners is the notion that people who are empowered to assert their interests in a collaborative yet forceful manner are able to advocate for themselves effectively and to make good decisions about complex problems. From the empowerment of individuals, socially constructive outcomes will ensue. This implies a belief in and a commitment to *deep democracy* as a foundation for social and personal change. Building this deep democratic foundation means providing not only a format for democratic decision making but also the tools and skills to make such decision making a vital part of people's everyday lives. It means giving people access to a significant voice in all the major decisions that affect their lives. For this kind of democracy to be a reality, people need to be protected from oppression, coercion, and violence from those in more powerful positions. Conflict intervention as a field is thus implicitly and usually explicitly committed to empowering people as individuals and to extending democracy and freedom from oppression to everyone.

Power is a complex phenomenon that operates in many often contradictory ways. The use of power can escalate or de-escalate a conflict. It can create resistance or overcome it. People can employ their power to create momentum for constructive dialogue and collaborative negotiations, or they can use it to accomplish their goals in the face of resistance and even to prevent cooperation. Everyone in a conflict has choices about how to use power and how to respond to power. But there is one choice none of us has, whether we are disputants, mediators, or decision makers—we cannot choose to have no power.

Everyone brings power to a conflict. Everyone also brings a set of values, beliefs, and approaches that are rooted in his or her culture. To complete an understanding of the nature of conflict it is necessary to consider the impact of culture on the individuals involved in a dispute and on the conflict process itself.

CHAPTER FOUR

CULTURE AND CONFLICT

Sometimes we are blind to the impact of culture on the conflicts we are dealing with, and sometimes we are overwhelmed by it. Even though culture is the medium within which conflict plays out, to most of us it is as invisible as the air we breathe. As a result it is often easy for us to overlook the critical role cultural norms and practices play in creating conflict, affecting its course, and influencing the way we try to deal with it. Conversely, when we do focus on culture, it is easy to view it as the overarching determinant of what will occur. As conflict interveners, we often feel hopeless about altering the ways disputants from different cultures approach conflict. When we view a particularly destructive approach to conflict as being rooted in cultural practices, we may feel powerless to change its course. We also often have a difficult time distinguishing the impact of culture from the dynamics of dominance.

Part of the challenge arises from how we think about culture and conflict. We often focus on the many culturally based differences in how people approach conflict that have the potential to exacerbate a conflict or make communication more difficult. We tend not to look at the similarities or continuities among different cultures, or at how differences can actually benefit us over the course of a conflict. And it is not just the difficulties that different cultural practices put in the way of communication that are instructive but also the ways in which people transcend those difficulties as they work across cultural boundaries to handle conflict productively. The truly amazing thing is not that cultural differences intensify conflict but that people so often manage to relate and communicate well across cultures, often under very difficult circumstances.

Although conflict theorists have given a great deal of thought to the interplay of conflict and culture and much has been written about how conflict plays out in different cultural settings, our understanding of how to deal with cross-cultural conflict is still underdeveloped. The challenge we face is to take the enormous impact of culture on conflict into account without becoming either overly deterministic (culture determines conflict behavior) or relativistic (everything—values, behavior, communication, and needs—varies by culture). Cultural norms and practices are critical forces in conflict, but culture does not tell the whole tale. Furthermore, each culture contains many subcultures, and each subculture contains many groups. Each has a different set of values, customs, and views about conflict, just as does each of us as an individual. And culture is not static. Just as culture affects the course of conflict, conflict affects culture.

WHAT IS CULTURE?

What do we really mean when we refer to culture? We speak of organizational culture; gender culture; the culture of a region, community, or town; generational culture; and of course ethnic culture, among others. For our purposes, culture may be considered as the enduring norms, values, customs, historical narratives, and behavioral patterns common to a particular group of people. In this sense each of us belongs to multiple and overlapping cultures, a situation that creates internal conflict at times. Which cultural identification we are most influenced by at any particular moment depends on the context and the nature of the interaction in which we are involved. One prominent approach to understanding culture and conflict suggests that culture is best understood as residing in the changing and evolving set of discourses that individuals adopt or operate on the basis of as they interact with others (Winslade and Monk, 2008). This approach to culture emphasizes the histories we create, the values embedded in how we communicate with each other, and the stories about who we are that are constantly changing and that we cocreate with those we are communicating with. For example, as a U.S. citizen living in Canada, the degree of my "Canadianness" depends on whom I am talking with and in what context. Interestingly, the more I am in a Canadian context, the more the U.S. element of my identity tends to be prevalent; the more I am in the United States, the more my Canadian affiliation seems paramount. But it also depends on what kind of conversation I am engaged in, what values or customs are being articulated or enacted, and which self seems most significant to me at the moment.

The overlapping pattern formed by all these cultures, our cultural matrix, affects our behavior in conflict and our ability to handle conflict. However, our own cultural patterns are often invisible to us because we experience these as a natural part of our environment. We therefore generally act within the confines of our cultural matrix without an awareness that this matrix strongly affects our perceptions of ourselves, of others, and of our behavior in conflict—as participants or as third parties.

CULTURAL VARIABLES AND CONTINUITIES

Perhaps the most essential challenge in working across cultures in conflict is to recognize that the presumptions we have about what is normative behavior in conflict are just that—presumptions. We tend to believe that what we consider logical, appropriate, even moral in dealing with conflict and communication are universal beliefs and therefore that deviations from these are signs of bad faith, bad character, or bad training. For example, if we ask someone whether we have upset him or her in some way, and we are assured that we have not, we may feel that a universally held norm of behavior has been violated when we later find out that this person has complained to others about our behavior. We may not understand that the question itself could have violated a behavioral norm, or that to have told us to our face that we did upset him or her might have been deemed profoundly disrespectful. Unless we have some handle on how to deconstruct the beliefs about conflict interactions under which we operate, we will find it very difficult to appreciate just how powerful an influence culture can be on our approach to conflict. And yet we can overdo this as well and assume that everything is contextual and culturally derivative, leaving us without a clear sense of how to handle ourselves in a cross-cultural context (which increasingly is just about every context).

It is useful to consider the variables that can help us look at different cultural norms and practices concerning conflict, as well as the continuities or similarities that exist among most cultures and that are the basis for successful cross-cultural communication and conflict engagement. It is clearly debatable (and often debated) to what extent these continuities stem from human nature; the common characteristics of the economic, social, and physical environment of most cultures; the increasing impact of a global culture; the high degree of intercultural interaction; or the structure of conflict itself. For conflict interveners, however, the more important questions are practical ones—How can we recognize the most significant cultural variables in how conflict is understood and approached that may not be obvious to us? How can we identify the common values and approaches that can assist us in working across cultural boundaries?

No culture is characterized by one specific conflict style that all its members exhibit. Because individuals differ, each culture will contain a range of behaviors and approaches to conflict. But different cultures do have different norms about conflict behavior, and acceptable behavior in one culture may be deviant in another. For example, in a typical middle-class American community one is likely to encounter a conflict style that tends to be direct, ostensibly rational, and linear. In contrast, many other cultures have a style that tends to be indirect, emotional, and intuitive. This does not mean that everyone in these cultures has these typical characteristics, or that these characteristics are operative at all times and under all circumstances. Rather, this suggests three important considerations: first, although the same *range* of individual styles might be found in almost all cultures, the *distribution* of these styles varies, so that compared to some other cultures, the middle-class American community has a greater percentage of people whose approach to conflict tends to be direct, rational, and linear; second, the norms of each culture *reinforce* one conflict style over other styles; and third, the behavior that predominates in a conflict *usually* exhibits certain characteristics. Some cultures may suppress individual differences more than others or provide harsher sanctions for exhibiting behaviors different from those acceptable according to the dominant social norms or enforced by a dominant group. Moore and Woodrow refer to the dominant constellation of cultural norms and practices in a particular culture as the "culture cluster" (2010, p. 6). No matter how well defined or dominant a particular cluster is, however, a range of approaches to conflict exists in all societies, even if some of these approaches are more circumscribed or undercover. This is one important continuity across cultures—each handles conflict in a multiplicity of ways.

The existence of a range of styles inside a culture is often essential to promoting effective interactions among individuals from different cultures, especially those involving conflict. In each cultural grouping, certain individuals exhibit a conflict and communication style that either varies in some significant ways from that group's normative style and is closer to the "cluster" of other groups, or is emblematic of an ability to use a broader range of styles. These individuals can therefore act as natural *translators* or as *bridges* to other cultures. Furthermore, because of this range of approaches, every culture has some experience in dealing with different styles, even those it labels deviant. The more rigid a culture and the less it allows different approaches to be employed or different values to be openly articulated, the less experience and the fewer translators it will have to assist in resolving conflict with individuals or groups operating from different cultural norms. For the same reason, a more constrained and rigid culture—whether or not it is the dominant one in the conflict setting—will have more difficulty dealing with cross-cultural conflict than one that is more tolerant and acknowledging of its own diversity. It is notable that the most enduring empires have been those that allowed different cultures to flourish under their jurisdiction.

Conflict analysts have suggested a range of variables to describe different cultural approaches to conflict. Moore and Woodrow (2010) offer a conflict map that suggests eight key variables in how different cultures might approach conflict. They discuss the critical importance of different views of outcomes, relationships, competition and cooperation, communication, time and space, participation, third parties, and the overall purpose of negotiation. The development and expression of these variables are significantly influenced by the natural environment, history, and social structures of the culture. Social psychologist Geert Hofstede (1991) suggests five dimensions for understanding cultural differences: power distance; uncertainty avoidance; and individual/collectivist, masculine/feminine, and long-term/short-term orientations. Other variables that have been offered to characterize different cultural approaches to conflict include orientations toward nature and human nature, social relations, high- and low-context communication styles, and the complexity of social identity, to name a few (Brewer and Pierce, 2005; Hall and Hall, 1990; Kimmel, 2006; Kluchohn and Strodtbeck, 1961; Pedersen, 2006).

Any of these variables can offer important insights into the impact of culture (and gender) on conflict. But it is also easy to become overwhelmed by the sheer number of variables that we might want to consider. So let's look further at three of these concepts, which I have found particularly useful because they seem to reflect communication styles and relationships that I have observed in many different cultural contexts. These three variables are especially useful in understanding what happens when people from different cultural backgrounds engage in a conflictual interaction.

- *High-and low-context cultures.* Have you ever experienced a group interaction in which everyone seemed to understand what was being said or why something was funny—except for you? When a significant part of the communication is implied or understood rather than expressed overtly, a high-context interaction is occurring. When the predominant meaning is directly and overtly expressed, the interaction is low-context. Some settings are characterized by high-context interactions (many indigenous groups or adolescent peer groups), and others are more likely to employ low-context communication (large-business or court settings). Moore and Woodrow describe this concept as follows: "In high-context cultures, communication and much of the rest of human interaction is highly contextualized—in other words, the ways that people talk and deal with each other are culturally coded and dependent on prescribed patterns of relationships that in many cases are obscure to the outsider. . . . Communications among people . . . are often imprecise, nuanced, and oriented toward saving face, preserving relationships, and allowing flexibility. . . . People in low-context cultures are much more explicit in speech and action. Discussions are more overt, detailed, specific, and clear" (Moore and Woodrow, 2010, pp. 49–50).

One of the challenges we face in working across cultures is to decode context in order to translate forms of communication that are often much higher-context than we realize into more explicit or low-context forms.

- *Power distance.* Our beliefs about what amount of power differential is acceptable in different contexts is a reflection of what Hofstede (1991) refers to as power distance. Low-power-distance cultures, on the one hand, value equality in communication, decision making, social status, and access to power. High-power-distance cultures, on the other hand, are ones in which those with less power accept the differential of power and the right of people in authority, of elders, or of leaders to make decisions without the same level of participation from those with less power. In the public culture of the United States, Canada, and much of Europe, there is an implicit assumption that we deserve to be consulted about and have input in the decisions that affect our lives. A position of leadership and authority is not assumed to give someone the unilateral right to make decisions without consultation. The developing field of public participation is organized to provide assistance in just how to do this. And this belief underlies much of the work done in the conflict field as well. For the most part, conflict practitioners operate from a low-power-distance set of assumptions. But in high-power-distance cultures a much more deferential approach to those in power characterizes how input can occur and how decisions ought to be made.

I often observed, when I worked in Eastern Europe in the years immediately after the fall of Communism, that one of the most important values Westerners seemed to bring, often without realizing it, was the belief that public officials could be held accountable, lobbied, and asked to listen. At the time I thought of this as "procedural entitlement"—as Westerners, we feel we have the right to a fair process, whereas many of the people we worked with, who had lived under a dictatorship for most of their lives, did not operate from this set of assumptions. In family contexts, some cultures presume the right of elders to make decisions for their family and children (for example, whom they will marry), but most of us who have grown up in the United States, Canada, or Western Europe operate from a much more egalitarian set of values about family roles.

- *Linearity.* Many of us like to think in stages: stages of development, stages of mediation, negotiation, facilitation, and problem solving. We assume that the best way to communicate is to focus on one issue at a time, for one person to speak at a time, and to attend to one task at a time. Others are more comfortable with (and may prefer) juggling many tasks at once, circling through a discussion of many different aspects of many different issues, and approaching problem solving in a nonlinear, more intuitive, or at least less structured way. This has sometimes been identified as a polychronic as opposed to a monochronic approach to time (Hall, 1959; Hall and Hall, 1990).

   Of course, most of us have a range of linear versus circular communication styles that we are able to adopt in different circumstances. But there are different cultural norms about how linear or nonlinear it is appropriate to be under various circumstances. One source of cross-cultural tension can arise when people from more polychronic cultures are forced to engage in more monochronic or linear communication (for example, when people from an indigenous background have to deal with the court system, with hospitals, with banks, or with government agencies).

When we are engaged in cross-cultural conflict, as participants or interveners, the factors which seem most cogent to us and that best assist us in understanding how different cultural patterns may be operating may vary considerably. But what seems essential in almost all contexts is for us to remain aware of the fact that our norms and beliefs about conflict and communication are rooted in our own cultural experience and are not necessarily normative for other individuals or in other cultural contexts. To maintain a perspective on this, it is helpful to consider some of the unspoken norms and approaches we take to conflict and to remind ourselves that these are not necessarily universal.

However, we should not fall into the relativistic trap. There are continuities among most cultures, and these are what help us bridge what sometimes appear to be enormous cultural differences. So although it is important to be aware of the differences that might exist and to be sensitive about either assuming our approach to be universal or imposing our way of addressing conflict on others, the worst response to this awareness would be to avoid engaging with others with whom we may have conflicts because we are intimidated by our differences in approach.

The wheel of conflict presented in Chapter One (Figure 1.1) offers an approach for understanding both the impact of culture on conflict and the relationship between cultural variables and cross-cultural continuities. Roughly speaking, the closer to the center of the wheel we look, the more cross-cultural continuities we will find, and the more we focus on the perimeter, the more cultures will vary. The more we focus on the genuine human needs at the core of conflict, the more we will see patterns that are constant across cultures. As we shift our view toward the surrounding dynamics and move further away from a focus on human needs, the differences among cultures become more dramatic. Cultural gaps are best bridged when people find a mechanism to focus on the fundamental needs at the heart of a conflict. Let's consider each element of the wheel from this perspective.

NEEDS

Needs are the key area of continuity across cultures. All humans have survival needs. In all conflicts, disputants have interests. We all have identity needs. People understand their needs in very different ways, and the ways in which these needs are expressed and addressed vary tremendously. For example, in some contexts identity needs are mostly experienced as individual concerns, but in others the experience of meaning and purpose is a more collective phenomenon. But the needs themselves are for the most part universally present in one form or another. One key to reaching out across cultures is to understand how people experience and satisfy these needs in their cultural context.

EMOTIONS

It is not uncommon for people from one culture to believe that those from a different background lead emotional lives that are entirely different from their own. Many people seem to think that someone who comes from a very different background is unlikely to respond to conflict or loss with the same range of emotions that they do. In fact, human beings across a wide range of cultures exhibit similar emotional responses. If people are insulted or attacked, they respond with anger or fear. If they experience a major loss, they grieve. If they accomplish something very important to them, they rejoice. For all practical purposes, people from different cultures experience the same range of emotions in conflict, and for conflict to be dealt with, mechanisms for the release and validation of feelings are necessary.

But which emotions are considered acceptable and how they may be expressed vary tremendously. In some cultural contexts any overt display of strong feelings violates important norms, and therefore feelings either are suppressed or are expressed only subtly and indirectly. In others the ability to express emotions strongly and dramatically is valued. Expressing anger or upset may be more or less acceptable than expressing excitement or love. In some contexts it is accepted that emotions can change rapidly and that there is no loss of face in expressing a feeling and then letting it go. In other settings the expression of strong emotions is more likely to lead to a serious loss of face or a permanent change in a relationship. This is related to how acceptable it is to acknowledge the existence of a conflict at all.

COMMUNICATION

Given the extreme variations in the ways people communicate, which depend on age, gender, ethnicity, and other factors, it is amazing that we ever understand each other at all. People from different cultures vary in how directly they communicate, how they use verbal and nonverbal cues, how they develop rapport, and how long they take to establish a personal connection before moving to substantive discussions. Their communication may vary in pace, in loudness, in whether it tends to be linear and sequential or circular and multifocused, and so forth.

We are aware of many of these differences. They fuel much of our humor and literature. From Mark Twain to Garrison Keillor, American humorists have used stereotypes about the ways people from different cultural backgrounds communicate and interact to create vivid characters and to poke fun at human foibles (or consider such movies as *Annie Hall, Borat,* or *My Big Fat Greek Wedding*). Outlandish though these depictions may be, they demonstrate the wide variation in communication styles, the stereotyping that occurs as a result, and the difficulty this causes in handling issues that arise across cultures.

One way of understanding cultural differences in communication is to look at the themes that underlie people's varying styles of communication. We find these in people's metaphors and narrative style and in the worldview these imply. This method of understanding provided a colleague and me with the key to overcoming an impasse when we were asked to mediate a dispute between a Native American group and a large corporation.

> The disputants could have been speaking two different languages (and maybe in a sense they were), given how little each seemed to understand of what the other was saying. The Native Americans, who were representatives of the tribal government, and the corporation, which had a large facility located on tribal land, had many common interests and a lot to offer each other, but every time they communicated the conflict seemed to escalate. The members of the Native American group employed a normative or value-based style of communication; they focused on their identity needs, particularly on the importance of preserving the tribe's sense of autonomy and community. Their language was full of references to the tribe's sovereignty, its dignity, and its efforts to preserve the Native American heritage in the face of continuous pressure to conform to the business and legal practices of white, middle-class America. The corporation used a more utilitarian, or interest-based, style of communication. Its representatives were outcome

focused, concentrating on what made "business sense" for both groups. Their language was replete with references to "sound business practices," "mutual economic advantage," "costs and benefits," and so forth.

Each group, in its own way, was trying to understand and address the other's concerns, but this was not working. When the business representatives discussed their interests, the Native Americans felt that their culture and values were being dismissed and that they were being urged to sacrifice their heritage for money. When the Native Americans discussed their identity concerns, the corporate representatives felt that they would never "get real" and focus on the issues that had to be resolved. They felt that they could spend forever listening to and validating the cultural concerns of the Native Americans but that they would never get around to working on the business questions that were important to them.

The key to our getting a handle on this case was to listen to the language and terminology that each group kept using. The differences were dramatic. So after listening to both sides long enough to get a feel for the communication obstacles, we shared our observations with both groups. We expressed our sense that the members of one group were communicating about their values and the members of the other about their business concerns, and we suggested that both were important. We also very explicitly discussed the different types of language they were using. This seemed to strike home for both groups. Their challenge, we said, was to understand and acknowledge both issues in language that made sense to each other. We discussed with the groups how they might do this. I am sure these communication styles continue to this day to pose challenges to their relationship. But during this particular interaction they displayed some understanding of their different approaches to communication and were able to translate from one communication style to another well enough to draft a set of proposals to take back to their respective leadership.

Individuals from different cultures communicate their thinking in very different ways during conflict. In some cultures meaning is conveyed through stories, anecdotes, metaphors, and comparisons. Others use logic and analysis. In other cultures so-called objective presentations, heavily loaded with facts, charts, supporting documentation, and the symbols of professionalism, are highly valued.

But there are many cultures in which such an approach appears cold, manipulative, and unreal. In these cultures the personality, values, life experience, and commitment of the speaker are the keys to establishing credibility.

These communication challenges can be present when people are talking in the same language, but when their languages are different there is an added dimension of complexity. The structure of language varies greatly. For example, Americans tend to use the conditional tense much more than is usual among people in parts of Europe. To certain Europeans, therefore, Americans often sound as if they are beating around the bush, whereas to Americans Europeans sometimes seem rude and blunt. This is to some extent a result of their respective languages. Words that have similar meanings in different languages often have very different emotional impacts. When people must communicate through translators, the richness, nuances, and emotional complexity of a message can easily be lost, and the intent of the speaker can easily be misinterpreted.

With all these differences in how people communicate, it is easy to overlook the commonalities. The most basic constant is that everyone fundamentally wants to be understood and will usually respond well to others who are making genuine, respectful efforts to grasp what is being said. In fact, even in conflict, people will usually try to help each other understand and be understood. If they sense that others are sincerely trying to listen and to connect, people will usually try to find ways to clarify, explain, or simplify to facilitate communication. In the middle of a conflict the need for this can be exasperating, and it is easy for people to doubt each other's sincerity of purpose, but the natural desire to understand and be understood often comes through even under very difficult circumstances.

VALUES

Basic value differences can cause conflict among cultures, including differences in values about conflict itself. Three types of culturally specific values about conflict are important to consider: values concerning content, process, and outcome. Content values concern the subject of the conflict itself. About what kinds of issues is it appropriate to engage in conflict? For example, in some cultures it is fine to argue openly about religion and politics, but in others it is considered inappropriate and disrespectful (and of course it can be dangerous). Process values concern how conflict is conducted. How should issues be raised, and with whom? Is it all right to raise a conflict directly with an elder or a superior? Should one negotiate with one's subordinates? How transparent should disputants be about their feelings, thoughts, and plans? When should they suggest solutions? Outcome values suggest what kinds of results are acceptable. Do people value compromise, collaboration, winning, or self-sacrifice?

Despite the many differences in values, disputants almost always share values as well. These concurrences of values can be links that help people get beyond their differences. Some values are almost universal, but any two cultures are also likely to share many values that are less widely held. For example, consider the Smiths and the Nelsons, who had very significant value differences about who should rear Jonah, but who were able to overcome these as they began to realize they also shared some very important common values.

Jonah, a half–Asian American, half–African American boy, was four years old when his parents' rights were terminated as the result of a history of severe abuse and neglect. He had been placed for two years with the Smiths, Caucasian foster parents who now wanted to adopt him. Shortly before the adoption process entered its final stages, the Nelsons, a maternal aunt and her husband, who had previously been unknown to the adoption agency, were located. They said that they were interested in adopting Jonah. A study of the Nelsons by the adoption agency indicated that this African American couple was also able to provide Jonah with a good home. The Nelsons felt very strongly that they should be given preference because they were relatives, and because they shared a racial identity with Jonah. The Smiths were equally adamant about the importance of keeping Jonah in the only stable home he had ever had. The differences between the families were reflected in similar discussions among the staff members of the adoption agency. This had the makings of a very destructive and potentially protracted court battle. The conflict was referred to me for mediation. Because of the ethnic issues involved, I co-mediated it with an African American colleague of mine.

Whenever the Nelsons and the Smiths discussed the relative importance of biological family, race, and continuity of care, they found themselves in deep conflict. They simply did not agree, and their different values about these issues were a source of great contention. But there were two very important unifying factors. One was that both couples cared deeply about Jonah. The other was that they shared many more values than they disputed. Both were very committed to children, marriage, and family. Both took a hard line against the use of drugs and alcohol. Both were very religious. In mediation they were able to see that their value differences were more about priorities than about fundamental disagreements. That is, all felt that Jonah needed continuity, stability, and connection with his biological family. All felt that racial identity was an important issue. When they were able to find a way of talking about and sharing their common values, they were able to begin to relate to each other more effectively. Eventually an interim agreement was reached. During the time this agreement was active, the Nelsons visited with Jonah, with the participation of the Smiths. As time went on the Nelsons took on the role of aunt and uncle, and an agreement about ongoing contact was worked out. In the end the Smiths adopted Jonah, but the Nelsons assumed an active role in his life.

STRUCTURE

All cultures establish structures for handling conflict, but these structures can be very dissimilar. People accustomed to one structure may feel alienated or exploited when they are forced to use a very different one. Some cultures promote a democratic and rights-based approach to dealing with conflict, whereas others use a more hierarchical and power-based approach. Cultures vary in the degree to which they rely on systems rooted in formal authority and position, compared to systems focused on personal prestige and influence. They also differ in whether they have mechanisms for counteracting differences in power and prestige, or whether they believe that such differentials form a legitimate basis for determining outcomes. Some societies have well-established legal systems that can be accessed relatively easily to address conflicts. Other societies have few such formal structures, and those that exist are widely mistrusted.

Despite structural differences, there are important and sometimes surprising cultural continuities. Almost all cultures have some type of rights-based framework within which certain types of conflict can be handled. They also always have informal mechanisms for handling conflict. Even in societies like the United States that have highly developed formal structures for addressing conflicts, the vast majority of disputes are handled on an informal basis. Without the natural mechanisms for conflict resolution that are embedded in families, communities, and other small-group structures, any formal system would be quickly overwhelmed. When investigating how conflict is handled in different cultural contexts, one can usually start by asking two key questions: What are the formal and informal mechanisms for addressing conflict? And what are the structural inducements to use—and obstacles to using—those mechanisms?

HISTORY

Cultures are not bound by their historical patterns, but how conflict is handled in a particular cultural context often cannot be understood without an appreciation of the historical experiences with conflict of those who are part of that culture. In the countries that emerged from the former Soviet Union and its satellite states, even as people adjust to a more democratic and participatory approach to decision making, it is easy to see the impact of a long history of centralized, hierarchical, and often repressive means for handling conflict. The impact of the Holocaust on Jewish cultural attitudes toward conflict is profound. It affects attitudes toward conflict engagement, avoidance, compromise, and social justice, among other things. All cultures carry with them historical experiences about what works in conflict and what does not, and what the likely outcomes of conflict might be. In the history of most cultures there are key events that have come to symbolize cultural values and beliefs about conflict. In understanding cultural approaches to conflict, it is important to understand both the general historical context and the key events that form the common cultural memory or experience of conflict.

History also can provide the bridge by which different cultures can begin to understand each other better. Different cultures often share certain historical experiences. When I worked in Poland a number of years ago, I was very grateful when some of my colleagues there took me on a tour of the Warsaw ghetto. My Polish associates and I were all children or grandchildren of people who had suffered very much at the hands of the Nazis. This element of shared history was an important bond, despite the fact that they and I had grown up in completely different circumstances. Even when individuals from different cultural groups have very little shared history, the process of learning about each other's past and the ways this history has influenced each party's approach to communication and conflict can be an important tool for building increased understanding among them.

A WORD ABOUT GENDER

Gender differences are not the same as cultural differences. Gender cuts across almost all cultures. There is virtually always a significant power dimension to the different ways in which men and women approach conflict. Although many people may not have much experience relating to very different cultures, all of us have considerable experience with gender differences. And then there is biology. There is considerable literature devoted to gender, conflict, and communication (see, for example, Kanter, 1977; Kolb, Williams, and Frohlinger, 2004; Tannen, 1990). Much of this emphasizes the different approaches men and women take toward cooperation and competition, communication and conversation, and individual and collective orientations. Clearly many of the variables that can be used to understand different cultural approaches to conflict can also be used to understand gender characteristics as well.

Just as belonging to a culture does not automatically mean that someone behaves according to the dominant norms about conflict that are characteristic of that culture, one's gender does not determine one's approach to communication or conflict either. But as with culture, gender provides a (more or less influential, more or less conscious) normative framework for our thoughts and actions. As with all differences among individual approaches to conflict, gender poses the challenge of deconstructing our assumptions so that we don't automatically believe that what is normative for our approach is normative for the approaches of others. Sociolinguist Deborah Tannen popularized the concept of "rapport talk" and "report talk": "For most women, the language of conversation is primarily a language of rapport: a way of establishing connections and negotiating relationships. Emphasis is placed on displaying similarities and matching experiences. . . . For most men, talk is primarily a means to preserve independence and negotiate and maintain status in a hierarchical social order. This is done by exhibiting knowledge and skill, and by holding center stage through verbal performance such as story-telling, joking, or imparting information" (Tannen, 1990, p. 77).

One manifestation of how this affects conflict can be seen when women raise concerns with male colleagues, say about an unequal division of workload. According to Tannen's concept, the most important thing a woman might want from this communication would be for her colleague to understand her concerns, sympathize with her, and relate to her. But for the man, the more important task might be to come up with a solution, address the problem, or offer advice. In this way, his best-intentioned efforts to be responsive can end up increasing the tension between them. In one way or another we have all experienced such interactions whenever we have felt that the other person "missed the point." The most important element of this challenge is to recognize that many different assumptions about an appropriate response to conflict coexist and to not assume that one approach is superior or natural for everyone.

A separate question is how to understand the norms of different cultures about gender and gender roles in conflict. Particularly important is the approach that different cultures take to power differentials between men and women. In some cultures men are assumed to be in charge of decision making, and this belief governs at least the formal ways in which conflicts are dealt with. In other circumstances women are granted equal rights in decision making and in conflict (at least in theory), but are expected to conduct themselves in accordance with male norms. Cultural contexts in which male and female styles of engaging in conflict are equally valued and supported may be fewer, but evolution in that direction is discernable, if slow.

We should not make the mistake of thinking that women for the most part have one style, men another. All of us are individuals, and men have a need for rapport talk just as women have a need for report talk, for example. Gender may incline us in one direction or another, and we have often been socialized in different gender groups, but women and men, as humans, have the same basic needs. The question that gender poses is not about our fundamental needs but about the messages and skills we have each learned concerning how to meet these needs.

Handling Culture in Conflict

Given all the different ways culture influences people's interactions in conflict, how does it happen that most of us normally succeed in overcoming these differences? Although cultural differences breed conflict and complicate communication under many circumstances, most of the time people bridge these gaps fairly well. Despite the publicity and focus that is so often placed on ethnic conflict, in most parts of the world different ethnic groups are able to work through their differences well enough to live, work, and play side by side. International commercial negotiations are successful across many diverse cultures. Spouses from different cultural backgrounds find a means to handle conflicts. Diverse workplaces succeed as employees and managers learn to handle conflicts well despite the different ways they have been socialized toward conflict. There are several sometimes paradoxical approaches that help people handle cultural differences successfully.

Cultural Sensitivity and Cultural Obliviousness

Being attuned and open to ethnic, class, gender, and other cultural differences can be essential to handling conflict effectively. Conflict engagement is a continuous learning process that in part involves becoming familiar with other people's cultural norms and beliefs about conflict and communication. The more open and respectful disputants are about the approaches others take to dealing with conflict, the more successful they will be in dealing with conflict across cultures. Increasing one's cross-cultural awareness and competence is a lifelong challenge.

However, sometimes people handle cultural differences best by ignoring them and reaching out on a simple person-to-person basis, focusing on the individual rather than the culture. Sometimes being too focused on cultural issues or differences can undercut a person's basic ability to interact with others. Our desire to connect with others is a fundamental human trait. We are social beings. An overemphasis on cultural differences, particularly on the part of someone from a dominant culture, can feel patronizing and controlling. Moreover, if we are too fearful of violating some norm or custom of which we are unaware, we may be inhibited from reaching out or using the intuitive interpersonal skills that normally serve us well. The ideal is for conflict participants to synthesize these two approaches, to be both sensitive to and respectful of cultural differences and to relate to each other as individuals, not just as carriers of particular cultural patterns.

FOCUSING ON ONE'S OWN CULTURE TO LEARN ABOUT ANOTHER

I did not really understand English grammar until I studied a foreign language. Similarly, I do not think people can really understand their own culture until they spend time in a different one. Unless someone has something with which to contrast his or her patterns of behavior and beliefs, it is hard to recognize what these are and to understand how culturally specific they may be. In learning to deal with conflict in other cultures, the first key is to recognize the conflict patterns that characterize our own. Once we can identify the many different cultural norms about conflict from which we operate, it is easier for us to become aware of how our norms might differ from those of others. A good place to start is by looking at our beliefs about conflict and communication and asking just how universal these are. For example, consider some of these norms that many of us hold:

- *Transparency:* If we have a concern or a disagreement, we should not beat around the bush; rather, we should find an effective way to raise the issue. But for some cultures transparency is less important than harmony, saving face, and preserving relationships.

- *Open-mindedness:* We should remain open to other points of view and consider different ways of achieving our goals. But in some cultural contexts open-mindedness is equated with moral relativism or weakness.

- *Equality:* Everyone deserves to be treated with respect, and the same standards of fairness should apply to everyone. But in many cultural contexts different standards of respect and deference are applied to elders and leaders.

- *Third-party impartiality:* Third parties should not behave in any way that advantages one party over another. But in some cultures third parties are expected to act in a way that respects and maintains existing power relations and community values—which may mean preferring one party or narrative over another.

- *Honoring agreements:* We should not agree to something unless we intend to follow through. Yes means yes, and no means no. But in some cultural contexts saying no to someone's face is not acceptable, and it is better to agree but not follow through than to openly refuse an offer.

The issue here is not whether our values about conflict are "right." We can continue to believe, for example, in the value of treating everyone equally. But unless we recognize that this is not a universal norm, we are prone to seeing others' behavior as inappropriate or even unethical, whereas they may understand themselves to be adhering to accepted principles of behavior.

STORIES AS A WINDOW INTO CULTURE

Culture is passed on and expressed through the stories we tell, our common fables, legends, and history. When I work or travel in a new cultural setting, I have found that the best way for me to prepare is to read a novel or story that originates within that culture. Histories, sociological or anthropological descriptions, and current newspapers are also helpful, but novels or stories that derive from that setting offer a particularly rich picture of worldviews, attitudes toward relationships, and communication patterns that are characteristic of that setting. Music, dance, art, theater, and cinema are of course other windows into new cultures. It is also interesting to think about what we might recommend to others who wanted to learn more about our own culture.

We also can bridge cultural divides by sharing our own stories and hearing the stories that others have to tell. We are a species of storytellers. We pass on our values and beliefs through stories, and we connect to others through the stories we tell and the stories we hear. Of course, as I discuss elsewhere (Chapters One and Seven), stories can also divide us, especially when we construct stories that objectify others and exclude the essence of their narrative. But to really grasp another culture we have to get beyond the analytical into the realm of meaning. Michelle LeBaron explains the importance of symbolic tools for bridging cultural differences: "We need creative tools because they have currency in the places where meaning is made and where expression is symbolic—levels not easily accessible through analysis. . . . Metaphor, ritual, and story are tools to access this level. They give us a window into each other because they convey not only thoughts but feelings, not only facts but perspectives about facts, not only ideas but values" (LeBaron, 2002, p. 181).

Part of our challenge as mediators is to help people tell their stories so others can hear them—and to help people hear the stories that others are telling with an open spirit. One important challenge we face when we find ourselves trying to bridge cultures is to find the means to exchange our stories. When I experience a free exchange of stories, both personal and cultural, I know that an important bridge has been crossed.

BEYOND SENSITIVITY: ENJOYING CULTURAL DIFFERENCES

When I think of what has helped me bridge cultural differences, it is more than just sensitivity; it is enjoyment of the differences, even when they manifest themselves in conflict. For the most part people are curious about each other's background and culture. When we are upset or angry, this curiosity may not be what is in the forefront of our consciousness, but it is still there. Differences in the ways people in conflict approach a situation, although these are potential sources of frustration and complication, are also stimulating and engaging. Furthermore, they provide an interesting and valuable mirror to our own natural tendencies. If we can cultivate a sense of humor and fascination about this, we can approach cultural differences as a source of strength and creativity as well as recognize the obstacles they can impose.

RECOGNIZING REALISTIC LIMITS—AND PUSHING THEM

Although we can do a great deal to educate ourselves about how other cultures approach conflict and prepare ourselves to interact across cultural boundaries—and although we often work through disagreements with people from vastly different backgrounds—there are also limits to how fully we can understand the world through the lens of a culture that is not ours. We cannot completely grasp what another culture is really like unless we have lived inside it for a long time (and maybe not even then). We can peel the outer layers of cultural practices, but there is a limit to how deep we can go in our understanding, just as there is a limit to how far anyone can go in completely understanding another person.

The more we understand our own culture, the deeper our understanding of others can be. The more we work with other cultures, the greater our sensitivity and understanding can become. In the end, however, we must recognize the limits on our understanding and plan accordingly—especially when conflict is high and much is at stake. By respecting the limits of our ability to comprehend other cultural realities, we show respect for other cultures. We cannot totally abandon our own culture to adapt to another; and we should not demand that others abandon their culture. We must instead find a way of respecting other approaches and opening ourselves up to different ways of communicating, without abandoning ourselves in the process. How can we do this?

We can recognize limits, and we can push them at the same time. For example, if we come from a culture in which communication is generally linear and one person speaks at a time, but we find ourselves dealing with a culture in which polychromic (that is, multiple and simultaneous) conversations are the norm, we may want to develop our tolerance for this new communication style. But we may find it necessary at times to express a need for more linear communication as well to be effective and present in an interaction. People from different cultures must frequently enter into a de facto and often unconscious or unintentional negotiation to develop an approach that allows everyone to participate fully and with power. This was a lesson driven home to me by my own inability to ignore a television.

> When I was a youth worker in New York and Colorado I would frequently visit people in their home. Many of the families I visited had a norm that allowed polite and focused discussion while the television was playing in the background. I found that I could not communicate effectively under these circumstances. Either because of my own cognitive limitations or because of the culture I came from, I found the TV extremely distracting. Initially I thought people were being rude or dismissive of me, and maybe some were, but I also experienced genuine warmth and interest from many others.
>
> At first I did not feel right asking people to turn their TV set off so I could focus because, after all, I was entering their home. I tried ignoring the television, sitting so I could not see it, and increasing my concentration. Sometimes this worked; usually it did not. Finally I found myself, somewhat apologetically, explaining that I was having a hard time focusing and asking whether the TV could be turned off or down or whether we could talk in a different room. Mostly people were fine with my request, but I am sure that several of them felt I was being bossy or controlling. It was a dilemma I struggled with repeatedly, and if I were in the same situation today I am sure it would still be a challenge. But if I had not taken care of my own needs, I would have been less able to bridge other more important differences and I would have been less effective.

RESPECTING AND SEEKING DIVERSITY

Those of us who work across cultural boundaries—and that essentially is everyone—should be aware of the need for diversity within our own groups, teams, or organizations. A commitment to respecting this diversity is not simply about being "politically correct"; rather it is about increasing everyone's ability to be effective in a multicultural world. It is also important to recognize when it is time to enlist the aid of people from different backgrounds to work successfully across cultural boundaries. Sometimes cultural, class, ethnic, gender, or other barriers mean that it is necessary to bring in third parties to help disputants resolve conflicts. But respecting diversity involves a lot more than bringing in people from diverse backgrounds. It means engaging in an ongoing effort to understand the ways in which organizational structure, communication patterns and norms, and language invite or discourage a diversity of styles and participation. The most important inhibition to genuine diversity is often to be found in the sometimes rigid and frequently exclusionary norms of interaction and participation that dominate many organizations, communities, and groups.

Separating Culture from Exploitation

Are some cultures racist, sexist, violent, abusive, rigid, or immoral? All cultures probably are at times. Or, more precisely, all dynamic cultures have to deal with issues of power, exploitation, violence, prejudice, and the like. Different cultures have different ways of handling these tendencies, but to see them as embedded in individual cultures rather than as possible products of human interaction within most social structures is not accurate, helpful, or fair. It is not German culture that produced the Holocaust, American culture that produced the My Lai massacre, Indian culture that produces honor killings, or Native American culture that produces high rates of alcoholism. It is important to understand the social forces that have led to these developments and how they interact with culture, but this is different from attributing them directly to a culture itself. Otherwise, when involved in a cross-cultural conflict, it is easy for us to focus on the opposing culture and to see ourselves as in conflict with an entire culture.

For the past decade we have been involved in an intense, costly, and divisive effort to combat political violence against civilian populations, which we have described as terrorism. Because some of the most horrendous of these acts have been carried out in the name of Islam, this has frequently been labeled as "Islamic terrorism" and the terrorists as "Islamists." Although there have also been efforts made to distinguish these attributions from mainstream Islam and from the genuine aspirations of the peoples of Afghanistan, Pakistan, Saudi Arabia, Palestine, and other primarily Muslim countries, the idea that these acts are somehow specifically encouraged or abetted by Islamic teachings or the associated cultures of these regions has been widely embraced. There is currently an almost hysterical fear that Sharia law will take root in the United States—despite the fact that there is no evidence that Sharia law has been afforded special status in any case before any U.S. court or that North American Muslims support the courts' imposing Islamic law (Macfarlane, 2012). Zareena Grewal, a professor of American and religious studies, has discussed how we interpret violence or other criminal acts in a way that both reflects and reinforces our cultural stereotypes: "The assumption is that in *our* culture [referring to non-Muslim cultures] violence is an exception so we must investigate the perpetrator's psyche or life experience, while in *their* culture [Muslim culture] violence is the norm, so what is relevant is their entire culture or religion" (Grewal, 2009, p. 5).

There are very grave political and policy consequences of this notion. People with an Islamic- or Middle Eastern–sounding name or Middle Eastern appearance are more likely to be challenged at border crossings, to be questioned closely by police, or to face discriminatory treatment in a host of other ways. Muslims have become the new target group for bias in many parts of the world. Of course, the perpetrators of violence who use the name of Islam and call for a holy war against the West encourage this bias—in fact, they cultivate it and make use of it to recruit adherents. But this is no more the true teaching of Islam than anti-Semitism is the true teaching of Christianity. Ethnic violence is often justified by an appeal to religion or to other cultural identities. But to say that a particular religion or culture is what generated or perpetuated the violence is unhelpful, inaccurate, and unfair.

To understand the roots of this violence we have to look at the nature of the power relationships and systemic forces that promote violence or that encourage one group to suppress another in this manner. In general I do not think explanations of racism, exploitation, or violence that rely on assertions that particular cultures or religions are inherently evil, crazy, or stupid make any more sense than explanations of individual human behavior that rely on these analytical "crutches" (see Chapter Two). To take the most intense example of the twentieth century, consider the Holocaust. There is no doubt that there was evil and craziness aplenty in the Nazi leadership, for example, but that does not explain the Holocaust. It is too easy, too comforting to resort to such simplistic analyses. The truth is much more complicated, significant, and scary.

To begin to understand how such atrocities could happen, we have to look at the historical factors, the structure out of which these developments arose, the values that were in play, how people interacted and communicated, and above all the fundamental needs that people were asserting or defending. We have to look at the forces promoting a genocidal response and the reasons why restraining forces were inadequate. Looking at things in this way is frightening because we are forced to face the possibility, even the likelihood, that such behavior will occur again. Such an approach pushes us to confront the most disturbing and challenging elements of these events, which we avoid to some extent when we label other people or cultures as crazy or evil. When we can understand these horrors without resorting to such easy explanations, we begin to see how they could happen again. Only by having the courage to look at these events in this way can we start to develop the understanding that will help us prevent such atrocities in the future.

CULTURE AND POWER

Much of what appears to be cultural conflict is really an attempt at cultural domination or forced acculturation. When one culture or group is in a more powerful social position and can impose many of its norms and structures on other cultures, the dynamics of dominance and submission should be considered. Under these circumstances the dominated culture is likely to know a great deal about how to operate within the more powerful culture. It is less likely, however, that the dominating culture will learn as much about how to work with the less advantaged group. But dominance and influence are different phenomena. The less powerful culture may in fact intrude many of its norms into the more dominant group, despite its weaker position.

A clash of cultures is usually about conflicting norms and values. Past conflicts in the United States between the view of the majority and the view of Mormons about polygamy, or between the view of the majority and Hmong views about child marriage, may be understood as examples of a genuine clash of cultural values in a context of cultural dominance. Many other so-called cultural wars, however, are probably less about values and more about dominance. For example, it can be argued that the history of U.S. drug laws is less about culture than it is about efforts to provide a social control mechanism for dealing with immigrant groups (for example, the enactment of opium laws was related to Chinese immigration, and marijuana laws to Mexican immigration). In seeking to understand cross-cultural conflict it is important to distinguish between issues of values and dominance. Mixing them together makes it harder to focus on the issue of power and can unnecessarily entrench people in a dispute about values. But separating them can also be very difficult.

Dominant cultures often try to strip less powerful groups of many of their cultural practices and symbols. In its simplest form, this action involves enforcing a certain style of communicating, dressing, or interacting. We see this playing out today in Europe and Canada in the movements to ban the use of the burka or the hijab (shawls or cloaks covering parts of women's bodies, heads, and faces). Although efforts to do so have been done in the name of cultural integration, the protection of women, and security, it seems clear (at least to me) that the real goal is the assertion of the supremacy of the norms of the dominant culture—otherwise a different kind of discussion would take place about how to achieve the goals that are supposedly promoted by these efforts. At other times this effort at domination involves an all-encompassing effort to prevent people from practicing their religion, speaking their language, or continuing to live in their own community. Such efforts strike at the core identity needs of the dominated cultural group—their needs for autonomy, meaning, and community. Occasionally cultural differences genuinely fuel such conflicts, but more often the driving force is the threat that a privileged or elite group feels from a subservient one. These conflicts are more often about power and social justice than about the clash of cultural values.

HOW CULTURAL DIFFERENCES HELP

It is easy to focus on the ways cultural differences complicate and confuse a conflict. But perhaps the more profound impact of diversity on conflict is positive. So much about effective conflict engagement involves a learning process. Conflict provides an opportunity for all of us who are involved to learn more about ourselves, the people with whom we have a conflict, and the issues in dispute. If we can make use of this opportunity, we will be more effective as conflict participants and conflict interveners. When we are operating on familiar territory, it is often hard for us to fully embrace this learning (or at times the opportunity to unlearn presumptions and stereotypes), to reflect on ourselves, and to take a broader view of our situation. All too often we are far too sure of ourselves when we are involved in a conflict. But when there is conflict across cultural boundaries, we cannot rely on the easy explanations or set responses we sometimes use in other circumstances, and we are often forced to be more self-reflective. Furthermore, the interplay of different cultures can increase our creativity, allowing us to expand the options that we bring to bear on a particular conflict.

This discussion is not meant to diminish the difficulty and sometimes the tragedy that are the consequences of cultural conflict. The most serious conflicts in our world, with the gravest consequences, involve cross-cultural issues. They cannot be ended by easy solutions that simply involve goodwill, sensitivity, and open-mindedness (although these qualities always help). But even in grave situations (for example, in Bosnia, the Sudan, Afghanistan, Palestine and Israel, Rwanda), the ultimate resolution must involve something other than the simple separation of the cultures. Engagement and dialogue must involve a new approach to interaction in which the reality of diversity becomes a source of strength in creating durable and fair approaches to conflict.

PART TWO

ENGAGEMENT AND INTERVENTION

CHAPTER FIVE

RESOLVING CONFLICT

Although the resolution model may not be applicable to every conflict, conflict resolution is still the most commonly articulated goal of those who seek third-party assistance. It is also the goal around which conflict professionals are most likely to organize their practice. And for all the limitations of the resolution model, helping disputants resolve those conflicts, or elements of conflict, that are amenable to resolution is an important aspect of what conflict specialists have to offer. But what do we mean by resolution, how do we achieve it, and what role do resolution efforts play in enduring conflicts?

In the field of conflict intervention, we often assume that resolution is equivalent to agreement about particular issues underlying a dispute. If the parties to a dispute can agree on an outcome that is mutually acceptable, then the conflict has been resolved. When a divorcing couple agrees on a parenting plan or the division of assets, a resolution has been attained. When environmentalists, government officials, and industrialists agree on regulations for controlling emissions, a resolution has been achieved. When a manufacturer and a plaintiff in a product liability case agree on a settlement, the issue has been resolved. When the different parties or blocks elected to a parliament agree on the formation of a government, there is resolution of a conflict.

But in each of these situations resolution is limited at best. Is the divorcing couple still in conflict? Do disagreements remain among environmentalists, regulators, and industrialists? Do product liability issues remain? Does conflict continue to characterize the relationships among political factions? Of course. Even when comprehensive agreements are reached it is likely that not all the parties experience genuine resolution. The image of disputants coming together to consider a major conflict, arriving at an agreement that adequately satisfies their essential concerns, and thereby fully resolving the conflict suggests a very misleading goal for conflict interveners. Most serious conflicts do not have such neat resolutions. Often the disputants cannot even imagine an outcome that would constitute such a complete and liberating resolution. That is because resolution and agreement are not the same.

Resolution has many aspects, and serious conflicts are seldom resolved in simple ways. Resolution occurs through a series of different activities over time, usually with many setbacks along the way. Resolution requires a process of letting go of conflict; of moving past it; and of gaining the energy, lessons, and growth that a conflict has to offer. This process can be liberating because it frees up energy that has been tied up in conflict, but it can also result in a feeling of loss when a conflict has provided meaning and focus for people. Achieving a resolution involves work and movement along several dimensions.

DIMENSIONS OF RESOLUTION

The dimensions of resolution parallel the dimensions of conflict, with the process of resolution occurring along cognitive, emotional, and behavioral dimensions. We can think of each dimension in terms of the individuals embroiled in a conflict or in terms of the conflict system as a whole. The cognitive dimension concerns how disputants understand and view a conflict, and whether they believe it to be part of their past or an ongoing process. The emotional dimension relates to how disputants feel about a conflict or about those with whom they are in conflict, and to what extent they are still emotionally engaged in a conflict. The behavioral dimension reflects the degree to which conflict behavior is ongoing or the behavioral agreements that have been reached and are being carried out. Let's consider each of these dimensions in more detail.

COGNITIVE RESOLUTION

Whether disputants have reached resolution in a conflict depends to a large extent on how they view the situation. If they believe that the conflict is resolved, perceive that their key issues have been addressed, think that they have reached closure, and view the conflict as part of their past, then an important aspect of resolution has been reached. Sometimes people make a deliberate decision that it is time to move beyond their conflict. They are resolved to be done with it, and if they can hold to that resolve, they have to some extent willed themselves to resolution. Resolution at this level can precede or result from resolution of the emotional or behavioral components. Mostly, however, the cognitive dimension of resolution develops in tandem with the other dimensions.

In considering the conflict system as a whole, we need to look at the beliefs and perceptions that seem to dominate the interactions among the different parts of the system. For example, there often comes a time after a divorce has been finalized when former family members no longer define themselves as being in conflict. Sometimes gradually, sometimes suddenly, a change occurs and the situation is redefined in the family system from one in which conflict is the predominant theme and defining characteristic to one in which cooperation or minimal involvement is the model. Individuals may arrive at this at different times and to different extents, but when this change becomes the dominant ideology within the new family system, the redefined family as a whole will begin to operate in accordance with this new belief.

Resolution on the cognitive dimension is often the most difficult to attain because people tenaciously hang on to their perceptions and beliefs about a conflict. Disputants may be locked into a set of behaviors and anchored in an emotional response as well, but people can decide to change behavior, and emotional responses often vary quickly and repeatedly. Beliefs and perceptions are usually more rigid. They are the cornerstone of a person's sense of stability and order, particularly in the midst of confusing and threatening situations. People cling to their beliefs and perceptions because to question them threatens to upset their sense of themselves and their world, and this sense is an essential guide through difficult times. Also, many people equate changing their views of a situation with admitting that they were wrong, something most of us do not readily do.

The cognitive arena provides some of the best opportunities for profound change to occur during the process of conflict. When disputants change their essential view of the people with whom they are in conflict, the nature of the conflict, or the issues themselves, a long-lasting type of resolution can occur. This possible result underlies some very interesting and important conflict intervention activities, such as victim-offender mediation, ethnic reconciliation processes, restorative justice programs, and citizen diplomacy initiatives. These efforts are all founded on the recognition that if people do not change their view of each other, if they do not learn to see each other as fully human, and if their basic beliefs about a conflict remain locked in an adversarial frame, genuine resolution is unlikely.

Working directly or exclusively to promote a change in disputants' attitudes about or understanding of a conflict can be very difficult. If the perceptions of a person in conflict are to change, they are most likely to do so through progress on the other dimensions of resolution, through a variety of healing and confidence-building activities, through events that force the person to reevaluate his or her views, and through time and maturation. However, there are a number of approaches conflict interveners take that directly deal with the cognitive dimension. The narrative approach to mediation as described by Winslade and Monk (2000, 2008) is an explicit effort to work directly with the cognitive dimension of conflict. They suggest, for example, that mediators attend to the double meaning behind almost any story or expression to allow people to give voice, and therefore focus, to not just what they are angry about but their hopes for something better. Thus they can begin to understand and experience a conflict in a different way. Another take on this comes from John Paul Lederach, who discusses what it takes to transcend a cycle of violence: "Transcending violence is forged by the capacity to generate, mobilize, and build the moral imagination. . . . [This] requires the capacity to imagine ourselves in a web of relationships that includes our enemies; the ability to sustain a paradoxical curiosity that embraces complexity without reliance on dualistic polarity; the fundamental belief in and pursuit of the creative act; and the acceptance of the inherent risk of stepping into the mystery of the unknown that lies beyond the far too familiar landscape of violence" (Lederach, 2005, p. 5).

Two specific techniques that conflict interveners sometimes use (although not always intentionally) illustrate how change along this dimension can be fostered—fomenting cognitive dissonance and facilitating successive reframing. Cognitive dissonance occurs when two values or beliefs held by an individual come into conflict with each other, forcing some level of change in that person's belief system (Festinger, 1957). When mediators say to divorcing parents, "You have to decide whether you love your children more than you hate your ex-spouse," they are attempting to invoke cognitive dissonance that will move people away from their embattled stance. The hope is that a new cognitive framework will result that will be more amenable to a resolution process.

Reframing (which I discuss more fully in Chapter Seven) is an attempt to recast how the conflict is presented to increase the likelihood that disputants will constructively communicate with each other. When a mediator helps two business partners redefine the issue of how to divide up work responsibilities into a question of how to work together to keep the business from going under, an effort is under way to create a new cognitive framework. However, because one single reframing effort is seldom powerful enough to change an entire narrative structure, interveners generally have to work with disputants in an iterative and interactive process if a significant reframing is to occur. Introducing cognitive dissonance and engaging in successive reframing are efforts to encourage disputants to take a new look at their perceptions about the nature of the conflict, the issues, the choices, and the other participants. These approaches are not effective unless they are part of a larger resolution strategy, and they lose their power when used in a manipulative or overly facile manner. But they are often a critical element in moving toward resolution because of how they address the cognitive aspects of a conflict.

EMOTIONAL RESOLUTION

The emotional dimension concerns the way disputants feel about a conflict and the amount of emotional energy they put into it. When people no longer experience the feelings associated with a conflict, or at least not as intensely, an important aspect of resolution has been reached. This is an especially volatile dimension of resolution because emotions can change rapidly and repeatedly. Disputants may have achieved a considerable degree of emotional closure in a conflict, but then an event or interaction occurs that reawakens their feelings and suddenly they are right back in the middle of it.

People experience emotional resolution in very different ways. Some disputants process conflict primarily through this dimension. If they feel better, the conflict must be resolved; if they do not, then no matter what else has occurred the conflict remains as alive as ever. Others, however, tend to minimize or suppress this aspect of conflict and are often unaware of whether or not they feel emotional closure. In any multiparty conflict there is likely to be a variety of different approaches to this dimension. This was an essential challenge I faced in dealing with an annexation dispute.

Some years ago, through the actions of several industrial facilities, the water supply of an unincorporated community in the midst of a midsize city was contaminated. An agreement was worked out providing for the city to construct a sewer and water infrastructure for the neighborhood at no charge to the residents. The city would then be reimbursed for its costs by the industries that had caused the contamination. However, in accordance with the city's long-standing policy, water could be provided only if the neighborhood were incorporated into the city. This led to a complex mediation about the terms of the annexation.

Although the neighborhood residents recognized that they were receiving valuable services that would significantly increase their property values, they were not pleased with many of the regulations they would be subject to once they were incorporated. Residents felt that they were being forced to incorporate in order to receive clean water and should therefore be afforded flexibility about zoning, planning, transportation, and related regulations. The city staff felt the neighborhood was already getting a very sweet deal and much greater financial and planning flexibility than any other newly incorporated area.

To reach the complex and comprehensive agreement finally attained, residents, city officials, and I spent considerable time working through the emotional, procedural, and substantive issues. We held neighborhood meetings, conferences with city officials, a variety of negotiating sessions, and many problem-solving sessions. The final agreement was approved by virtually the entire neighborhood and the city council. The neighborhood is now incorporated, receiving water and other services, and there appear to be no outstanding issues related to this conflict.

Despite what appeared to be complete agreement on all the issues, however, there was great variation in how much resolution different participants felt. Representatives of both the neighborhood and the city were unhappy that they had had to spend so much energy coming to an agreement. People on all sides felt disrespected, nitpicked, and misunderstood. There were also significant disputes within each negotiating team. In the end virtually everyone agreed that the outcome was a positive one that met everyone's essential interests. However, not all felt that the broad range of their needs had been met. Some believed that the outcome justified the effort and that the conflict was over. Others continued to see themselves in conflict for a long time. They alluded to how exhausted they were and said that they never should have had to work that hard to receive a reasonable response from the other side.

Over time, as the agreement has held and many participants have moved on to new issues, new jobs, or new neighborhoods, this conflict has gradually receded, and for most people resolution has been reached on all dimensions. For some this was a relatively quick and complete process; for others it took much longer, and perhaps residue from the conflict still lingers. This variety of reactions to a multifaceted conflict is the norm rather than the exception, even when almost all the substantive issues have been settled.

One of the best clues as to the degree of emotional resolution we experience in a conflict is the amount of emotional energy we continue to put into it. If we continue to spend a great deal of time thinking about a conflict, cannot discuss it without considerable emotional intensity, or need significant amounts of ongoing support to cope with the emotional aftermath, we have clearly not reached much resolution along this dimension.

Emotional closure is to some extent a natural result of time and distance, but it also occurs as disputants become more convinced that their essential needs have been addressed. Sometimes people cannot arrive at an agreement until they experience progress on this dimension, but at other times it is only through a settlement that they can gain the perspective and distance from a conflict that allow for emotional resolution.

The tension between the dimensions of resolution can be seen in a paradox facing many people going through divorce. The legal and practical demands of a divorce process require that people make some of the most difficult and far-reaching decisions they will ever have to make at a time when they may be emotionally the least able to make such decisions in a wise and thoughtful way. For conflict interveners working with divorcing couples, this can make things challenging. Should we assist couples in working through the emotional dimension so they can make practical decisions in a less reactive way, or should we focus on developing a divorce agreement, believing it will provide a stable platform for a longer-term process of emotional healing? Or should we work on both at once? The answer, of course, is "it depends"—on the individuals, the circumstances, and the alternatives they face. And what makes this even more complicated is that different parties are often in very different places. Sometimes we see that the more one party wants to focus on reaching a behavioral agreement, the more another asserts the emotional element of the work to be done, pushing the first party even more deeply into a desire to focus exclusively on the behavioral dimension.

Although it may be easier to think of emotional resolution in terms of the experience of individuals, the concept applies to systems as well. Conflict systems are containers and transmitters of emotional energy. If a system is characterized by a high degree of emotionality, this may overwhelm the individuals involved, regardless of their personal feelings. Similarly, as a conflict system moves toward resolution, individuals who are still very emotionally involved may be carried along toward closure, or their emotionality may be marginalized.

This is not an abstract concept. We see it all the time. In a conflict between union and management, the level of emotional energy may be so high that individuals who are not experiencing or expressing a great deal of emotionality about a conflict may be distrusted or pressured to join the emotional mainstream. But when the union and the management are ready to move to a less intense emotional relationship, those individuals who continue to be wrapped up in the emotional drama of the conflict become less influential and are often pressured to "relax."

How do people attain emotional resolution? This is usually a complicated process, and we do a disservice to our understanding of resolution by oversimplifying it. Disputants do not often reach resolution simply by "working through their feelings." Having an opportunity to express feelings and have them acknowledged by others is frequently an important part of reaching emotional closure, but this is seldom enough for those who are experiencing a great deal of emotional distress.

Often emotional resolution requires a period of escalation during which people experience a conflict more intensely. Sometimes disputants also need a cathartic release of some kind, but this can escalate a conflict to the point where resolution becomes more difficult. Although everyone has his or her own way of working on the emotional dimension of conflict, people seem to experience several common elements as they move toward emotional resolution. These include

- Feeling accepted as individuals and that their personality and values are not under attack (or are no longer under attack)
- Feeling that they can maintain their dignity, or "face," as they move toward resolution
- Feeling that their core needs are respected and taken seriously
- Having time to gain perspective and experience healing
- Having others accept their feelings as valid and their values as legitimate
- Feeling genuinely heard in a nonjudgmental way
- Feeling that they are being given a real choice about whether to move forward toward resolution

The role of forgiveness and apology in reaching emotional resolution is often critical. Both apologizing and forgiving, when done genuinely, are acts of emotional resolution. They provide mechanisms for us to put some part of the emotional aspect of a conflict behind us. By offering an apology or forgiveness, we move ourselves toward emotional resolution, even if our action does not have that effect on others. The most powerful apologies or acts of forgiveness are in fact those offered without any expectation of reciprocation. They can, of course, have a big impact on the cognitive dimension as well. When we apologize for our own actions (if the apology is authentic) or when we forgive others, we begin to understand and think about a conflict in a different way.

To be genuine and effective, apologies must be unconditional. If we are genuinely sorry about something, we are remorseful regardless of whether someone else forgives us or has an apology to make in response. It is more effective to offer a narrow but genuine and unconditional apology than a broadly framed but conditional one. Becoming clear about what we are really sorry for is therefore essential for an apology to be effective. However, this is not to say that one person's feelings of remorse cannot be triggered or released by another person's apology.

Forgiveness is also potentially very powerful, but it can sometimes be seen as patronizing or self-righteous. In terms of emotional resolution, genuine forgiveness is important not primarily because of what it does for others but because of what it does for the forgiver. Although it can be very healing to be forgiven, a person has to see himself or herself as having done something that merits forgiveness in order to accept it. Forgiveness is an act of letting go and of accepting the essential humanity of people with whom we are in conflict. Genuine apologies or forgiveness cannot be forced, orchestrated, or bargained for, but conflict interveners can often help people separate their hurt or anger at others from what actions of their own they genuinely regret. We can also help them consider what resentments they are holding on to that they would like to let go of and move beyond. Simply resolving to forgive and forget does not necessarily mean that this kind of letting go has actually occurred, but it is often an important step in that direction.

Some of the post powerful experiences I have had as a conflict intervener have occurred when genuine acts of apology and forgiveness have taken place. For example, for me, my time with James and Ray was a gift.

James and Ray worked in a manufacturing facility. James had been Ray's supervisor for several years, and the two had been friends, with Ray looking at James as somewhat of a father figure. The management of the facility saw Ray as a difficult employee, and James often acted as a peacemaker between Ray and others. Their relationship took a dramatic turn during a tense labor dispute when Ray openly criticized the management and needled James about being a manager. James, under a great deal of pressure during this period, lost his temper and called Ray a "loser, troublemaker, and asshole to boot."

Ray filed a grievance, and James asked for a medical leave of absence. The grievance was never acted on because James was gone, Ray's requests were somewhat vague, and neither the union nor the management was sure how to proceed. James's leave lasted more than a year, but then he had to return or lose his job. For a variety of reasons, he had to be placed in the same position, returning as Ray's supervisor. I had been working with this facility on designing a new grievance process, and as James's return approached, both the union and the management asked if I would be willing to mediate this dispute. Both felt it was a no-win situation, but one with which they were stuck.

I met with each of these men, listened to their stories, and discussed the possibility of mediation. James was ready to do anything to put this behind him, but Ray was very reluctant. He told me how painful the incident had been and was not sure there was anything James could do or say that would really help. I asked whether he wanted an apology, and he said that might help—if he believed it.

Clearly, putting pressure on or simply encouraging Ray to mediate would have been counterproductive. Instead I just asked him to think about it and let me know if he had other thoughts or questions. I also told him that I did not feel a mediated conversation was necessarily the "right" thing for him to do, but it was an option to consider. That is where things stood for over a month. Finally, the afternoon before the last day of my final trip on the project, I got a call from Ray saying he had decided he did want to meet with James. Hastily, I scheduled individual meetings with each of them and then a joint meeting for the following morning.

I first met with Ray. He wanted an apology, and we discussed what would make it feel genuine to him. All he could say was that he would have to see how he felt—he did not know whether anything James could say would make a difference. He also wanted to tell James how he felt. I asked Ray if there was anything he was sorry he had done. His first response was that he was the victim in this interchange. I said that this might be the case, but that it did not necessarily mean there was nothing he regretted. He acknowledged that he could be pretty provocative and that he could tell he was getting to James. At this point I delivered a little homily about apologies, explaining my view that they could not be bargained for and that the only meaningful apology was one freely given. I said that if there was something Ray felt sorry about, it would be valuable for him to say so, even if he felt that James's apology was incomplete or insincere. I also asked Ray to think about how he could express the effect that James's statement had had on him in a way that James might understand. I had a similar discussion with James, encouraging him to think about what he was really sorry about and also to think about what he needed to say about Ray's behavior.

The joint meeting resulted in one of the most emotionally intense—and rewarding—interchanges I have experienced as a mediator. At first both James and Ray were very tense and nervous. There was some small talk, and then I asked James to say what was on his mind. James talked about how horrible this whole experience had been for him, how much he had enjoyed having Ray as a friend, and how bad he felt about losing their relationship. He then looked at Ray and said how sorry he was about what he said and how hurtful he knew it had been to Ray. At this point I suggested that James give Ray a chance to respond. Ray accepted the apology and said that he knew he could be a "pain in the ass" and that he understood that this had been hard for James as well.

Ray then talked about how hard it was for him to trust an older man, especially one in a position of authority, and how bad it felt when this trust had been violated. James listened carefully to this and reiterated how sorry he was. He then went on to say how hard it had been for him to have Ray as a friend one minute and to be needled by Ray in front of his unit the next, especially because he felt he was always defending Ray to other managers. Then they went on to talk about what they had each gotten out of their friendship and how much they missed this.

In the end they agreed they wanted to try to work together, and they even set up a time to go out for a cup of coffee. Almost as an afterthought Ray agreed to drop the grievance. Both of these rather tough-looking working-class men had tears in their eyes—as did I—and they both looked as if some enormous burden had been lifted from their shoulders.

BEHAVIORAL RESOLUTION

When we think of resolution, it is the behavioral dimension we usually have in mind. We think of resolution as being about what people will do (or will not do) and the agreements they make about this. Behavioral resolution has two aspects. One has to do with discontinuing the conflict behavior, the other with instituting actions to promote resolution. Stopping fighting is one part of behavioral resolution. Taking steps to meet each other's needs and to implement a new mode of interaction is another.

Sometimes there is a specific act that symbolizes or actualizes the cessation of conflict behavior and the initiation of resolution behavior. Formal agreements, peace treaties, contracts, and consent decrees are examples of this. Sometimes less formal or less institutionalized acts function in the same way—shaking hands, having a drink together, offering a hug, initiating a joint activity, giving flowers, and so forth. At other times conflict behavior simply ceases, sometimes gradually and sometimes abruptly, and resolution behavior begins, without any obvious demarcation between the two. There are conflicts in which all that needs to occur is the cessation of conflict behavior. This is particularly true when the disputants will not have any relationship after the end of the conflict.

Agreements and solutions operate primarily along the behavioral dimension. Although a solution can affect our emotions and perceptions, we cannot really agree to feel different or to have different perceptions about the situation. Feelings and perceptions change, but not simply through agreeing to change them. Although an agreement to behave in a certain way does have meaning and can be enforceable, if efforts at behavioral resolution are too far out of sync with where disputants are on the cognitive or emotional dimension, then even the most tightly worded agreements are unlikely to hold. We have witnessed, for example, quite a few agreements intended to move the peace process forward in the Middle East that have proved ephemeral. A divorcing couple may have a very detailed parenting agreement, but court dockets are full of divorced parents who are not ready to move beyond a conflict, often despite having apparently arrived at comprehensive divorce agreements.

Long after the 1995 Dayton accords that ended the fighting in Bosnia, the ethnic conflicts that fueled that war continue. The provisions of Dayton provided a mechanism for the warring parties to disengage from their conflict behavior and instituted certain guarantees that this behavior would not restart. To this extent, behavioral, if not cognitive and emotional, resolution was reached. But the conflict is clearly not over on the behavioral dimension either. Attempts to create an effective joint government, resettle refugees in their respective former communities, deal with severe economic dislocation, and bring the perpetrators of some of the worst atrocities to trial have met with mixed results. The problems in making progress toward resolution on the emotional and cognitive dimensions have led to a significant erosion of progress on the behavioral dimension, and the remaining behavioral issues have in turn exacerbated the emotional and cognitive aspects of the conflict. There are some hopeful signs despite these remaining problems. Recently, some of the most sought-after war criminals, most notably Ratko Mladić, have been arrested and transported to the war crimes tribunal in The Hague. This move reflects an attitudinal change among the Serbian leadership and has the potential to promote movement toward cognitive and emotional resolution for the people of Bosnia, Croatia, and Serbia. In Northern Ireland, which provides another hopeful example, movement along the behavioral dimension was supplemented by efforts to promote dialogue and interactions among activists on both sides of the dispute and among Catholics and Protestants in Northern Ireland more generally. Although this conflict is by no means completely over, the work along each dimension has clearly enhanced the work on the other dimensions.

Finding a means for making progress on all dimensions is one way of understanding the central challenge we face in most significant conflicts. Full resolution of conflict occurs only when there is resolution along all three dimensions: cognitive, emotional, and behavioral. But such closure does not often happen in a neat, orderly, synchronized manner. Sometimes disputants are happy to call a conflict resolved when they have achieved significant resolution on one or two dimensions. Not that people think of resolution in this way, but this is often how they experience it. There is nothing wrong with this. Accepting a conflict as resolved, even if resolution along all three dimensions is not complete, can itself be an important step.

Although resolution along one dimension encourages resolution along the other dimensions, the reverse is also true. Disputants may experience a significant setback in their progress toward resolution on one dimension when they do not experience progress along another. Furthermore, different disputants in a conflict often experience differing degrees of resolution along the various dimensions. Sometimes this difference becomes the basis of a trade-off that allows individuals to reach an agreement. People will often make a psychological concession, for example, in exchange for a behavioral agreement. Enduring resolution of deep conflicts, however, generally requires significant progress toward resolution along all three dimensions.

Pursuing Resolution at the Appropriate Level of Depth

I have suggested that genuine resolution of complex conflicts requires emotional, cognitive, and behavioral resolution. It also requires that people's essential needs be addressed at an appropriate level of depth: that is, deep enough to address the real concerns people have that are motivating their engagement in a particular conflict, but not so deep as to require them to work through fundamental life issues that are beyond their practical motivation. Thus one major challenge for conflict interveners is to find a way to address people's needs at the appropriate level of depth. Another is to handle the different dimensions wisely, so that each is approached when possible and as appropriate.

These challenges may be met in many ways, and to suggest that one outcome or one approach is superior to all others is to erect a barrier to understanding the nature of conflict and of resolution. Resolution is not really a fixed end, but a process that we go through when we are in conflict. It occurs in stages, with setbacks, and in many unpredictable ways. Sometimes the quickest way to reach a tangible outcome is to help disputants put agreement aside as an immediate goal and concentrate on analyzing the conflict and communicating with each other. At other times the quickest road to empowerment and transformation is to help the parties succeed in resolving smaller or more immediate issues. The art of conflict intervention requires an analysis of each situation, and the most powerful practitioner is the one who can apply different approaches based on this analysis.

Beyond analysis, effective intervention requires a willingness to wade into a conflict knowing that there is often no "right" way to intervene and that by entering into a conflict we are becoming part of a complex and unpredictable system. Our ability to be effective depends on our ability to adapt to rapidly changing circumstances. Staying attuned to the different dimensions and levels of conflict and to parties' evolving relationship to these can help us be effective, but one of the interesting things about being conflict interveners is the unpredictability of the path we are taking.

In most circumstances resolution is a dynamic process that can feel like a moving target to those involved. As conflict interveners, we need to listen to the people involved in a conflict and to understand the level at which they are experiencing the dispute. We then need to search for the right level of depth at which to intervene or to engage disputants. Because an appropriate level of intervention for one person or at one stage of a process may be wrong for another, and because this can change for people as they go through the process, we can never be sure whether we have found the optimal level, and we have to keep attuned to this search throughout the intervention process.

If we look at Bosnia, Northern Ireland, or South Africa, we can see these dynamics demonstrated on a very large scale. In each of these places agreements were made that settled some aspect of a deeply rooted dispute but fell short of resolving all the fundamental issues or satisfying the identity needs of the people involved. Yet each of these agreements allowed the parties to at least temporarily disengage from an extremely destructive pattern of conflict behavior. Will this lead to longer-term, more profound peace and to a more just society, or has each situation been patched over in a way that will cause greater conflict later? One of the dilemmas of conflict intervention is that we can never clearly know the answer to questions of this nature.

Fundamental resolution of enduring conflicts and the achievement of social justice require long-term efforts. Conflict intervention activities can be part of this process, but only a part. They are one element in a much larger picture, and unless we see them in that context it is impossible to have a reasonable and flexible approach to choosing how and where to apply them.

IN DEFENSE OF OUTCOMES

In the following chapter I advocate as I have elsewhere (Mayer, 2004a, 2009b) for the importance of moving beyond an agreement or outcome focus when we work with conflict. But this does not mean that the search for good agreements or for a resolution to a conflict is not in itself an important effort. Indeed, it is probably the most common reason why people seek out the help of conflict specialists. And it is not for us to tell disputants that they should be working at a deeper or more profound level than an outcome focus can provide. So before making the case for moving beyond a resolution focus, let's consider why people so often focus on outcomes, and why they often should.

Although we should not preclude a broader focus by how we frame our purpose or structure our intervention, we should not insist on it either. If we are alert to the different levels at which a conflict may be operating, and if we provide disputants with the framework and opportunity to look at the longer-term elements of an issue or the ongoing relational components of a dispute, we will sometimes find that this opens up an important and profound interaction that goes well beyond a resolution focus.

But at other times disputants will want to focus on achieving whatever agreements are possible at the moment—and they may want to devote their full attention (and ask that we do the same) to hammering out agreements to the issues they have defined. As someone who has suffered from a medical error, for example, I might find the way that medical administrators or their representatives treat me to be disrespectful, defensive, manipulative, and arrogant. But I may, nevertheless, want to devote all my energy to getting financial compensation for what I have suffered. If dealing with the relationship issues or the systemic problems that might be involved helps me do that, great, but if not, that may be less important to me, at least in the immediate situation (and especially if I do not expect to have an ongoing relationship with these particular individuals). Of course I may later feel a lack of genuine resolution because these other issues were not dealt with. And often the kind of outcome one disputant is looking for may very well be out of sync with what is important to another. One divorcing parent, for example, may want to achieve an agreement about child support and parenting time, and the other may want to focus on how to communicate more effectively about parenting issues. Part of the challenge conflict interveners often face is working on these metanegotiations (negotiations about how to negotiate and to what end; see Chapter Eight).

The importance of outcomes to people and the frequency with which we are asked to devote our energies to arriving at agreements rather than to looking at underlying conflicts raise several questions. Why are people so fixated on resolution, even when significant elements of the conflict are not easily amenable to resolution processes? When is this a healthy approach (and when is it not)? What is the role that agreements play in dealing with more enduring elements of conflict?

WHY PEOPLE FOCUS ON RESOLUTION

On one level, this is obvious. We focus on resolution because we want our problems solved, sooner rather than later. Tangible outcomes, whether in the form of voluntary agreements or imposed decisions, offer an end (or at least seem to do so) to problems we face. We have all wished at times for a decisive conclusion to a conflict, no matter what that might be, because we haven't wanted to continue to devote energy and time to an issue. We end marriages, leave jobs, and sacrifice important goals because we no longer want to stay in a conflict, with all the anxiety, uncertainty, and energy drain involved.

The challenge is to understand why we so often remain preoccupied with outcomes, even when by doing so we avoid important issues and sacrifice major goals. For example, why do divorcing parents sometimes focus on a precise and detailed parenting schedule even though their more important conflict is about parenting styles and values? Or why might an employer and employee focus exclusively on resolving a dispute about overtime pay when the real concerns of both are about bad communication and poor working relationships? Four interrelated sets of reasons seem to be significant factors in promoting an outcome focus. These relate to our fears, our hopes, our calculations, and our self-image.

Fears

To explore the underlying dynamics of a conflict, especially with those we are in conflict with, can seem not only scary but also dangerous. We often feel almost desperate to reach an agreement—not necessarily any agreement, but one that seems at least minimally adequate—to avoid what can feel like dangerous territory or uncharted waters.

For example, we fear that

- This is the best deal we will ever get.
- Things will get worse if we don't reach an immediate agreement.
- We will "open up a can of worms" by delving more deeply into a conflict—that is, we will open up issues, feelings, attitudes, and differences that we will not be able to handle.
- We will not feel good about our own behavior or feelings if we push a conflict.
- We will not have the energy or resources to continue to engage in a conflict.
- Relationships will be permanently damaged.

Hopes

On the flip side of the emotional coin, we also hope that an outcome will solve our problems, lead to a brighter future, and allow us to put an unpleasant or painful experience behind us.

In particular, we hope that an outcome will

- Genuinely make things better
- Solve real problems
- Make other issues irrelevant or less problematic
- Be a significant first step in a more far-reaching conflict resolution process
- Improve relationships significantly

Calculations

We don't just gravitate toward agreements for emotional reasons, we also engage in a kind of cost-benefit analysis about whether we ought to pursue a conflict or reach an accommodation. We may calculate that

- The immediate benefits of an agreement outweigh the long-term costs of not dealing with broader or deeper concerns.
- We have done as well as we can reasonably expect to do.
- We will have a chance to deal with other concerns at a more opportune time.
- Others involved will not be willing or able to engage on a deeper level.

Self-Image

Perhaps paradoxically, we may be motivated to focus on immediately achievable outcomes because of underlying issues of identity and sense of self. Most of us do not like to view ourselves as highly conflict-prone people. Instead, our self-image is often that we are

- Problem solvers
- Practical minded
- Focused on the present
- People of action
- People who dislike (or are not good at) negotiation or emotional exchanges

And these are just a few among many self-attributions about our approach to conflict.

Frequently our fears are justified, our hopes reasonable, our calculations wise, and our self-image accurate. Sometimes avoidance of more enduring and deeply rooted issues is the wisest approach for us to take. At other times, of course, we are engaged in destructive avoidance. Perhaps the fundamental reason we focus on outcomes is that these provide the most tangible and easy-to-understand challenge we face in conflict.

When to Focus on Outcomes

Our fundamental challenge in conflict is to find a way of engaging with our most important issues or concerns in a constructive, powerful, effective, and ethical way. So the question we have to consider is whether a focus on outcomes, agreements, resolutions, or decisions at any given time contributes to this purpose. If by working toward a specific agreement we can solve particular problems—thereby opening the door to working constructively on other issues or, at the very least, removing these problems as obstacles to further effective engagement—then by all means let's focus on outcomes. And of course there are those situations in which key issues can really be resolved through a focus on tangible agreements. In divorce, for example, often an agreement about parenting or financial arrangements removes the most important issues parents face and allows them to go forward with a minimum of conflict. At the very least, an agreement provides the platform for a more constructive engagement with longer-term issues.

Sometimes clearing up a specific grievance in a workplace (for example, about a job assignment or promotion decision) not only settles a troubling conflict but also opens the door for discussions on broader issues of working relationships or other more fundamental problems (such as communication, work expectations, or teamwork). For some people, focusing on a specific outcome is the only way they can intentionally and constructively engage a conflict. Focusing on a specific agreement can provide people with hope, reinforce the most constructive elements of their approach to conflict, and make it less likely for their more destructive tendencies to dominate an interaction or even to emerge. For those who feel less empowered, achieving progress on a specific issue, even if minor, can help them realize the potential power they do have. Perhaps the main reason conflict interveners end up focusing on specific agreements or outcomes is that these are what the disputants we are working with—or the people we are in conflict with—want to focus on.

THE ROLE OF AGREEMENTS IN ENDURING CONFLICT

Perhaps the biggest mistake we make in seeking to understand the role of agreements or outcomes in conflict is that we view these as the end of the process—the final stage of the journey. We see all of our efforts as leading to a successful conclusion as determined by the achievement of an agreement that solves all significant issues and thereby ends the conflict. Of course this sometimes happens, but a more realistic and, in my view, hopeful approach is to view agreements as steps along the way and as part of a larger, ongoing process. If we view agreements in this way, then we evaluate their worth in two ways. One is to assess whether the agreements successfully and wisely resolved specific issues of concern to the parties. The other is to consider how they moved the overall conflict engagement process forward—how well they helped establish a better framework for a constructive approach to the ongoing conflict. Agreements can assist in setting the stage for a more extensive conflict engagement effort in a number of significant ways. They can do the following (Mayer, 2009b, pp. 183–185):

- Contain a conflict through creating behavioral guidelines for interaction
- Focus the conflict by taking distracting issues off the table
- Create new processes for engaging in conflict
- Build and solidify relationships among disputing parties
- Promote ongoing dialogue
- Promote a more constructive conflict narrative
- Protect the rights of vulnerable parties
- Alleviate the worst fears of disputants
- Deal with immediate problems demanding attention
- Memorialize and solidify progress that has been made

By advocating that we look beyond outcomes and beyond resolution, I am by no means suggesting that achieving agreements to difficult problems is not a valuable, even critical aspect of effective conflict engagement. I am instead suggesting that we need to understand this in a larger context. Within that context there is still a vital role for pursuing immediate agreements, even partial, short-term, and sometimes not very satisfying ones. If they deal with immediate concerns effectively (or at least as effectively as would a no-agreement alternative), and if they set the stage for a constructive approach to future conflict engagement efforts, then something very important has been achieved. However, our work in conflict, as interveners or as participants, ought not to begin and end with a focus on outcomes. Agreements provide a new opportunity, maybe even an excuse, for doing the real work of conflict engagement. In the next chapter I consider that larger context and how we can expand our self-definition as conflict interveners to encompass it.

CHAPTER SIX

ENGAGING CONFLICT

Perhaps the most important decision we make as conflict interveners is one we often don't even realize we are making. Our whole approach to conflict is governed by what we sense our purpose to be. The default position most conflict interveners take is that our mission is to resolve conflict, reach agreements, or settle disputes. This belief is embedded in how we market our services, name our organizations, and identify our profession. Our field is often referred to as the field of conflict resolution or alternative dispute resolution. In the United States our two most prominent professional organizations are the Association for Conflict Resolution and the Dispute Resolution Section of the American Bar Association.

The implications of this identification are very significant and in my view very limiting. If we see our purpose in entering into a conflict as being essentially about finding a way to settle or resolve the issues in dispute, then we will inevitably limit our potential involvement to situations that are ripe for such an intervention or to disputants who are amenable to this goal. But what about the conflicts that are not ripe for resolution, or the disputants who are more committed to carrying on a conflict and perhaps to deepening and broadening rather than resolving or de-escalating it? Can

---

Note: This chapter summarizes the concepts developed in B. Mayer, *Beyond Neutrality: Confronting the Crisis in Conflict Resolution* (San Francisco: Jossey-Bass, 2004), and in B. Mayer, *Staying with Conflict: A Strategic Approach to Ongoing Disputes* (San Francisco: Jossey-Bass, 2009).

we play a useful role in these circumstances as well? I believe we can, and furthermore I believe that if we embrace a broader view of our defining purpose and potential contributions, new opportunities for participating in a wider range of disputes will open up.

Changing our view of ourselves and our core purpose is not such an easy task. For the past several years I have presented myself as a conflict specialist and thought of our profession as the conflict intervention field, but this is swimming against the current of how conflict professionals usually think of themselves, how they present themselves, and how they are generally perceived by the public. Many of the institutional frameworks within which our work is conducted are defined by the goal of reaching a resolution or developing an agreement, and our services within these programs are often evaluated in relation to these goals. As a participant in a discussion of child protection mediation said: "None of us [child protection mediation program administrators] thinks that getting an agreement is the most important thing for us to focus on. More important is to get parents, social workers, and lawyers talking. But you can't go to a judge and say, 'We had a great discussion but didn't get an agreement' and expect a great response." This means that many of us face the challenge of how to address short-term goals with a long-term sensibility.

Complicating the picture of our self-image is the narrow way we present the roles we play in conflict. We have, for the most part, identified our field with the third-party role—an important role, but not the only one relevant to helping people through conflict. When making presentations to mediators, I often ask to whom they go for assistance when they are involved in a significant conflict. Interestingly but not surprisingly, they seldom indicate that they seek out mediators or conciliators. Like almost everyone, their first (and second and third) choice for assistance is someone who will act in some way as an ally rather than someone who will take the role of a third party or neutral. And these are mediators I am asking! Clearly, as important and valuable as third parties can be, disputants choose to use them in very limited circumstances only. And yet when we try to explain what we do, who we are, how our field differs from other professions—law, counseling, organizational development, public relations, or human services, to name a few—the easiest shorthand we can use is to identify ourselves as third parties, usually as mediators but sometimes as arbitrators, facilitators, or conciliators. I feel this pressure myself, especially in informal interactions. When I meet people in a nonprofessional setting and they ask me what I do, it is far easier to say that I am a professor or a mediator than to say I am a conflict specialist or a conflict engagement practitioner, especially if I don't want them to glaze over or change the subject.

One problem with this narrow self-identification is how it limits our focus. Abraham Maslow said: "It is tempting, if the only tool you have is a hammer, to treat everything as if it were a nail" ([1966] 2002, p. 15). If we approach every conflict that comes to our attention wondering what it is we can do to help resolve it and how we can bring the parties to the mediation table, we will miss the fact that many conflicts call for a different approach and purpose. For example, if faced with a dispute concerning job assignments between an employer and a manager, we may automatically assume that our job is to convene a discussion about this issue with an eye to resolving the specific conflict. What we could easily be faced with, however, is a much broader relationship problem or a systemic issue in the workplace that will not be amenable to resolution until circumstances change, power dynamics evolve, and a longer-term struggle is identified. We may have a very valuable role to play in this, and dealing with the immediate issue could be part of it, but we should be willing to consider whether there are other approaches we may want to consider (or recommend) so that the broader issues or underlying dynamics are addressed.

This is not just an abstract issue concerning how we might more accurately define our role. This challenge of self-identification and professional focus is central to the capacity of the field to grow, to address the most important conflicts of our time, and to help disputants with the most difficult aspects of their conflicts. It is also central to our credibility in dealing with enduring conflicts, those disputes that are not readily amenable to resolution efforts and are often the most important and troubling conflicts people and organizations face. None of this suggests that the traditional roles we play in trying to end or resolve a conflict should be scrapped; however, these approaches should be embedded in a larger sense of who we are and what we do.

The Challenge for Conflict Practitioners

One way of considering the significance of the limits we have placed on ourselves is to take a look at the overall status of the conflict intervention field. There is good news and bad news here. The field has grown tremendously in the past thirty years. Conflict resolution (as it is most commonly called) is an accepted field of practice. In one form or another it is prevalent in all parts of the United States, Canada, and Europe, and indeed throughout the world. Mediators are plying their trade in a wide variety of arenas from divorce and child custody disputes to large-scale policy issues. There is a proliferation of graduate programs offering degrees in dispute resolution, mediation, peace building, and conflict studies. Professional organizations exist on national, international, state, and provincial levels, many with an active and dedicated membership. Government agencies have been instructed to employ consensus-building processes for internal, interagency, and public issues. Many court systems mandate mediation for certain types of disputes, and many offer mediation as part of their services. There is a rich and growing literature informing the work we do.

But there are also warning signs that suggest the challenges facing our field. There is a significant imbalance between the number of people who are being trained as conflict interveners, particularly mediators, and the work available for mediators and other third-party interveners. Ours has always been a supply- rather than demand-driven field. Up to a point, this can be healthy. Conflict interveners are motivated to develop and market new services and to generate demand. However, when this imbalance becomes too great, people interested in developing their conflict intervention work can easily become disenchanted, and individuals and programs may be tempted to agree to constraints or approaches to the provision of services that are unlikely to be sustainable or effective. For example, some court-based programs allow only very limited amounts of time to mediate complicated disputes and rely on volunteers to conduct complex and delicate interactions. Prospective mediators eager to gain some experience may agree to work under these constraints even though this is not a sustainable approach to providing quality services. Of course, many volunteers are excellent mediators, but a primary reliance on volunteers is not the basis on which to build a field, any more than it would be for law, medicine, or psychotherapy.

Perhaps the most dramatic change in how conflict practitioners are currently being trained relates to the proliferation of master's programs (or graduate certificate programs) in conflict resolution, mediation, and related topics. The upside of this is that these programs provide more thorough and sophisticated training than the thirty- to forty-hour seminars that have previously made up the sum of the training received by most mediators, facilitators, and other conflict interveners. However, there are clearly more people graduating from such programs than there are jobs available. It is one thing to commit the resources and time to participate in a forty-hour program with no likely outlet for using these skills afterward, and another to make the commitment necessary to complete an advanced degree and then find that there are only a limited number of jobs available.

In short, the growth in interest in conflict resolution is not generally matched by a growth in demand for these services. Although government agencies are mandated to consider consensus-building procedures in a variety of circumstances, there is no evidence that there has been a significant growth in the use of these processes, especially for the most intense public conflicts. I am frequently struck by how seldom well-structured and well-facilitated consensus-building or conflict engagement processes are employed for the most significant disputes. Instead what we often see is an effort that is billed as an opportunity for public involvement in decision making but is actually a carefully orchestrated and very circumscribed procedure that allows for public comments but offers little genuine opportunity for dialogue.

When we consider where mediation is well established, growing, and institutionalized, we also see some disturbing patterns. For example, consider the growth of court-connected mediation programs and commercial mediation processes. Two related elements seem to characterize these programs. One is that they are very solution driven. The second is that they are predominantly rights based in execution (Welsh, 2002). Mediators in both of these arenas—in response to market demand and the requirements of the institutional setting in which they practice—are increasingly likely to conduct their sessions essentially as settlement conferences. The growth of court-connected mediation has been vital to the institutionalization of conflict intervention services for small claims, family disputes, and child welfare conflicts, but these programs are very vulnerable to changing economic circumstances and policies. In a number of jurisdictions, well-respected programs that have flourished for a number of years have ended suddenly or been dramatically curtailed because of budgetary crises or new political or judicial leadership. As budgetary pressures have increased, court-based mediators have either had to cut back their services or devote less time to each case, which often leads to a more evaluative and pressured approach to mediation.

The mediators who are succeeding in private practice, particularly in family, commercial, and labor-management disputes, are ever more likely to come from a legal background. A legal background is very valuable for mediators and other conflict professionals, but law is only one of many professional backgrounds that can help prepare one for conflict work. The more the conflict field is dominated by any one profession, the more it is that it will lose the multidisciplinary character that has been so important in its development. Furthermore, the more that legal professionals dominate the field, the more likely it is that rights-based approaches will come to the forefront, because that is what lawyers are trained to offer. (For an analysis of how this might be changing within the legal profession, see Macfarlane, 2008.)

These warning signs are not indicative of poor services being delivered. Nor should we conclude from them that disputants "ought to" want something other than outcome-focused mediation. But they do suggest that we may be operating with a limited and limiting view of what disputants want and need. They also suggest that the scope of what conflict practitioners are offering is limited, perhaps increasingly so, and that the potential we have to work with significant conflicts in a more profound and lasting way is not being fulfilled.

The advice I have heard given to prospective mediators for many years is to market effectively, to treat mediation as a business, or to work on developing a strategic business plan. This is sound advice, but it may fail to address the most significant source of the problem—the disconnect between what we claim to offer to those in conflict and what is actually most important to them. Identifying what people want (not just what they need) and how we can best help accomplish this is critical to a strategic approach to marketing. In this sense, we do need to think about how to market ourselves more effectively.

What People Want in Conflict (and What We Offer)

Obviously we want many different things when in conflict, and this varies person by person, conflict by conflict, and even moment by moment. And what we want can change dramatically over the course of a conflict. As a conflict escalates, for example, we often experience a change in what we believe we need to end the conflict. At lower levels of intensity or escalation we tend to be most concerned about meeting our own needs, but the more a conflict escalates, the more concerned we become about imposing consequences on those we are in conflict with. Rubin, Pruitt, and Kim describe this process of escalation: "In the early stages of many conflicts, Party is simply out to do as well as it can for itself, without regard for how well or how poorly Other is doing. . . . As conflict escalates, however, Party's simple interest in doing well is supplanted by a clearly competitive objective. Now doing well means outdoing Other. Finally, as escalation continues and the costs for Party begin to mount, the goals tend to shift again. The objective now is to hurt Other. . . . For every drop of blood that Party has shed, a far more terrible bloodletting must be forced on Other" (Rubin, Pruitt, and Kim, 1994, pp. 70–71).

This is of course just one of many ways in which what we want in the midst of a conflict changes in accordance with our experience in conflict. Sometimes we start out with a goal of repairing a relationship and end up with a desire to end it (or the reverse). Sometimes we find that what we think we need (for example, custody of our children) is not what we really want (for example, more time with them but less responsibility for day-to-day caretaking).

Sometimes we change our understanding of those with whom we are in conflict and of what we are in conflict about. In other words, conflict is a coevolving process among disputants and others, and as the process evolves our sense of what the conflict is about, what we need, and how we visualize the long-term outcome necessarily evolves as well.

Any effort to generalize what people want in conflict is therefore going to be limited to very broad concepts. Nonetheless, it is worthwhile, I believe, to try to look broadly at what people generally want in conflict and to consider how conflict interveners, and in this case mediators in particular, tend to approach these needs. By comparison, it is interesting to consider the dominant ways in which litigators address these same needs, as discussed in the paragraphs that follow. Litigation provides an important counterpoint to mediation, and this comparison can illuminate why disputants are often more comfortable with litigators than with third-party facilitators or mediators.

In *Beyond Neutrality* (Mayer, 2004a) I suggested six broad needs that we generally have in conflict: voice, validation, vindication, procedural justice, impact, and safety. Different conflict intervention approaches offer different avenues for addressing these needs. By exploring the implications of these avenues, we can gain insight into the incentives and disincentives for using each approach and the additional ways of intervening in conflict we should consider.

VOICE

Perhaps our most fundamental need in conflict is to be heard in a powerful, meaningful way by people who matter to us—for example those with whom we are in conflict, decision makers, the public, people who seem to confer cultural or social legitimacy, or those to whom we want to deliver a message. In fact, one of the main reasons we initiate or escalate conflict is to establish or increase a meaningful voice.

Lawyers are often seen as vehicles for obtaining voice (one common nickname for a lawyer: "mouthpiece"). Their message is that they will help disputants to "make their case to those who matter"—that is, to be heard. In other words, they will become the voice of the disputants in court or in negotiations. The message of the mediator is that he or she will help people be their own most effective voice and will create a forum for them to deliver their message to other disputants. However, the confidentiality that defines most mediation processes also limits the volume and the reach of that voice. A conflict coach, by contrast, might assist disputants in developing their voice in a more effective way as they prepare for direct conflict interaction. Other approaches that allow for private discussions but public presentation of the outcomes (for example, sunshine settlement processes that provide for private negotiations of class action suits but require public disclosure of the results) address the need for voice in yet another way.

VALIDATION

When we are in conflict, we want to know that our beliefs and feelings have been understood and that they are accepted as legitimate, either by those we are in conflict with or by others whose opinion is significant to us. Furthermore, we want to know that we are recognized as having behaved in a way that is consonant with our values. This is different from being agreed with or being told that we are right.

As conflict interveners, we often talk about validating someone's feelings, but we often do this in a superficial way. Genuine validation requires living with someone's beliefs and feelings, putting energy into understanding them, and assisting with their effective expression. What we often offer as validation is a much shallower version of this—acknowledging and identifying feelings through a paraphrase or active listening statement (if we even offer that). Genuine validation takes time, is not always possible, and is hard to do from a neutral stance.

Lawyers often don't see this as their job at all, and the desire for validation is a need people have that is often dealt with superficially or not at all in conflict intervention processes. Yet the more profound the conflict, and the more significant the emotional dimension, the more essential effective validation becomes. One of the greatest sources of frustration many disputants have is that they have never felt fully validated and have in effect been asked to ignore or swallow their feelings and beliefs. Allies can validate disputants in a way that third parties generally cannot and litigators do not. They can use the fact that they are not impartial to go deeper and stay longer with the beliefs, feelings, and narratives of disputants. (For a discussion of the opportunities and challenges of functioning as a legal representative and a conflict ally, see Mayer, 2004a; also see Cameron, 2004; Tessler, 2001.)

VINDICATION

Vindication is the desire to be proven or acknowledged as having been "right," "justified," or "victimized," or as having in some other way acted correctly in conflict. How we get vindication (even in theory) is complicated. We can get it by winning our case in court (although the dispute often goes on), by receiving a meaningful apology, by achieving an outcome that we desire, by attaining public recognition, or by observing or experiencing events that appear to show the correctness of our approach.

Part of vindication is distributional in that it requires one side to be "proven right" in a conflict, which can seem to require (and sometimes does require) another side to be shown to be "wrong." Of course, all parties can turn out to be "right" (or "wrong") in some way—and perhaps that can lead to vindication of a sort, but at the height of conflict that is often not the type of vindication we want. We want unambiguous vindication. Intervention processes often involve an effort to encourage disputants to give up their need for vindication, particularly of the distributive sort. And in consensus-building processes such as mediation, this type of vindication is particularly hard to even envision. In fact, in most serious conflicts the type of powerful vindication people want is seldom achieved. But in litigation, it is at least imaginable. The image of the judge speaking from the bench, telling those on one side that they are completely right and justified in all they have done and those on the other that they are completely wrong—or of a jury ruling decisively for one side over another—presents a model of vindication that many people seek, that lawyers sometimes promise, and that impels many toward adversarial processes. Such unambiguous vindication is rarely achieved (even if the court case is won), and most of us have to either give up this need or find it internally and informally. An interesting contrast to this is how restorative justice programs address this need. A critical part of many of these efforts, such as truth and reconciliation programs, is the expectation that the perpetrator of an injustice will speak the truth and take responsibility for his or her actions in front of victims and the community at large. Thus the need for vindication is partially addressed, and this is often critical to promoting a healing process.

PROCEDURAL JUSTICE

Most of us have a sense of what constitutes a fair process for dealing with a dispute. Sometimes, of course, we conflate a fair process with a desired outcome. If we get what we want, the process was fair; if not, it wasn't. I have yet to mediate a grievance in which someone got what he or she wanted but objected to the process. Yet grievances are almost always couched as though they are about mistaken, unfair, or illegal processes. For us to have a sense that a process is fair generally requires that we believe that it is not stacked against us; that it is relevant to the conflict or complaint we have; that it is managed in a credible way, in which we have some opportunity for having a voice or otherwise participating; and that it has the capacity to deliver what we want.

Although what is "fair" varies from person to person, culture to culture, and situation to situation, we usually equate fair processes with ones that reflect a clear set of standards, that are transparent, and that are applied in an equitable manner. Litigation offers an approach grounded in a centuries-old set of evolving principles, an established set of procedures, and a recognized mechanism for selecting decision makers. Of course, the process is not necessarily fair by other standards. Not everyone can afford to hire effective representation or to wait out procedures that sometimes seem interminable. But litigation does offer a very robust answer to how procedural justice will be delivered. Mediation addresses this need through the commitment of the mediator to impartiality and an even-handed approach. In fact, mediation can often address the need for procedural justice very effectively, but it lacks the clear societal sanctioning that litigation offers, and whether the need for procedural justice is successfully met is entirely dependent on how disputants feel about the way the process was conducted and about the mediator's approach. These are liable to be questioned or doubted if one is dissatisfied with the outcome. (For a critique of how concerns about procedural justice are addressed—or not addressed—in mediation, see Welsh, 2002.)

One aspect of our desire for procedural justice, which we may not be in touch with when we are in the middle of a highly charged conflict, is a need to believe that we have behaved fairly and in accordance with our own procedural values. We don't want to be treated in a manner that is unfair, but we also don't want to treat others in such a way. We may tie ourselves up in logical and emotional knots at times to justify our behavior, but this is in itself a reflection of our need to believe that we have treated others fairly. One of the strengths of collaborative processes is that they offer a mechanism for addressing our need to feel that we are treating others fairly even as we advocate for our own interests. In litigation, we cede much of our responsibility for how we treat others to the litigation system and instead focus on advocating for our own interests. As a result, when we go through litigation we may not feel great about how we have behaved, even if we feel justified. The need for procedural justice is something that informs the work of dispute system designers and managers, and to some extent the measure of the effectiveness of such systems is how well this need is addressed.

IMPACT

Of course, we don't just want to be heard, validated, vindicated, and treated fairly by the process—we want to have an impact on what happens. We want to make sure our needs are met, our interests addressed, and our goals furthered. Those of us in the conflict field have focused so much on establishing fair and legitimate processes that we sometimes don't adequately speak to people's need for substantive results. And when we do, we assume that the best way to do this is through aggressive efforts to get agreements. Sometimes that is the best way. But the need to have an impact is broader than the simple desire for agreements.

Disputants want their efforts to mean something, to make a difference—and sometimes third parties, in the service of making progress toward an agreement, can actually interfere with the potential for a substantial and lasting impact. This is something that we have in common with litigators. Litigators almost automatically equate having an impact with obtaining a victory in court or a satisfactory settlement in negotiation. A clear example of this regularly occurs in medical malpractice cases. Plaintiffs in these cases frequently desire to influence how medical practice will be conducted in the future, partly to give meaning to their experience, but in these cases negotiations usually devolve into questions of compensation. (For an example of how this plays out in the arena of human rights disputes, see Macfarlane and Zweibel, 2001.) Litigation offers a clear, if often ephemeral, approach to achieving impact. In collaborative processes, the potential for impact can be very significant but the route to it is less clear, less straightforward, and more dependent on the cooperation of those with whom we are in conflict.

SAFETY

A final fundamental need, often in contradiction to some of the others, is for safety. We want to be able to engage in conflict in a powerful way but to be safe at the same time. Mediation offers safety in a number of ways—through the <u>confidentiality</u> of the process, the impartiality of the mediator, and the manner in which the interchange is conducted. Nonetheless, having to deal directly with someone we are in conflict with, especially if we feel vulnerable and unempowered, can feel very unsafe.

In litigation the lawyer offers the safety of direct representation. This may not in fact be safer. There is no evidence, for example, that victims of domestic violence are more endangered if they participate in mediation as opposed to litigation. But it can feel more unsafe (and at times it may be more dangerous) because disputants may be forced to interact in person in an informal process. Those in conflict ally roles, such as collaborative practitioners or community organizers, attempt to address safety concerns by providing advocates while keeping disputants in the center of the conflict engagement effort.

The more serious the conflict, the harder it is to meet all of these fundamental needs effectively, no matter what process is being used. Although people may feel their voice is louder, their potential for vindication greater, the opportunity to make an impact more profound, and their safety more protected in litigation, for example, this is often simply not the case. Mediation may offer a more meaningful voice, an interpersonal interchange that can fulfill the need for vindication in a more constructive manner, a greater long-term impact, and a more genuinely safe setting than litigation. But what people feel about how well different approaches will meet their needs is very important to which processes they will chose to employ, and there are genuine limitations to how far mediation and other consensus-building processes can go to address these needs.

As third parties, we can only go so far within the constraints of our role to assist disputants in having the powerful voice they want, achieving the depth of validation they are looking for, or getting the vindication they feel they deserve. And we cannot always provide the clear, codified approaches to procedural justice that disputants may feel are available elsewhere or offer a recognizable path toward impact or safety. As mediators, we can work on all of these, but we will find in many conflict circumstances that our ability to address these needs is genuinely limited. And even when we can address these needs effectively, the ways in which we do so are often not clear, transparent, or familiar. This is one reason why we often find that disputants are more likely to be satisfied with the outcome of mediation than willing to enter into it to begin with. The challenge this poses to conflict specialists (and the potential it offers) is to identify other ways to help people meet these needs, separate from the third-party role. By expanding the roles we play in conflict and, more important, by broadening how we view who we are, we not only can significantly improve how we help people meet their needs but also can begin to overcome some of the barriers that keep people from using our services at all.

CONFLICT SPECIALIST ROLES

Mediation offers one set of answers or approaches to address the fundamental needs people have in conflict, but as I have discussed, this approach does not always address the full range of these needs. The solution to this dilemma is neither to give up on mediation nor to try to stretch it to do more than it can reasonably be expected to do. Instead we need to widen our sense of the potential roles we can play as conflict specialists so that at different times and in different ways we are better positioned to assist people to meet these needs in an effective and constructive way. As we look at some of the most interesting developments in the conflict intervention field, this is exactly what we see happening. Collaborative practitioners, conflict coaches, dispute system designers, and conflict strategists are examples of roles we can play in conflict, but not necessarily as third-party neutrals.

As I discussed in *Beyond Neutrality* (Mayer, 2004a), I think we can profitably play three broad types of roles in conflict—third party, ally, and system intervener. We can't play all of these at once, in the same case, or with the same clients, but to maximize our possibilities for working effectively with people in conflict we need to develop all three approaches in our field.

THIRD PARTY

We have built the field of conflict intervention around the role of the third party, especially the roles of mediator, facilitator, and arbitrator. These provide essential services to help people approach conflict more constructively, and all of us have at times taken on third-party roles or benefited from someone else who has adopted them, whether formally or informally, consciously or unconsciously. During the past thirty years we have formalized many of these roles and created a body of theory, practice standards, training protocols, and professional organizations to define and organize them. We have also seen these roles become institutionalized in organizations and policy. Although I have suggested that the conflict intervention field needs to expand beyond the third-party role, I am by no means suggesting we abandon it. It is a critical component of what we have to offer.

We have often confused ourselves and others by conflating the concept of neutrality with the definition of third party. Third parties are sometimes in a structurally neutral and impartial role, as in formal mediation, but often they are part of the system and inevitably represent some of the interests of the system—for example, mediators who work for government agencies or universities, or managers who mediate between coworkers. The concept of neutrality is a complex one, consisting of structural elements (Do we have any relationship with either party? Do we stand to gain depending on the outcome?), psychological elements (Are we biased? Do we feel impartial? Do we like one side more than another? Do we have strong opinions about the issues involved?), behavior (Have we acted in a way that promotes the interests of one side or disadvantages another?), and perception (Do we appear neutral? Have we done anything that can be seen as one-sided?). Neutrality may best be understood as aspirational—that is, we intend to be equally attentive and respectful to the needs and concerns of all parties. But pure neutrality is not achievable and not necessarily desirable—part of our job as third parties is to create an environment in which everyone can participate in interactions in an effective and secure way. That often means taking action to prevent a very powerful party from intimidating or bullying a less powerful party—which sometimes entails departing from a purely neutral stance.

One of the problems we face as third parties, therefore, is that although we have claimed credibility based on our skill, experience, and commitment to impartiality and neutrality, neutrality is a confusing and to some extent ephemeral goal, and many disputants are suspicious of our claims in this regard. So even when people are open to third-party intervention, claims of neutrality are not always the most effective way to clarify just how we can help or why we should be trusted. The commitment that third parties can most genuinely make is one based on their intention to remain fair, unbiased, and impartial, rather than one that suggests they will not have an impact that may favor one side more than the other.

ALLY

When dealing with a significant conflict, most people will first look for assistance from someone who is in essence an ally or advocate. This may be a friend or relative to whom they can ventilate and who may give them advice, an advocate or agent who can represent them, a coach who can prepare them to participate more effectively in conflictual interactions, or a strategist who can help them plan an approach to a particular dispute. A conflict ally, like a third party, is a natural role that we all play at some times and seek at others. And there are many formal, professional expressions of this role—lawyer, labor relations specialist, community organizer, bargaining agent, conflict coach, and many more. The conflict field has generally not seen this as its bailiwick, although in recent years, with the development of conflict coaching and collaborative practice, that has begun to change.

Allies are often in the best position to help guide a conflict in a more constructive direction. By helping disputants view their situation from a broader and longer-term perspective, by helping them consider both the integrative and distributive elements of conflict, and by encouraging constructive communication—all the while operating from a commitment to help a particular disputant further his or her interests—allies can promote an effective approach to conflict.

Some of the most interesting developments in conflict intervention during the past ten years have involved new applications of the ally role. Conflict specialists have worked with policymakers as advisers on how to deal with difficult disputes. Organizations are making increasing use of conflict coaches to help with grievances. The growing field of collaborative practice, applied most widely to divorce negotiations, has sought to view advocates as representatives, advisers, and coaches in a collaborative problem-solving effort. Labor relations specialists and union representatives often see themselves as conflict resolvers and advocates at the same time. And of course the most dominant of all conflict intervention professions, law, is increasingly influenced by conflict intervention processes, practices, and theories, with changes in the actual practice of law outstripping adaptations in the structure of legal education (Macfarlane, 2008).

For many conflict professionals who primarily operate from within a third-party framework, the role of the advocate can seem almost diametrically opposed to their professional identity and values. We tend to see our role as one of bringing people together to communicate and collaborate, whereas we see the role of the advocate as one of conducting combat and confrontation. Or, to use our own conceptual framework, we tend to see our role as one of encouraging disputants to take an integrative approach to conflict, whereas we believe advocates promote a distributive approach. But effective conflict engagement requires being able to work both of these dimensions, often at the same time. An effective advocate must be able to look at how to create value and pursue joint gains, and an effective third party has to know how to facilitate the distributive elements of a negotiation as well. If we truly grasp this, we can see that the best advocates promote constructive—and powerful—approaches to conflict using many of the same concepts and techniques as do third parties, although from a different vantage point.

System Intervener

Organizations, groups, and communities inevitably have systems for dealing with conflict, whether specifically designed and formally organized or informal and unrecognized. For example, organizations may have grievance systems, consumer complaint processes, public input procedures, and litigation departments. Even in small organizations there is often someone who is either formally designated or informally recognized as the person to whom to take certain types of problems, and as the person who will either deal with the issue or take it up the decision-making hierarchy. Courts may have settlement conferences, mediation programs, special masters' processes, or victim-offender reconciliation programs. Many universities have ombuds offices, student mediation programs, processes for dealing with disputes between students and faculty, mechanisms for appealing tenure and promotion decisions, and even restorative justice programs. These are all systems designed to prevent or manage problems or disputes. The people who design, manage, and staff these systems have a significant impact on how conflict is dealt with in that setting. System interveners or managers are therefore extremely important conflict specialist roles.

Sometimes people in these roles are specifically mandated to manage conflicts and to create conflict intervention systems. Ombuds are usually charged with the task of dealing with specific conflicts or complaints that arise in their organization, but they also are generally expected to help design and maintain conflict systems. Human resource specialists are generally expected to deal—both individually and systemically—with personnel conflicts, labor relations specialists with labor-management issues, and corporate counsel with legal disputes with external organizations or individuals (and are often also responsible for overseeing internal conflicts that have legal ramifications). Federal agencies in the United States are mandated to have a plan for dealing with public policy issues in a collaborative way and to have an office or officer responsible for developing and implementing dispute resolution programs.

At other times the creation and management of conflict falls to certain people without a specific mandate or recognized responsibility. For example, the decision of whether to use mediation in conflicts around land use, water, transportation, or development often falls to project managers or their supervisors—who can have a key role in guiding how a conflict will play out but are not necessarily depicted (or trained) as conflict managers or interveners.

Whether formal or informal, these system interveners are often critical to determining how conflict will be handled across a wide range of cases. When a group of specialists in child protection mediation gathered in a series of "think tanks" to discuss lessons learned about how to deal with child protection mediation, one of the points repeatedly emphasized was the necessity of having a systems manager with the time and support to design and oversee child protection mediation and family group conferencing programs. (Kathol, 2009; Mayer, 2009b). Similarly, a project initiated to discuss how dispute systems could best be implemented in unionized workplaces identified as one key factor the importance of a specifically identified person whose job it is to champion and oversee the system (Pearlstein, Robinson, and Mayer, 2005). In the courts, a new case manager role has evolved for judges and masters who are responsible for nudging forward—via case management and settlement conferences—the progress of a case through litigation. For example, the master or judge may propose a schedule for the exchange of information between the parties or an exchange of offers to settle. In family courts, a similar role is sometimes played by a family counselor or court social worker.

These three broad types of roles are not meant to provide an exhaustive description of all the ways in which specialists can intervene in conflict, and certain roles overlap several of these categories (ombuds, for example). Other potential roles may not neatly fit into one or another of these approaches—such as trainer, evaluator, resource provider, or therapist. (See *The Third Side* by William Ury, 2000, for another take on the range of roles that conflict interveners might play.) What is essential for understanding the nature of conflict intervention is to recognize the broad range of approaches that conflict specialists can and do take. We are not just third parties, and some of the other roles we have the expertise and ability to fulfill are essential to promoting constructive approaches to conflict. A healthy system of conflict intervention offers a multiplicity of roles to assist people and systems in dealing with conflict.

Six Faces of Conflict

Almost all conflicts are multifaceted, having many different elements and potential ways of being understood and characterized. How we explain a conflict and what aspect of a conflict we choose to focus on—or simply name—have a profound effect on how we engage with the conflict, or help others to engage. Often we focus on the element of a conflict that aligns best with the way we are most comfortable engaging with it. So, on the one hand, if we are comfortable as third-party problem solvers, we will gravitate toward characterizing conflicts as problems begging for cooperative solutions. If, on the other hand, we are more comfortable in the role of advocate, agitator, or activist, we are more likely to see conflict as a problem that has to be taken to a higher level of awareness, as an issue that needs to be escalated. How we characterize and describe a conflict inevitably directs us toward a particular way of thinking about and intervening in it. And we often choose how to characterize a conflict unconsciously and unintentionally.

One way we do this is by emphasizing the elements of conflict that are preventable or resolvable at a particular moment in time. Almost all serious conflicts have elements that are open to problem solving and other elements that are likely to endure. In

Staying with Conflict (Mayer, 2009b), I suggested that we consider six faces or aspects of conflict—latent, low-impact, representative, transient, stubborn, and enduring. Most conflicts have several, if not all, of these faces, and as participants or interveners in conflict, we tend to focus our attention on one or two of these faces at any given time. This is usually unavoidable, but we should at least be conscious of the choices we are making. Let's consider each of these faces.

LATENT

The latent face refers to an element of conflict that has not yet crystallized or manifested itself, but for which conditions are ripe. Ethnic tensions that may lurk beneath the surface in a community, organization, or school, for example, or growing distance and distress in a marriage that has not yet erupted into open conflict, are both examples of conflicts that in a sense are waiting to happen.

We are often faced with a choice when considering latent conflict: is it wise to try to find a way to raise these issues, to make them manifest and deal with them in a transparent and intentional way, or is it better to try to hold the lid on the situation in the hope that tensions will lessen? We frequently espouse the view that it is better to be proactive in dealing with potential conflicts—and often it is—but sometimes, when the conditions are not right for engaging with a dispute, it may be best to let latent conflict stay latent a little longer.

LOW-IMPACT

Sometimes conflicts erupt over relatively minor issues—minor even to the disputants, although irritating or upsetting nonetheless. Perhaps most of our everyday conflicts (for example, which parent gets the children during a particular holiday, whether to buy a new car or not, who gets a particular job assignment or vacation slot, who is responsible for a fender bender, how housework is divided) have this characteristic. Issues that seem enormous at the time may upon reflection actually be low-impact in the larger scheme of life. Whether a conflict is truly low-impact is clearly a matter for those involved to assess. Nonetheless, we can all think of conflicts we have been involved in that at least in retrospect just don't seem that important. I think the worst argument I ever had with one of my sons was over when he was going to unload the dishwasher. Why do low-impact conflicts seem so important?

I believe there are two related reasons that often make what might appear to be a trivial conflict into something that can take up a lot of time and emotional energy. One is that the conflict may trigger a previous conflict or issue that has been important to us in the past. For example, if there is a long history of my having futilely requested help with housework from my children, then perhaps I am bringing to the present situation all the weight of the past interactions about this. The other is that this particular conflict represents a larger or deeper concern (see the next section). The decision we often have to make is whether to deal with a low-impact conflict at all, whether to deal with it in isolation from other issues, or whether to connect it to the historical or underlying issues it represents.

Representative

Virtually all conflicts represent other conflicts, and we always have to draw the line somewhere in terms of how large or deep an issue we are ready or able to take on. Some of the most challenging decisions I have had to make as a conflict intervener have revolved around how far to go in looking behind a presenting conflict to understand and address the other issues it might represent. A grievance about overtime represents resentment about the authoritarian atmosphere of the workplace. A dispute over exchange times between divorced parents represents concerns about parenting standards and styles. A complaint about the location of an Islamic center near Ground Zero represents questions about American identity and religious freedom.

My own inclination in my personal and professional life is to err on the side of going beyond the presenting issue to discuss at least some of the underlying conflict that might be involved, but this is not always the best move. Sometimes people are not prepared to explore issues beyond their immediate scope, and sometimes efforts to delve beyond the immediate issue will only lead to unnecessary and unproductive escalation.

TRANSIENT

There is generally some element of every conflict—including more complex and deeper ones—that is amenable to resolution or that will fade in a relatively short time. When we frame a conflict as a problem to be solved, particularly a problem that can be solved through a negotiation or problem-solving process, we are generally focusing on the transient or resolvable element: How will assets be divided in a divorce? How will a suit be settled? Will a facility be sited as proposed? Will a treaty be negotiated and ratified?

Because we have mostly identified ourselves as conflict resolvers, we look for that aspect of a conflict that can be resolved, and therefore we gravitate to this face. Often, by focusing on this element, we can make overall progress on a larger conflict, but sometimes we substitute work on this face for considering and engaging with the more serious and significant elements of a conflict.

STUBBORN

Just because a conflict has the potential for being resolved does not mean that it is easy to discover a resolution. Those elements of conflict that might in principle be transient but are very resistant to resolution are the stubborn face of conflict. Will a dam be built in a wilderness area? What will the status of Jerusalem be? How will new health care policies be implemented? What will be done about nuclear weaponry in North Korea?

It may take a while, a long while, for these issues to be resolved, but to the extent that they can be framed in terms of negotiable issues—for example, how to minimize the impact on the wilderness of building the dam, how to establish a multiparty governing authority for the Old City of Jerusalem, what pilot projects can be rolled out in specific sites to implement new health care policies, when the North Koreans will agree to next meet with international mediators—they are still transient by nature (but difficult). The more stubborn the issue, the more we have to ask ourselves whether it is better to work on the resolvable potential or to delve into the sixth face—the *enduring* face of conflict.

ENDURING

We have all experienced conflicts that are likely to continue for a long time and for which it is hard to even imagine a resolution. Many of our most profound conflicts, as individuals, organizations, or societies, have this characteristic. For example, disputes about climate change (and what to do about it), disputes concerning the role of government versus the market in dealing with economic and social problems, ethnic conflicts, disputes between highly conflicted divorced parents or between labor and management in a polarized workplace, or conflicts in a community over growth usually have at least an element that is not really amenable to comprehensive resolution. There may be agreements that can ameliorate or resolve an aspect of the conflict or move the dispute to a new stage, but there are also likely to be elements of the conflict that are going to continue over time. This is the face of conflict that may be hardest to accept and address but that also offers the greatest opportunity for making a lasting impact. To understand the challenges and opportunities presented by enduring conflict, it is important to consider its nature and the ways in which we can help address it.

ENDURING CONFLICT

Why do some conflicts seem to endure? Why can't we even imagine a resolution to these conflicts? For example, can we imagine a resolution to the conflict in the United States over immigration policy? We can imagine immigration reform, but can we imagine an end to the dispute over the fundamental stance that should be taken toward immigrants? In one form or another, this is a dispute that has been going on since Colonial times. We could ask the same question about race relations, the relationship between the federal government and local governments, or the role of regulation versus the market, to name just a few conflicts on the policy level. Each of us can probably identify conflicts in our respective families, communities, or organizations that have lasted for many years and are likely to last for many more, perhaps into future generations. For example, there may be conflicts in university departments, perhaps about philosophical emphasis or admissions criteria, which existed before any of the present faculty were part of the department and will continue after they have all departed.

Are these conflicts fundamentally different from what I have called transient or stubborn conflicts? Yes and no. Although they may cover many of the same issues and exhibit many of the same power, communication, and relationship characteristics, there are significant differences as well. Enduring conflicts tend to be rooted in structure and reflect fundamental value differences. They are often based on identity needs and almost always involve concerns about power and trust. These kinds of conflicts do sometimes end or morph into something very different, but this usually only occurs when the environment or structure within which they exist changes, or the individuals involved significantly mature or evolve. These conflicts are less likely to be concluded through an intentional process of resolution. Consider this not uncommon family dispute:

> Fred and Lee have been divorced for ten years after having been married for seven. They have two children, Pete and Ann. Ann is currently in college and has been a relatively easy child to rear. Fred thought Lee was too lenient in her parenting of Ann, and Lee thought Fred was at times harsh and judgmental of Ann, but because there were no major stresses in Ann's development they were able to handle parental decision making with her fairly easily. Pete was another story, however. He was diagnosed with ADHD, disliked school, was frequently in trouble, and demanded a great deal of energy. Pete is now fourteen and continues to be a source of a great deal of parental concern and tension. Fred believes that Pete demands a firm hand and clear limits, and he thinks Lee rescues Pete every time he gets in trouble rather than having him face the consequences of his behavior. Lee feels Pete needs support, love, patience, and understanding and thinks Fred is exacerbating the problem by being rejecting of Pete. Pete is a master at playing them off against each other. Whenever Fred and Lee try to talk about Pete, as they have done with teachers, principals, and counselors, and directly with each other, they inevitably bring up all the past instances in which they feel the other has proven to be a bad parent. This has been going on in one way or another since before they were divorced.

Fred and Lee might agree on specific steps that need to be taken at any given time, but they seem unlikely to resolve their basic differences over parenting. Will this dispute end when Pete leaves home? Perhaps, but not necessarily—it could easily migrate to new issues or manifest itself in new ways. Can their interactions improve? Certainly, and one of the challenges conflict interveners face is how to help people engaged in enduring disputes handle them better, even when the disputes themselves are unlikely to end.

Why does this dispute endure? It is based in the structure of their relationship. They have fundamentally different values about parenting. Each of their identities is wrapped up in their parenting—and their narratives about who is responsible for the problems that exist between them are very entrenched and very different. Furthermore, Pete has become the focal point for a long-term struggle between Fred and Lee about power, trust, and communication. Perhaps family therapy can help. Perhaps mediating specific issues can help. But this conflict is unlikely to change until something changes in the structure in which it is embedded, or until a change occurs in how Fred and Lee experience their identity and understand the values that are most important to each of them.

We all know of disputes like this. The challenge they pose for conflict interveners is how to help people engage in these disputes in a constructive way. In *Staying with Conflict* (Mayer, 2009b), I suggested six basic challenges that have to be faced if we are to help people find a constructive approach to enduring conflict:

- Helping people overcome their avoidant tendencies and face the enduring aspect of the conflict
- Framing the conflict in a way that is constructive, realistic, and hopeful and that recognizes the enduring element
- Working to build effective and durable systems of communication
- Helping find constructive ways to employ power
- Making the appropriate use of agreements to move an enduring conflict to a more constructive place and resolve important issues, but not as a means to avoid the key conflict
- Developing the resources and mechanisms to sustain people through the course of the conflict

None of these challenges is easy or straightforward when dealing with deeply rooted conflicts, but the skills and procedures necessary to face them are what effective conflict intervention is about—and accepting these challenges opens up many new opportunities for conflict professionals to work on serious disputes in a meaningful way.

Resolution, Transformation, Engagement, and Social Change: The Purpose of Conflict Intervention

There is a rich and ongoing debate about the goals of conflict intervention. Should conflict interveners have a purpose beyond helping disputants attain an agreement? What is the intervener's responsibility for protecting the weak or unrepresented? Is conflict intervention about ending disputes, building peace, achieving social justice, or transforming relationships? Although these discussions can seem self-conscious or academic in the abstract, they are critical to guiding us in our work. We may think that our purpose ought to be to address whatever needs the people we are working with have, but embedded in the approach we take to discerning these needs are our own assumptions about our role and our goal. If we are to be intentional and transparent in how we approach our work, we need to be aware of the different purposes that might define our work, the arguments supporting them, and some of the criticisms that have been leveled against them.

Belief: conflict intervention is about helping people reach agreements to end their disputes. Conflict intervention is neither a therapeutic nor a political movement. Although solid agreements that genuinely meet the interests of the parties to a conflict can lead to both personal and social change, this is a by-product of effective dispute resolution activities, not a direct goal. Were this the primary purpose of conflict interveners, they would become just one more advocacy group trying to impose their own agenda on a problem-solving process. The strength of collaborative approaches to conflict is that they empower participants to advocate effectively for their own interests in a safe and constructive environment.

This potential is diminished if those who conduct collaborative processes are imposing their own agenda for social change or personal transformation. People come to dispute interveners for help in arriving at a settlement to a conflict. They want this help to be powerful and effective. They do not come to experience personal growth or transformation, to clarify their feelings, or to deepen the level at which they are engaged with a conflict. Any agenda beyond those that the parties have explicitly brought into the process is manipulative and disempowering.

Critique: focusing on agreements, outcomes, or solutions is also an agenda, and it ignores some of the most important elements of conflict with which disputants have to contend. At the extreme we see the all-too-frequent practice of dispute resolution through arm-twisting, in which people are pressured to agree through relatively coercive means. Practitioners of this approach are often more focused on getting an agreement than on finding a way to meet disputants' essential needs. Even those who practice a gentler approach within this framework often fail to understand that each conflict is frequently a symptom of an underlying concern that the parties are either unwilling or unable to articulate. Furthermore, this approach often overlooks the cognitive and emotional dimensions of resolution. Even when disputants want to deal with the conflict in a fuller and more profound way than can be accomplished through an outcome-focused intervention, practitioners coming from a resolution-oriented perspective often direct the effort to the more tangible aspects of the dispute—to its transient face. Unless conflict practitioners offer people the opportunity to work on the deeper and broader issues they are facing, it is likely that they will focus on a shallow resolution that will not genuinely address their needs. This approach can be as upsetting and alienating as traditional legal processes but without the procedural safeguards.

Belief: dispute intervention has a great potential to encourage personal transformation, and such transformation is often essential if conflicts are to be effectively addressed. Mediation in particular has the power to transform the way people relate to each other and to a conflict. This point of view is forcefully presented in the work of Bush and Folger (2005). Transformation happens primarily through the process of empowerment and recognition that is a potential part of every conflict intervention effort. A significant obstacle to achieving this potential is the narrow focus on outcomes that is typical of much mediation. Opportunities for empowerment and recognition are lost when the process is so focused on achieving an outcome that more profound communication is not encouraged and may even at times be actively suppressed. If the goal of conflict professionals is to arrive at an agreement no matter what, they are imposing that agenda on the process even as they claim to be impartial and focused on process. Ignoring the transformational potential of mediation not only denies participants and society an important opportunity for growth but also fails to address the real, underlying needs that people have in conflict. (For another, more broadly conceived—and profoundly moving—take on transformation, see Lederach, 1995, 1997, 2005. He focuses on the transformation of relationships and systems of interaction as well as on personal change.)

Critique: transformation often does occur as a result of experiences people have with conflict and its resolution, but not through a direct effort to make transformation happen. People may, paradoxically, be more apt to have fundamentally transformative experiences in mediation because the process does not promote personal growth or change as its primary purpose. Many people are willing to engage in mediation (as opposed to therapy, for example) precisely because it is a focused and limited intervention. Most skillful mediators look for opportunities to empower people and help them recognize each other's concerns and humanity. This is simply good mediation practice. But when changing people becomes part of an ulterior purpose, the potential of dispute intervention practices to give people power over decisions in the midst of conflict can get lost. The experience disputants have of reaching a settlement in a complex dispute is in itself empowering and opens the door to deeper levels of recognition among the parties, far more than does a direct focus of the mediator on empowerment and recognition.

Belief: dispute intervention cannot be conducted fairly without addressing power imbalances and issues of social justice. In the absence of a commitment to deal with power inequities, dispute intervention procedures may become just one more way in which victims of social injustice are further disempowered. Neutrality in the face of injustice contributes to the furtherance of injustice.

Conflict resolution as a goal makes sense only when coupled with an active commitment to ensuring that power inequities are corrected. There is no such thing as genuine neutrality, either structurally or personally.

Critique: if dispute interveners take on the task of eliminating structural inequalities in society, they not only will be less effective in dealing with conflict but also will add little to movements for social justice. This approach is patronizing to disputants in assuming that they need the assistance of a third party to make sure they do not make inappropriate choices. A credible process conducted in an impartial manner is often extremely valuable to disempowered people. Although there certainly should be screening procedures to make sure that only appropriate intervention processes are used, the choice of processes also has to be made in light of the realistic alternatives. For example, a woman who has faced violence from her intimate partner may feel that a structured and well-managed face-to-face discussion offers a better chance of safety over the long term than does a restraining order from a court. Or she may not—but ultimately this is a disputant's decision and not ours. Sometimes collaborative decision-making procedures give people the best opportunity to play a relatively weak hand. Practitioners of a social justice approach often deliver fewer real accomplishments than do well-constructed conflict resolution forums. These forums are designed to provide procedural justice, which in the end is the foundation of social justice. (For a spirited exchange about this approach, see McCrory, 1981; Stulberg, 1981; Susskind, 1981.)

Belief: the goal of conflict interveners ought to be deeper analysis and understanding of the identity issues that are at the root of most serious conflicts rather than negotiated agreements based on identified interests. Similar to the transformative belief but focused more on transnational issues and ethnic disputes, this approach critiques many international peacemaking efforts because they fail to address the root causes of conflicts. The most well-known advocates of this approach are John Burton and his colleagues at the Institute for Conflict Analysis and Resolution at George Mason University (Burton and Dukes, 1990). The critical importance of focusing on identity issues in conflict, as well as a methodology for doing so, has also been described by Jay Rothman (1997). Proponents argue that mechanisms are needed for helping people analyze the deeper levels of human needs, particularly identity needs, which are at the root of many profound conflicts. Unless disputants understand both their own needs and those of others, a genuine resolution of conflict is not possible. When a process places its major focus on solving a particular conflict, the underlying issues are often ignored, and instead of genuinely solving the conflict the process allows issues to continue to fester and often escalate. Advocates of the analytical approach sometimes refer to events in the Middle East, Northern Ireland, Bosnia, Rwanda, and South Africa as examples of this dynamic.

Critique: the analytical approach embodies an unrealistic view of the way progress occurs in resolving serious conflicts. There is a time for analysis and reflection and a time to seize the opportunity to make progress by arriving at agreements on divisive issues. As tangible progress is made on specific issues, people become better able to address the deeper and more complicated needs that drive their conflict. If people in Bosnia, Kosovo, Northern Ireland, and Rwanda had to wait for the identity needs of the disputants to be thoroughly discussed and addressed, many opportunities for progress toward resolution via trust-building and interim agreements would have been lost—and probably many lives as well.

Belief: disputes are resolved when key interests are addressed. The goal of dispute intervention, according to Fisher and Ury (1981), is to obtain a solution that addresses the most important interests of the different parties. This can be done through an interest-based approach to negotiation, in which disputants' interests and motivations are explored, as opposed to a positional or power-based struggle over whose position will prevail. The goal of dispute intervention is to arrive at a solution to the conflict, but one that addresses the key interests of the different parties. It is not necessary to distinguish between needs and interests because one is just a deeper expression of the other. Negotiated agreements are the major outcomes that should be sought in most conflicts.

Critique: most serious conflicts are based on a deeper level of needs than is captured through an exploration of interests. Furthermore, interests are not static—they change as people interact. This approach is too rationalistic and linear. It does not recognize the role of power and identity in the conflict process. Focusing on interests is a tactic, but it is inadequate as an overall philosophy of conflict intervention. As a tactic it can be very valuable, but it is not always appropriate. Disputants can often arrive at effective agreements without dwelling on their interests, and sometimes doing so can become an academic exercise divorced from what is really important to people. Furthermore, interests are just one element of the range of needs in play in conflict. By focusing on interests, we can easily overlook other critical needs, such as identity, intimacy, meaning, and survival.

Belief: our overall purpose as dispute interveners is to help people engage more effectively with the essential elements of the conflict they are facing. (This is the approach I have argued for.) This may involve an effort at resolution, but not necessarily, and we ought not to enter into a dispute with resolution, social change, or transformation as our single fundamental purpose. As conflict interveners, we should enter into a dispute without assuming that our essential goal is to strive for a resolution to a conflict that may not be ripe for resolution. There are many ways to help people deal with conflict more effectively that do not presume an agreement or resolution to be either possible or desirable. But we should also be open to the possibility, and maybe even the likelihood, that participants do want some resolution or agreements, even if the overall conflict may be an enduring one. We should not impose our own agendas about transforming individuals, organizations, or societies. What we can assume is that people want assistance with engaging with a dispute or problem in a more effective way (or with finding a constructive way of avoiding the conflict), and our job is to help them do so. When we enter into a dispute, we in fact have to negotiate with the parties we are working with about what their purpose is and how (or whether) we can help them achieve it in a constructive way.

Critique: we need a clear focus and a clear message about what we are doing in conflict. When we tell people that our job is to help them resolve outstanding issues or to achieve social or systems change, that message is clear, and we can be held accountable to it. When we say our goal is to encourage empowerment and recognition, and that out of that will arise the greatest likelihood that a transformation will occur, we are also clear about our purpose. When, however, we say our goal is to help people engage in conflict, we encounter several problems. This goal is more abstract. Disputants will find it harder to know whether, when, and how to use us. Our efforts, therefore, to market our services will be more complicated. And, perhaps most important, we will be operating counter to the instinct of most parties to do the opposite—that is, to disengage from conflict.

Although many skillful conflict interveners instinctively use the best insights from all these approaches—resolution, transformation, social justice, conflict analysis, interest based, and conflict engagement—adherents of each point of view handle conflicts in somewhat different ways. To explore this further, consider how each might approach a typical community conflict. This example is based on an unmediated dispute that took place several years ago.

> The Beechwood County Department of Human Services (DHS) plans on establishing a group home for teenagers in a middle-class residential neighborhood in the town of Holmes. A group of neighborhood residents has circulated a petition opposing this plan and threatening court action. The petition raises concerns about traffic, the impact of the teenagers on the local school, and the effect on property values. One of the supporters of the group home, an advocacy group for youth, has countered with a statement that suggests the real problem is racism; Holmes is a predominantly white community, and many of the teenagers will be members of minority groups. The Beechwood County Board of Supervisors has asked for help from a conflict professional to deal with this dispute. This professional might pursue one of the following approaches.

- *Get an agreement.* The neighbors, the teen advocates, and the DHS need to come up with an agreement that everyone will accept. In this way the neighbors' concerns can be met, a plan for the group home can be formulated, and a negative court battle can be avoided. To saddle this process with an attempt to work through everyone's feelings about community, race, and the needs of teenagers would overwhelm it and throw a considerable obstacle in the path of finding a solution.
- *Encourage personal transformation.* These people need to hear each other—to understand and recognize the underlying concerns everyone has. This process presents a wonderful opportunity to

break through some serious stereotypes and misunderstandings. There are at least three major reasons why this should be done. First, if the group home is to move into the neighborhood, these folks will have to live with each other. If they do not recognize the legitimacy of each other's concerns, the stage will be set for a long-term problem. Second, no workable agreement is likely to emerge unless efforts are made to encourage empowerment and recognition. Third, the neighborhood residents and group home staff and clients can do much for each other if each group can change its perceptions of the other side.

- *Address social justice issues.* Unless the disparity in power between these wealthy residents and the potential group home clients is addressed, the victims in a negotiated solution are likely to be the teens. Compromises may be agreed to that will negatively affect the youths and perhaps the workers staffing the home, and these are the people most likely to be underrepresented in a conflict intervention process. The intervener should ensure that the outcome does not exploit the unempowered.
- *Provide conflict analysis before attempting conflict resolution.* The disputants should concentrate on understanding their deeper needs and how these are in play in the conflict. An appropriate analytical process will get to the deeper issues that people have concerning the group home proposal and the neighborhood reaction to it. If the parties instead try to arrive at a negotiated agreement, either there will be no resolution at all or, if there is one, the conflict will continue to emerge in various new forms, to the detriment of the teenagers, the neighborhood, and everyone else involved.
- *Address everyone's procedural, psychological, and substantive interests.* Rather than focus on the various positions people have taken, it is important to help people express their interests, consider the principles that should govern an agreement, and evaluate their alternatives. If this is done, a creative problem-solving process that genuinely addresses the interests of those involved can lead to a solution that will maximize joint gains. The question should therefore be: How can the neighborhood residents' concerns about safety, property values, and traffic be addressed, while the DHS's need for a suitable group home in an appropriate neighborhood is also met?
- *Encourage constructive engagement.* An agreement may or may not be possible, but to assume that agreement making is the sole purpose of the intervention is likely to pose significant obstacles

to obtaining participation and encouraging a frank and open dialogue. Instead, it is critical that disputants be provided with an opportunity to give voice to their most significant concerns and that the longer-term elements of the issues involved be addressed (the enduring face of conflict). This will allow disputants the chance to develop the capacity and mechanisms to deal with the many manifestations of this conflict that are likely to arise over time in a more constructive way and to identify whatever immediate agreements are possible or advisable.

Probably any of these approaches, if skillfully applied, could prove beneficial to the group home and the neighborhood residents. And, of course, these are not exclusive approaches. There are elements of overlapping goals and strategies among all of them. In the end the best guidance about which approach to take in such a conflict and how deep or extensive an effort to make will come from the parties themselves: the neighborhood residents, the youth advocates, the group home staff, and the Department of Human Services.

There are of course other approaches to conflict intervention, and there are variations on each of the ones I have described. Also, many other critiques have been made. There is truth in each of these points of view and each of the critiques. But there is also a great deal of confusion generated when proponents of one approach mischaracterize others or attack an extreme version of an approach as though it were representative. For example, on the one hand, critics of the transformative approach have argued that transformative mediators have pushed disputants to achieve empowerment and recognition even when those individuals are clearly eager to arrive at a settlement of their particular dispute and do not want to delve into deeper issues. However, the advocates of transformative mediation have gone to great lengths to address this concern through how they contract with people at the beginning of the mediation process. On the other hand, transformative mediation proponents have criticized other mediators, suggesting that they are generally so focused on achieving outcomes that they will not allow the parties to communicate genuinely with each other, even when the disputants want to do so. Many proponents of other approaches are very committed to and skilled at encouraging rich and effective communication among parties, even as they search for resolution.

We should not be discouraged by the differences among these approaches. To the contrary, we should encourage more debate and dialogue about these issues. Having different philosophies and frameworks is entirely healthy for the conflict field. What is not healthy is either avoidance of interaction and discussion among proponents of different approaches or unfair and extreme characterizations of each other. In other words, we should encourage constructive engagement among different schools of conflict intervention.

I have argued in this chapter and elsewhere for an expanded view of the role of conflict interveners so that we do not focus exclusively on either the work we can do as third parties or on the goal of achieving immediate outcomes or resolutions. I believe our ability to expand our practice and to reach our potential as conflict interveners depends on our taking a broader view about who we are, what our purposes are, and how we can best work to pursue them. But whatever approach we take to conflict intervention, there are certain key skills that we need to bring to the table. None is more important than helping disputants communicate more effectively. This is the challenge to which I turn in the next chapter.

CHAPTER SEVEN

COMMUNICATION

Effective communication is the key to constructive conflict engagement. We engage in conflict through communication processes that are direct and indirect, purposeful and accidental, verbal and nonverbal, symbolic and concrete, interactive and unidirectional. Good communication is deceptively simple and yet extremely complex. It is the most important skill for conflict professionals to develop and nurture. The good news is that communication skills can be learned, applied, and enhanced. But good communication is harder than most people realize. Most of us who work as conflict specialists believe we are effective communicators (at least when we want to be), and most of us are able to articulate the essentials of good communication. But like everyone else, we are only sporadically effective as communicators, particularly in the midst of highly charged situations. For the purpose of understanding communication dynamics in conflict, we need to consider five questions:

- What makes for good communication?
- How can disputants connect with one another so that everyone feels heard?
- What are the most challenging obstacles to effective communication?
- How can disputants deliver difficult messages in a constructive and effective way?
- How can conflict interveners help turn ineffective, destructive, or nonproductive communication into more constructive interchanges?

These questions are relevant across cultural boundaries and at all stages of a conflict. This does not imply that complicated issues, deeply bitter feelings, or long-lasting antagonisms can be made to go away simply by communicating effectively. Communication is only one part of constructive conflict engagement, but it is a critical part. Without effective communication, it is hard to do much about conflict.

Intention

THE BASIS OF EFFECTIVE COMMUNICATION

Good communication stems from intention, not technique. If we put our full and focused energy into communicating, we can make lots of mistakes and still be effective. Conversely, no communication technique will substitute for a lack of commitment and desire to hear or to be understood. Communication is often characterized and taught as if it were essentially a set of behaviors or procedures—as if good communication automatically flows from the use of the right techniques or words. But most of us have had the experience of communicating with someone who is intentionally using a recommended approach to communication, such as an "I" message or active listening, and have come away feeling patronized or not genuinely heard. We can also recall interactions in which we knew we needed to listen and tried our best to do so, but in which our hearts were not in it. We may have been distracted, upset, defensive, or even bored, and despite our trying to be effective listeners or to communicate our concerns constructively, our efforts fell flat or even made things worse. *Commitment Focus*

However, we can probably also remember occasions when effective communication occurred despite the use of supposedly poor communication techniques. People might have interrupted each other, asked either-or questions, made self-referential statements, tried to problem-solve too quickly, or injected humor when someone else was trying to make a serious point. Yet they still genuinely connected and felt heard. Why? The key is intention and focus. If we genuinely want to understand what another person is saying and are willing to work at it, that intention is likely to come through, despite behaviors that might not seem desirable when considered in the abstract. Similarly, if we want to express ourselves respectfully and clearly and are willing to work at it, the chances are that a successful interchange will occur. But all the good techniques in the world will not make up for a lack of genuine interest in what someone else has to say or the absence of a sincere desire to communicate effectively.

This does not mean that behaviors and techniques are unimportant. We can learn to be better listeners, to deliver difficult messages more effectively, to reframe toxic language, and to be attuned to nonverbal communication. But these techniques are not at the heart of effective communication. When our attitudes are not conducive to communicating, our behaviors cannot help but convey this.

Effective communication starts with an understanding that none of us is always effective at listening to others or conveying ideas clearly. Although effective communication may come more naturally to some than to others, we should never take it for granted. Being attuned to the possibility, even the likelihood, that we have not communicated effectively may sometimes feel unnatural, but it may also be the most important thing we can do to improve communication.

I believe that the following attitudes or mind-sets are essential for successful communication, particularly in conflict.

- *Caring about what others are saying is the heart of good communication.* If we genuinely care about what others have to say, our desire to understand will get communicated. If we do not genuinely care, that too will be communicated.
- *There is always new information to learn from a communication.* When we listen with one ear while composing a response to what we think others are about to say, genuine communication has not occurred, even if our conjecture is correct.
- *Good communication requires focused energy.* When we focus our attention, energy, and best listening efforts on an exchange, others generally feel respected, even in the midst of conflict. Communicating clearly in an intense interaction is tiring for a very good reason—it takes a lot of work.
- *Effective communication always goes two ways and requires a joint effort between speaker and listener.* Effective communication is interactive and iterative. People have to work together to make a complex interchange successful, particularly in stressful

circumstances. Directly or indirectly, people have to verify whether they have really understood each other. But even more important, we have to teach each other (mostly unconsciously) how to best communicate as both speakers and listeners and how to adjust our communication process as we go. (See the discussion of the communication loop in the next section.)

- *Communicating is different from persuading, evaluating, and problem solving.* When we are focused on communicating, we are trying to understand what others are saying and we are helping others understand what we are trying to convey. When we focus instead on convincing others that we are "right" or on evaluating the merits of what others have said, effective communication is less likely.

- *Tolerance of people's difficulty in communicating (including our own) is essential.* These principles are all ideals and goals to strive for. However, we do not become better communicators by setting up a new orthodoxy about human interaction and then judging each other in accordance with it. No one can always be focused and completely attentive. Everyone mixes up communicating, persuading, and problem solving at times. It is important to be respectful of others who are trying to communicate effectively and to avoid becoming so conscious about the rights and wrongs of good communication that we cannot interact in a natural and unselfconscious way. Thus the final principle . . .

- *The best communication occurs when we are genuine and* ~~Be real!~~ *natural.* Communicating is about interacting as human beings. This means being real, being authentic, speaking from the heart, and connecting with others on the basis of who we really are, with all of our good intentions and flaws wrapped up in an often confusing package.

LISTENING AND CONNECTING: THE COMMUNICATION LOOP

Although those of us who work as conflict interveners generally recognize the importance of good listening to dispute resolution, we often fail to understand the heart of what listening is about. We tend to think of listening as a sequential process in which one person talks while others listen and then another person talks while the first person listens. However, effective communication is seldom a one-way or linear process. Effective interpersonal communication is always interactive and requires those involved to form what is in essence a partnership in communication. We have to help each other communicate, especially when we are in conflict. We have to work together to create a rhythm of interaction and a common narrative framework.

COMMUNICATION AS TEAMWORK

What changes a conflict dynamic from an adversarial contest to a joint search for a way forward? Disputants do not necessarily start to feel different about their adversaries or to view the conflict differently. But they do start to feel a connection with them, almost a partnership, based on a different kind of communication than they have had before and an understanding that they need each other to find their way through the conflict. Mandela and de Klerk, Sadat and Begin, Rabin and Arafat, or McGuinness and Paisley did not necessarily change their views of each other and learn to like or even to respect each other. But they did connect, and they did come to view each other as necessary partners in a peacemaking process. Of course, good communication alone cannot resolve deeply rooted problems if other conditions are not favorable. Communication is a necessary but not a sufficient condition for constructive engagement.

The connections between these leaders did not happen through the simple process of good listening. They occurred through a complicated process of individuals' learning to communicate with each other. Each of these leaders had to learn how to decode the messages he was receiving, how to deliver his own ideas so that they would be understood, and how to develop a suitable atmosphere for communication. Beyond that they all needed to find a way to cue each other when they were grasping what was being said and when they felt they were being heard. This is no easy task to accomplish against a background of long and intense conflict and personal antagonism. As these leaders struggled to find a way to work together, third parties often played a critical role in encouraging this communication. This struggle to establish an effective connection is not just relevant to large-scale international conflicts. It happens every day in workplaces, families, schools, and, as in this example, communities.

> My plan for breaking an impasse came close to blowing up in my face. In the middle of a difficult policy dialogue about the use of wildlife control measures on agricultural lands, I asked two participants representing opposing interest groups to try to arrive at a set of proposals to present to the whole group. As one of the facilitators of this dialogue, I had noticed that these two seemed to be genuinely struggling with how to accommodate each other's concerns. I thought that if they could develop some principles of agreement, the whole group might be able to use these principles as a template for a broader discussion. They too were aware of this and were willing to give it a try. The problem was that they genuinely disliked each other.
>
> Jonathan, an architect, represented a local environmental group. Charles had been a rancher and was currently a lobbyist for farmers and ranchers. He was also well known as an auctioneer. Where Jonathan was terse, blunt, suspicious, persistent, and very creative, Charles was easygoing, gregarious, funny, and sure of himself, but Charles also had quite a temper. Jonathan would make a suggestion, lay out its merits, anticipate criticism, and suggest why the criticism was misdirected—all in one statement. To Charles this sounded arrogant and rigid, even when he thought there was merit in Jonathan's proposal.
>
> As Charles listened to Jonathan, his body language would become more tense, his brow more furrowed, and the few statements he made more clipped. When he responded, he tended to tell an anecdote or make an analogy; sometimes he would tell a joke. This was his way of stating his concerns about Jonathan's proposals (and perhaps his way of commenting on Jonathan's communication style). His most significant concern seemed to be about how hard it would be to sell these ideas to his constituents rather than about the ideas themselves.
>
> To Jonathan, Charles's responses seemed evasive, illogical, or irrelevant. Jonathan would react by leaning forward, speaking a little louder and more intensely, and occasionally pointing his finger (behaviors that almost always escalated the conflict). Even though the two were making progress on some joint proposals,

their communication was breaking down, and they were both on the verge of losing it with each other.

As tensions between them escalated, they each approached me to discuss their frustration about what was happening. Each interpreted what the other was saying as manipulative and unreasonable. Neither was picking up cues from the other about what was working and what was not in how they communicated. Yet both were really trying to communicate effectively. I asked Jonathan what he had noticed about how Charles reacted to his proposals—what kind of communication seemed to get through to Charles and what did not. It almost did not matter what Jonathan's answers to these questions were, because just being asked them was a bit of a revelation to him. They implied that he should pay attention not only to what he was saying but also to how he was saying it. He had been so focused on the substance of his ideas that he had not paid any attention to how he was conveying them. I also asked him to interpret the messages behind a couple of Charles's anecdotes. I suggested that he think about spending more time drawing Charles out and that he convey his ideas more slowly and in smaller segments. Jonathan was quite open to such coaching.

Charles was less interested in suggestions about how to communicate. He prided himself on his interpersonal skills. So instead of focusing on this, I asked him what he wanted Jonathan to understand about what he was saying. He told me a couple of stories, the gist of which was that he felt environmentalists did not understand the marginal economic situation of small farmers and ranchers. I expressed the hope that Charles would lay this concern out in no uncertain terms, and I suggested that Jonathan seemed to like bluntness. Neither of these two representatives fundamentally changed how they communicated, or what they thought of each other for that matter. But they did become slightly more attuned to each other's cues, and they were able to work out several helpful proposals to take to the group.

THE COMMUNICATION LOOP

Communication needs to be interactive to be effective. As listeners, we have to help speakers deliver their messages so that we are receptive to them. As speakers, we have to help others listen so we feel heard. This means that we have to listen as we deliver a message and deliver feedback as we listen. This communication loop is a necessary part of effective interchanges. People's ability to connect with each other, particularly in the course of an intense and significant interaction, is dependent on their ability to tune into the often subtle messages that reveal how a communication is being received. We also have to learn about when to speak and when to listen—when jumping in with an idea is conducive to constructive conversation and when it is interrupting. We don't do this, normally, through a direct discussion of how to interact, but we all send out and ideally pick up a lot of cues as to how to do this

We engage in *metacommunication* (communication about communication) in many ways, and we mostly do so unconsciously. We change our body language or tone of voice in ways that indicate whether we comprehend a communication or feel understood. We display our level of engagement, frustration, appreciation, or confusion in various subtle and not so subtle ways. Sometimes we will tell others directly that we are not feeling heard or understood. Sometimes we will say that we understand something or that we are confused. But more often metacommunication is less direct, overt, or intentional. Speakers have to learn to "read" their audiences. Students acquire very effective ways of letting teachers know when they are bored. Children are always training their parents in how to speak to them. This is critical to the success of human relations, which require complex, multilayered interactions to make communication work. Jonathan's and Charles's respective inabilities to pick up on each other's metacommunication were in large part responsible for their difficulties.

Deborah Tannen, in several of her best-selling books about communication (for example, Tannen, 1986, 1990), discusses the central role of what she calls "metamessages" in communication: "Information conveyed by the meanings of words is the message. What is communicated about relationships—attitudes toward each other, the occasion, and what we are saying—is the metamessage. And it's metamessages that we react to most strongly. . . . Whereas words convey information, how we speak those words—how loud, how fast, with what intonation and emphasis—communicates what we think we're doing when we speak: teasing, flirting, explaining or chastising. . . . In other words, how we say what we say communicates social meanings" (Tannen, 1986, pp. 29–30).

No one is always effective at delivering or decoding metacommunication. Frequently, one party to an interchange feels that she or he has successfully connected with another but this sense is not reciprocated. One complicated aspect of cross-cultural communication is the variation in how individuals from different backgrounds engage in the communication loop. Some groups need very active and clear messages of connection during a communication, with head nodding, verbal assents, and intense eye contact. Others prefer much lower-key and subtler feedback. Also, a form of metacommunication that indicates one thing in one culture could well mean something quite different in another. When cultures with different engagement patterns interact, interesting disconnects can happen.

Several years ago one of my colleagues was conducting a training program in Warsaw during which a lively discussion occurred as people expressed very different viewpoints. He was listening attentively to the discussion and nodding his head as different arguments were put forward. In North America this gesture normally signifies that we are being attentive and comprehending what is being said. It does not necessarily mean that we agree. But in Poland the participants interpreted it as a sign of agreement with the speaker. So when my associate responded to people with opposing points of view by nodding his head, he appeared hypocritical to the group. Fortunately, enough rapport existed that people were open about their perception, and an interesting discussion about cross-cultural communication ensued.

The failure to develop a successful communication loop is one of the main sources of communication breakdown, and building this loop is one of the primary ways in which conflict intervention can make a difference. When trust is low and animosity is high, it is often important for third parties to focus first on establishing effective communication with each disputant before focusing on how disputants communicate with each other. When effective communication loops have been developed between the intermediaries and each of the parties, these can then become the basis for establishing a workable system of communication among the disputants.

Successful communication in conflict is iterative. When we are in conflict, we need to try and try again to establish and enhance the communication loop. Unless we have the opportunity to do this, we cannot correct or refine our communication, we cannot work with other disputants to clarify what we are saying or learn how to interact, and we cannot achieve the richness of communication necessary to engage in a constructive interaction. We need to try to keep communication flexible and open. If we state an absolute position or belief firmly and publicly, then it becomes harder for us to modify it in accordance with others' reactions to it.

One of the problems with interacting primarily through formal written communication is that this medium of interchange introduces a major source of inflexibility into an interaction. Written communication tends to be more explicit than oral communication and certainly more committing because it so readily becomes part of a formal record. E-mails are such a fertile source for conflictual communication in part because although they can easily seem informal and impermanent, e-mails are in fact written forms of communication that can be treated as formal documents, maintained forever, and spread to multitudes instantaneously.

CHALLENGES TO COMMUNICATION

Communication can seem challenging under any circumstances, even for people who are supposedly trained in communication. My wife and I are both mediators, and every once in a while we look at each other and wonder how it is that two people trained in conflict intervention can sometimes do such a bad job of communicating. But the fact is that communicating, particularly under stress, is hard for everyone. In conflict situations, even the best of intentions and the most practiced use of good communication processes do not necessarily lead to constructive interactions. Our upset, anger, fear, or anxiety can interfere with communicating. Our capacity to be authentic, to attend to the communication loop, to clear out our mind so that we can really focus, and to remain open to hearing what someone else has to say can be compromised by the tensions and pressures we may be experiencing. That is why the very best of intentions don't always lead to effective interactions in conflict. Let's consider some of the specific challenges to effective communication that we face in conflict.

REACTIVE DEVALUATION

Groucho Marx is reputed to have said that he would never join a club that would have him as a member. When we are in conflict, we are likely to assume that everything we hear from those we are in conflict with is to be treated with suspicion at best and often with immediate and unambiguous dismissal. It is as if I were saying to someone with whom I am in conflict, "If you offer me what I really want, then it must not be what I really want." This is an example of what is sometimes referred to as reactive devaluation (Ross, 1995).

Disputants tend to discount the value of what someone may have offered in a negotiation simply because he or she has offered it. This is one reason why it is often not advisable for negotiators to make their best offer too soon, even if they know it will address the other party's concerns. Unless negotiators have experienced a certain amount of struggle in the attempt to arrive at an ostensibly satisfactory outcome, they may tend to think it is not really the best offer, that they could do better, or that somehow they are being manipulated. This is particularly true if the negotiations are taking place under conflictual circumstances.

> During the previous three years, the union had filed upwards of fifty grievances about the issue of overtime. Less than ten of these had been resolved, and every time the issue of overtime came up, tensions rose in the workplace. Managers felt they could not make even the simplest decisions about overtime without encountering a firestorm of protests over what they saw as minutiae, whereas the union felt that management was simply not willing to honor the letter or spirit of the collective bargaining agreement. These grievances were emblematic of the poor communication and embittered relationships in this workplace. A colleague and I were asked to work with both management and the union to improve their communication and to see if the overall relationships between managers and workers in this midsize factory could be improved.
>
> After some initial work on the broader communication and relationship issues, we thought, along with the factory manager and union president, that it would be useful to try to settle the outstanding overtime-related grievances, thereby removing what had proved to be a significant thorn in everyone's side. The

union and management had already agreed on a procedure to deal with future overtime decisions, but they had not yet decided how to deal with grievances that were still open. We knew that management was willing to agree to much of what the union was asking for, particularly because they were very satisfied with the future procedures that had been worked out. The union, however, was very suspicious of management and did not want to be manipulated by them. Every time management made a concession, the union dismissed it as if it were totally meaningless or unimportant. It seemed that even if management offered the union what they were asking, the union would not trust it and would find some reason to reject the offer. Yet we also had reason to believe that the union really did want these grievances out of the way, and the grievants certainly did.

To break through this very serious case of reactive devaluation, we asked management (in a private discussion) to stop making any offers at all for the moment. We then asked the union to outline very clearly what they needed to settle these grievances. We said we would see what we could do. Then, quite frankly, we manipulated the use of time. Over a period of about sixty minutes, we kept the groups in separate rooms. We kept coming back to the union to discuss a few specifics, and we asked management to consider exactly what they were prepared to commit to. In the end, management had essentially agreed to what the union had asked for, but we still played out the drama a little longer until we felt the time was ready to say we thought that management was willing to accept the union's proposal. The union was still suspicious—and we asked management not to be too effusive about the agreement. Fortunately, enough effort had been expended in getting an agreement that was in principle attainable almost from the beginning of the negotiation that everyone felt satisfied. Of course, a great deal of work still had to be done to deal with the underlying relational issues that made these negotiations so difficult, but having this particular set of issues off the table helped considerably.

Almost everyone who has mediated negotiations with highly distrustful parties has at one time or another had to contend with similar challenges. We did not like to manipulate the negotiations in the way described, but it seemed necessary in this case. Perhaps it would have been better to put the "Groucho Marx syndrome" on the table and discuss it, but our sense was that the timing was not yet right for this. Before they were ready to talk directly about their communication patterns and their general distrust, they needed to see that they could achieve an agreement on some substantive issues. This was not the first or last time that I felt my role as a mediator was akin to that of a theatrical director.

REPORT TALK AND RAPPORT TALK

Communication has multiple purposes, and sometimes we find ourselves at cross-purposes with each other because of this. One potentially problematic difference arises when the primary goal of one party in a communication is to convey information whereas another's is to build or experience a connection. As discussed in Chapter Four, this is sometimes described as the tension between "report talk" and "rapport talk" (Tannen, 1986). For example, many of us who are parents have the habit of asking our children as they arrive home from school to tell us about their day. Perhaps parents do want information, but at least for me this question is almost always primarily about connecting and relating. More often than not (at least with my children), however, this question is seen as a request for information—and as such as a bit burdensome or intrusive (except when they have a story they really want to tell). A typical sequence may go like this:

Parent: How was your day in school today?
Child: Fine
Parent: What did you do?
Child: Not much
Parent: How did your history test go?
Child: Fine, can I go and watch TV now?

Our different motives for engaging in conversation are at least an obstacle to overcome, and if we are embroiled in a significant conflict we can easily feel rebuffed, dismissed, or put down by the incompatibility of our communication aims. Tannen (1990) suggests that boys are more oriented toward report talk and girls toward rapport talk. My own observation is that men and women may have different styles of achieving each goal, but everyone engages in communication for both purposes at different times.

For example, discussions about sports are often a kind of rapport talk that is common among men.

Other differences in communication purposes can exacerbate conflict as well. As suggested by the dimensions of conflict in Chapters One and Five, communication can be focused primarily on achieving action (behavioral), conveying information (cognitive), or expressing feelings (emotional). Communication is sometimes about drawing closer and connecting and sometimes about maintaining boundaries (or both). In *Difficult Conversations,* Stone, Patton, and Heen (1999, pp. 7–8) suggest that all difficult conversations are really composed of three different types of interchanges, which they characterize as the "'What Happened?'" "Feeling," and "Identity" conversations. By unpacking and working in a different way on all these aspects, a more effective approach to difficult communication (which they characterize as a "Learning" conversation) is possible.

However we choose to characterize the different purposes we may have in conversations, it is readily apparent that they can exacerbate already existing communication problems. When we are in conflict or our relationship with someone is tense, the normal tolerance or flexibility we may have to accommodate different purposes or styles of communication is often diminished, and communication itself can therefore make a dispute worse.

ASSUMPTIONS (AND MISAPPREHENSIONS) ABOUT BEING UNDERSTOOD

When someone makes a statement to us, we tend to assume he or she means what we would have meant had we said the same thing in the same way. When we say something, we assume someone will hear it in the spirit in which we intend to communicate it. Even without the added complication of a conflictual relationship these assumptions are often erroneous, but in conflict, with the distrust, suspicion, tension, and fear that are often present, we are especially liable to be mistaken. I may make what I mean to be a friendly but teasing remark in an effort to lower tension and create rapport. You hear it as being dismissive and insensitive. My very effort to get past a barrier in fact reinforces it.

I often feel as if the most important advice I can give to people in conflict is "be less certain"—less certain about the facts, about what is "right," about what is really motivating others (and maybe them), about what their best alternatives are, about what might happen in court, and certainly about whether they have made themselves clear or understood what others have been trying to communicate. It's not the difficulty in communication that is most often the problem in conflict but the assumption that we really have communicated clearly when we have not. When someone does not embrace a concession, accept an apology that we believe to have been obviously sincere, or take a friendly comment in the spirit in which we intended it, we become resentful and often more entrenched. Perhaps we were not as clear as we thought. Perhaps our friendly comment was interpreted as a put-down, or perhaps our apology was accepted in a way that seemed to us halfhearted or dismissive. The problem that causes a breakdown in communication or an escalation of a conflict may exist not because we failed to communicate clearly but because we assumed our communication was accurately understood and reacted accordingly.

SPEAKING WITH POWER

Communicating clearly in conflict takes courage. Delivering difficult messages powerfully, clearly, and at the same time respectfully can be a daunting challenge. Because we are not usually eager to engage in conflict and are often insecure about how well we can handle conflict, we often raise conflict ineptly or unproductively. Probably our most common tendency is to not raise a conflict at all, to hope that an issue will go away, or to allude to the conflict indirectly, even surreptitiously. We are often more comfortable "taking shots" at each other, making snide or cutting remarks, or finding safer surrogate issues to squabble about than we are raising our real issues in a serious manner that demands a response. Sometimes we raise issues in a way that is dramatic, forceful, and clear but brooks no response, no dialogue, and no engaged interaction (as discussed in Chapter Two). A powerful stance is not one that attempts to forestall a reaction or disagreement but one that is offered with confidence that we have a right to our feelings, with an assurance that our needs are legitimate, and with a belief that conflict can be carried out with dignity. Even when we are in a seemingly powerless position, an effectively delivered message can have a strong impact.

In many parts of the world Roma people ("Gypsies") continue to be the targets of racism and discrimination. Unemployment is rampant, death rates are high, and many continue to live in horrible shantytowns. Common attitudes among officials of social welfare, education, and labor agencies reflect this racism. Roma culture and the Roma people are blamed for their situation, and overt expressions of racism are everywhere. Roman is a respected Roma leader in a small city in Bulgaria. I worked with him for several years as part of a multicultural cooperation project. On the outskirts of his town is an extremely poor Roma village that has received almost no services. At the time of our project, there were no sewers, water lines, or paved streets. Unemployment exceeded 90 percent. But the neighborhood had recently received electricity.

A community conflict arose when several families failed to pay their bills, and the municipal government responded by turning off electricity to the whole village, even though most households had paid for the electricity they received. The people in the village approached Roman for his assistance. He had grown up in this neighborhood and still had relatives living there. Roman, together with several colleagues from our project, went to the town hall to complain to municipal officials. Roman and his associates first had to listen to hostile and racist remarks about the people in the village—about how untrustworthy they were and how turning off electrical service was the only way to ensure payment. Roman was used to this. He had heard it all his life. After listening respectfully he made this statement, with a quiet voice but a great deal of fervor.

"Our people have problems, and we should take responsibility for them. It was not right that certain families did not pay their bills. But you too must take responsibility for your mistakes. It is not fair to punish the whole community for what a few families have done. You would never do that to your own community, but because we are Roma you think you can do it to us. We will not accept this, and you must find another way of handling this situation. We will work with you to find a fair way of dealing with this problem, but our community has so little, and this you must not take away from us." [Translated by his daughter]

Roman did not immediately get the response he wanted, but he persisted. After a number of meetings, during which he repeatedly conveyed this message, the municipality relented and installed mechanisms so that in the future just the electricity of those who did not pay their bills would be turned off.

Like listening effectively, raising difficult issues productively is often more a matter of attitude than of technique. For example, it is usually better to use "I" messages—that is, to speak in terms of one's own concerns, needs, experiences, or feelings—than to use "you" messages—to offer judgmental or prescriptive statements about what others have done or ought to do. But having the attitude that underlies an "I" message is more important than using a linguistic formula. If the underlying attitude is prescriptive or judgmental, then all the "I" messages in the world will not prevent others from reacting aggressively or defensively. Conversely, if speakers genuinely believe that more than one point of view is possible and that their story is not the whole story, this will come through even when they make an occasional prescriptive or judgmental statement. Roman delivered quite a few "you" messages in his statement, and he certainly did not frame his comments entirely in terms of how he felt. But he still managed to convey both power and respect, because he felt them. We convey strength, dignity, and respect when our approach embodies these attitudes:

- *All of us have a right to our opinions, needs, concerns, and wishes, and we have a right to have them heard.* If we need others to give us permission to express our views, we will find it harder to speak with constructive power. When we believe that we do not have to justify our concerns or our desire to be heard, we will find it easier to give voice to these concerns in a calm but forceful manner.
- *Others also have the right to their opinions and concerns, and they too have a right to be heard.* Asserting our own needs and views is not about shutting people up. In a conflict, we don't have to justify our feelings or defend our right to have an opinion. We may, however, have to explain and clarify our needs and beliefs, and we have the right to ask others to do this as well.

- *Other points of view are possible, and new information always has the potential to cast a situation in a different light.* In other words, it helps if we are open to the possibility that we might be wrong or at least that we might change our mind about some aspect of a conflict once we hear other perspectives.
- *Expressing concerns or raising issues is different from convincing people that we are right.* One of the surest ways to evoke a defensive or hostile reaction is to raise an issue as an argument. Expressing a concern and stating a point of view are very different from delivering the opening statement in a debate. If I say that I am upset with you for always being late and that this has caused me a lot of problems, that is in itself a powerful statement. If I then go on to list all the reasons why it is not fair for you to be late and to counter all your potential excuses even before you have raised them, then I am trying to shut off your reaction, and you are likely to find it hard to hear my real concerns.
- *Timing is important, as is taking the time necessary to deal with significant issues.* We do not have to unload all our concerns and ideas in one statement or interchange, and is it unwise to squeeze important communication into inappropriate time frames. Sometimes there is no ideal time to raise a difficult or painful issue, but there are often very bad times. When you are rushing out the door to pick up a young child who is waiting for you outside her school, it is probably not the best time for me to tell you how furious I am with you.
- *Presenting one's concerns is different from solving a problem.* One of the biggest mistakes we can make is to raise an important problem and then try to solve it in the same statement. Although this may at first appear to be a constructive approach, it has the effect of focusing others on deciding whether the solution is acceptable rather than on understanding our issues or needs. It may also be an attempt to impede people from expressing their reactions to the issues or concerns we have raised.
- *The fact that two people are involved in a conflict does not mean that there is something wrong with either of them.* There is a difference between being angry about what someone is doing and viewing her or him as a bad person. When we can hold on to

this distinction, it is easier for us to raise our issues forcefully without attacking others personally. Maintaining a sense of the essential humanity of the person with whom we are embroiled in a painful conflict can be very difficult, but it is one of the keys to productive communication.

- *Initial reactions are not necessarily final reactions. Everyone has the right to an emotional reaction to an issue that has been raised or a concern that has been communicated.* My right to express my views does not negate your right to get angry with me when I do so. If I believe you have been cheating me out of my fair share of a joint business, I have a right to express my opinion. That does not mean that you do not have the right to be furious at me for jumping to this conclusion. My raising an issue in a constructive way does not mean you have no right to be angry, upset, or sad in response.

- *Raising issues effectively does not automatically mean things will get better.* No matter how careful we have been to communicate respectfully, we cannot make an issue go away or guarantee that a relationship will improve. All we can be sure of is that we have done our best to set the stage for an effective conflict engagement effort.

- *It is important to communicate in a way that gives others the best chance of understanding what we have to say.* Attentiveness to someone else's communication style is important, especially in conflict. We should be aware of our language, the complexity of our presentation, the metaphors we use, and the buttons we might push. One of the arts of communicating is adapting our language to others' communication style without being patronizing or phony. I may not be able to authentically use teenage lingo when I am dealing with adolescents, but neither do I have to employ professional jargon.

- *Stating something clearly does not mean that others have understood it.* Conflicts escalate when we become convinced that the way we meant to express something is the only honest way in which someone else could have heard it. No matter how clear or careful we have been in expressing an idea or feeling, others can honestly misunderstand it or interpret it in different ways.

These attitudes are not concepts that most people can simply adopt or will themselves to have, but they are often key to effective communication. An important part of the work we do as conflict interveners is to help people raise their concerns in a powerful and respectful way. We do this in part by helping people act on the basis of these attitudes.

FRAMING CONFLICT CONSTRUCTIVELY

We can't solve problems by using the same kind of thinking we used when we created them.
—ALBERT EINSTEIN

We make sense of our world through language. How we describe an event not only influences our understanding of it but also affects how the event unfolds. Conflicts are both exacerbated and alleviated by the language we use to characterize them and by how we frame our issues, concerns, and views. One of the most powerful tools for promoting constructive communication is the process of *successive reframing.* Framing refers to the way a conflict is described, a concern presented, or a proposal formulated; reframing is the process of changing the way ideas are presented so that they maintain their fundamental meaning but are more likely to encourage productive communication. Successive reframing comes into play because complex ideas or issues cannot be effectively reframed in one clever effort. The process instead requires iterative efforts to refine the essential message so that those involved begin to see a greater potential for effective communication. (For another interesting take on reframing, see Bandler and Grinder, 1982.)

For example, a significant reframing is often essential to moving discussions about parenting arrangements subsequent to divorce in a more productive direction. Disputes over custody can be very divisive, partially because of the framing of the parenting decisions that need to be made. In particular, the concept of custody tends to call forth a distributive, all-or-nothing, either-or presentation of important parenting questions. Furthermore, the concept of custody promotes images of control and possession as opposed to responsibility. Mediators and others working with divorcing parents often attempt to reframe the issue of custody into a question of parenting rights and responsibilities. This promotes a more integrative and flexible response to the issue, and it emphasizes obligation rather than just control.

In many conflicts over natural resources, the issues are presented as a dispute about protecting the environment versus encouraging economic development or as a conflict between the government's duty to protect the environment and the rights of individuals to be free from undue governmental interference. Both of these formulations set up a value-based conflict that is difficult to resolve and present an either-or choice. Often it is more productive to consider how economic strength can be enhanced through wise environmental practices or how promoting a sound economy can help preserve the environment.

PRINCIPLES FOR EFFECTIVE REFRAMING

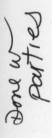

None of these changes in framing come easily when positions are polarized, people are angry, and issues are complicated. Reframing has to occur through an interactive communication process. It has to reflect the basic needs that are being expressed, and it has to be done with the parties, not to them. As with other elements of communication, effective reframing is more a matter of operating from a constructive set of attitudes than about applying a formula or set of techniques. These attitudes include the following:

- *How issues and ideas are framed is important.* Perhaps this is obvious, but if we think of reframing as simply word games or manipulation and not as an important key to unlocking troubled communication and enhancing our ability to understand each other, then word games are probably what we will engage in.
- *In all presentations of important issues there is truth and there are challenges.* Even in the most hostile, negative presentation of an issue there is information about a person's concerns and attitudes that can be useful in moving a communication forward. Likewise, even in the most collaborative-sounding

presentations there are challenges and obstacles to effective communication.

- *Constructive reframing is about clarity and honesty, not about smoothing over difficult issues.* Often a successful reframing will make a conflict seem more severe. Sometimes the hardest conflicts to discuss are those we present in vague, indecisive, and confusing ways to avoid confronting serious disagreements. Effective reframing must therefore occasionally start by highlighting the disagreements and the importance of the issue. If reframing is an attempt to minimize the seriousness of a dispute, it will not in the end be constructive.

- *Reframing has to honor the most important needs of the parties.* One of the keys to an effectively framed conflict is for the essential interests or needs of the main participants to be reflected in the framing. Reframing that does not include people's most important needs is not genuine and will not work. Reframing must capture not just the content of those needs but also the intensity with which they are felt.

- *Successful reframing is interactive and iterative.* Disputants will not change their way of thinking unless they are personally engaged in the reframing process. Significant reframing requires work, successive trials and refinements, and a gradual reorientation of both attitudes and perceptions. Although there will be times when one statement or intervention catalyzes or symbolizes change, such moments almost always rest on previous efforts.

LEVELS OF REFRAMING

Reframing works in different ways at different levels. As conflict interveners, we have to gradually work our way to deeper levels if we are to be truly effective. Often we start by trying to remove the toxicity and provocation from the presentation of an issue or proposal, but in the end we are trying to help people tell a different story, one that is more constructive, hopeful, and flexible. I have observed four essential levels at which reframing occurs. They are related to and intertwined with each other, but they operate at different levels of understanding. All have an emotional and a cognitive component to them. The descriptions that follow are accompanied by examples of a client's framing and a mediator's reframing. These examples (drawn from my mediation practice) show how the content of a framing might change. They are not meant to suggest that simple restatement, without an iterative and interactive process, will get people to look at things differently.

Detoxification Reframing

Reframing as detoxification is about changing the presentation of an idea, concern, proposal, or question so that a disputant's essential interests are still expressed but unproductive language, position taking, and accusations are removed. This is the simplest level of reframing, with the primary goal being to help people get past their inclination to discount what they are hearing because of its toxic presentation. The biggest challenge here is to make sure that the underlying concerns and the intensity with which they are felt do not get minimized or discounted in the reframing process. The most common tactic is to replace value-laden language and positional demands with interest-based formulations.

Framing: He could care less about our child. All he is worried about is how much of his precious money he is going to have to pay in support.

Reframing: You don't think that he is really motivated by your child's well-being, but you are clear that he wants to minimize how much money he has to pay.

Framing: Hell will freeze over before I agree to work with that jerk again. It was torture last time we were on the same team, and I won't subject myself to his arrogance and sadism again.

Reframing: You had a very bad experience working together, and you do not want to repeat it. In particular, you felt exposed to certain behaviors and attitudes that you do not feel you should have to deal with in the workplace (or elsewhere).

The effectiveness of the second reframe—and others—is dependent on not just the words used but the intensity and intonation with which they are expressed. The metamessage is as important as the message.

Definitional Reframing

Definitional reframing focuses on redefining the issue in a less polarizing way. Most definitional reframes emphasize the mutual or integrative nature of the problem to be solved or the interests to be reconciled. This involves a conceptual reframing and often takes the form of presenting an issue as a mutual problem to be mutually addressed. At this level the cognitive aspect of the conflict is usually the most significant target of the reframing effort. The key is to incorporate the essential needs or concerns of all the parties in a common problem statement or suggestion. Often definitional reframing involves changing the level of generality or specificity at which an issue or idea is presented and also altering the time frame in which it is being considered. When parents argue about where their children will spend Christmas Day, a mediator may suggest that they consider what principles they believe should govern decisions about where children will spend important holidays and birthdays. If this reframing reflects the key concerns of the parents, a successful redefinition may have occurred. If not, more work needs to be done. The challenge is to avoid defining the issue so generally or broadly that the immediate interests are lost, or so narrowly or specifically that underlying concerns are not addressed.

Framing: We have to decide who has custody, where the children will live, and how much time they will spend visiting the other parent.

Reframing: You have to decide how you will share your responsibilities as parents and what kind of time your children will spend in each of your homes.

Framing: Are we going to protect the unique quality of our community, or are we going to give in to the city's demands that we conform to regulations that will in the end turn us into just one more yuppie neighborhood?

Reframing: How can the uniqueness of your community be preserved within the city's regulatory framework?

Both detoxification and redefinition are involved in the second example. The danger with this example is that it implies a solution "within the framework." This might seem to rule out the option of remaining outside the city's regulatory control, which might be important to some community members. But in this instance the goal was to see if a satisfactory way of becoming part of the city might be possible.

Metaphoric Reframing

Metaphoric reframing occurs when we try to find a new or altered metaphor for describing a situation or concept, thus changing the way in which it is viewed. Sometimes this means finding a metaphor that all parties can use or translating one party's metaphor into a metaphor recognized by the other party. Sometimes it means making an implied metaphor explicit and exploring its implications. Metaphors are an essential tool that we all use to characterize our circumstances, feelings, and ideas. We also use analogies, aphorisms, proverbs, and quotes for this purpose (see the Einstein quote earlier). These devices can take on a life of their own, and they can constrict our thinking and define situations in ways that make communication difficult. Or they can open up our thinking and encourage greater receptivity to communication. What is a very clear and cogent metaphor for one person may be confusing, irrelevant, or irritating to another, or it may have a very different meaning. I may think "bluffing is part of the game," and you may value being "a straight shooter," but in the end we may all have to "face the music" and "step up to the plate."

Metaphors are not tools we occasionally choose to employ. They are an essential part of how we communicate and how we think. Abstract thinking occurs in great part through the use of metaphors (Lakoff and Johnson, 2003). In fact, reframing itself is a metaphor. It implies that the picture presented by the communication does not change at all, but that it appears to be different because it is presented in a different way. However, as with all metaphors, along with the truth there is some inaccuracy. Reframing inevitably does change some element of the meaning, although ideally not the most important element.

Metaphoric reframing is subtle and requires a great deal of sensitivity to the underlying meaning a metaphor or adage has. It also requires considerable perceptiveness about the ways metaphors can shut down or open up communication. But it can be a very powerful way of bringing about a new understanding of a conflict and encouraging a more productive interaction. A changed metaphor cannot be imposed, however, and third parties need to monitor the metaphors that they introduce as well.

Framing: He just wants to be a Disneyland Daddy while I continue to slave away like Cinderella, doing all the unpleasant grunt work of being a parent.

Reframing: Being a parent is like climbing a mountain. It can be an exhilarating experience, but it involves a lot of hard work. The more work you put in, the greater the exhilaration. It's important for each parent to participate in both aspects of the parenting experience.

Framing: You want to turn this into a hunter's paradise at the expense of a lot of defenseless animals who can't hire lobbyists or lawyers.

Reframing: Humans and animals need to live in balance with each other in this ecosystem.

Narrative Reframing

At the level of narrative, reframing addresses the fundamental ways in which disputants view or analyze a conflict. Normally this means changing how an individual sees herself or himself in the conflict system. It involves looking at the relevant world in a new way and influencing how people make sense of the conflict.

Narrative reframing involves working on the "story line," the dramatic view people have of their conflict. A number of writers (for example, Hale, 1998) have analyzed how people understand a conflict in terms of the dramatic framework they use. For instance, a tragic frame implies powerlessness to influence a conflict and a sense of fatalism or inevitability about how the conflict will turn out. A comic frame, however, implies a multiplicity of options over which disputants have considerable influence. By changing how the action is described, how different participants are characterized, and how the setting is presented, the dramatic frame can be altered.

Another characteristic of drama is the archetypical roles found in most stories. Most narratives at a minimum contain heroes, victims, and villains (Harper, 2004). As we listen to stories of conflict, we can almost always identify who is being cast in these roles. Sometimes the victim and the hero are all wrapped up in the same character. The way these roles are depicted is often an important clue as to how a narrative is fueling a conflict. There is usually no shortage of victimhood to go around, and often there is a potential to expand the story line so that all disputants begin to realize that they are in some sense victims. For example, both Catholics and Protestants were victims during the Troubles in Northern Ireland. For the peace-building process to move forward, it was important for people on all sides of this issue to begin to accept this. The change did not occur easily, but for many people it has slowly taken root, and this has been an essential aspect of the peacemaking efforts. Understanding that we all fill the hero and villain roles at times may also be essential.

However it is accomplished, the process of helping people tell a different story, one that is less hopeless, less polarized, and less populated by good guys and bad guys, is often essential to helping them view a conflict differently. This kind of reframing is not simple or facile. It requires that people listen to each other in new ways. It frequently requires establishing processes that allow disputants to tell their respective stories to each other in a rich and powerful manner and then work to create a new story that incorporates the main elements of each disputant's story line. Unless Palestinians and Israelis, for example, find a way to retell their stories to include the essential elements of each other's history, it is hard to imagine how significant progress can occur.

Many peace-building efforts (for example, dialogue groups, citizen diplomacy, peace camps) are aimed in part at creating a more constructive narrative framework (and establishing the relational ties to support this). Similarly, the power of restorative justice and victim-offender mediation programs is tied to their capacity to influence the narrative structure of those involved so that the pictures victims and perpetrators have of each other are more rounded and nuanced. Of course, the most powerful efforts to formulate a new narrative will not, in the absence of serious efforts to address disputants' most essential concerns, change the fundamental conflict dynamic.

Suggesting neatly packaged examples of narrative reframing is difficult—if not impossible—because narrative reframing is very much about a process and not just about its outcome. The example that follows is intended to show an aspect of narrative reframing but not the process by which this change in the narrative structure might be accomplished. The actual process takes time, is founded on the relationship that is built between the mediator and the disputants, and can only occur as people begin to sense that there might be a way forward to a more constructive type of interaction.

One framing: I have worked hard to make a good education available to my children. They are good students and have the test scores to prove it. But because of race-based admissions criteria, some minorities can get into law school, and get scholarships to boot, just because of how their ancestors were treated in the past. That has nothing to do with my children, and it is unfair.

Another framing: Our children have had to endure inferior schools, racially biased testing, and an ongoing pattern of discrimination. Yet when given a chance to receive a decent education, they have done very well, have become community leaders, and have begun to break the cycle of racism in education and employment. Affirmative action is merely a means of interrupting an ongoing pattern of institutional racism.

Reframing: Everyone has been hurt by the history of racism and discrimination in American education and employment. Minorities have been subjected to inferior education, and now the students of today are being forced to face the consequences of a long-term problem. The diversity of a student body is one of the greatest assets an educational institution has to offer as it prepares leaders to work in a diverse world. However, it is critical that this diversity not be achieved at the expense of any particular group. Our educational institutions need to develop the capacity to educate qualified students from all backgrounds and the evaluative tools to recognize the potential of students from very different educational settings.

This example shows how hard it can be to attain a genuine reframing of a conflict narrative. It also shows how hard it is to find a succinct way to express a complicated concept. Reframing, particularly at the narrative level, often takes time and many iterations to be effective. But encouraging such reframing is sometimes the most profound intervention a conflict specialist can bring to a dispute.

Reframing is an essential part of a constructive communication process. It occurs naturally, but it is also an area in which intentional efforts make a difference. However, reframing can also be manipulative. It can be used to talk people out of their concerns or feelings or to water down a conflict or issue. Although this may occasionally work in the short run to bring about agreements, it is almost never effective in achieving a significant level of progress on important issues. In fact, manipulative reframing leads to disputants' mistrust of dialogue efforts and of the third parties who conduct them. The art of reframing is to maintain the conflict in all its richness but to help people look at it in a more open-minded and hopeful way.

not to manipulate

Communication is a system of interaction. In some sense communication is always flawed because it is impossible simply to put our thoughts and feelings directly into someone else's head. In the struggle to communicate and to overcome the obstacles that get in the way of our truly understanding each other in tense situations, genuine creativity can emerge. When individuals in conflict view the truth as existing not inside them but among all the people involved in the dispute, they are more likely to achieve a higher level of understanding and empathy. This view is the foundation of all profound conflict engagement processes.

CHAPTER EIGHT

NEGOTIATION

It's not about WIN-LOSE

Negotiation is a basic life skill that we use every day in many ways. We use it in making business arrangements, family decisions, plans with friends, and commercial transactions. When we work out special arrangements about bedtimes and chores with our children, we are negotiating. When we decide which movie or restaurant we will go to with our spouse, we are negotiating. When we agree on a division of work responsibilities with our colleagues, we are also negotiating. Why is it, then, that when we think of an interaction as a negotiation it can suddenly seem tense, challenging, or tricky? Labeling an interchange as a negotiation seems to take it beyond the everyday kind of transaction we are used to and at which we are mostly competent. Suddenly we start thinking that there are going to be winners and losers, that a game is being played, and that people are out to take advantage of one another. We believe we will have to compromise on issues that are important to us, and we suddenly become concerned about how open to be about our needs and alternatives.

POPULAR ASSUMPTIONS ABOUT NEGOTIATION

Our approach to negotiation is guided by culturally based assumptions or beliefs about negotiation, which are not necessarily grounded in the structure of the negotiation process. Let's consider some of these common assumptions.

- *Negotiation is a game.* The metaphors we use in discussing negotiation often come from sports, poker, or other games. We talk about "putting our cards on the table," "upping the ante," "calling a bluff," "scoring a knockout," "reaching a stalemate," "playing hardball," and the like. Thinking of negotiation as a game implies a particular kind of structure and motivation. Games tend to involve a known process, standards of conduct, and a relatively clear goal. But games also are normally about winners and losers, about fixed-sum outcomes, and about being more competent or clever than the other players (who are viewed as opponents).

- *Negotiation is about compromise.* Many people resist negotiation because they think it implies having to compromise on important issues or values. Although negotiation may involve compromise, that is not its necessary result. In many (but not all) negotiations we do operate from a set of norms that promote compromise and the consideration of an adversary's point of view. Sometimes these collaborative norms may make us resistant to negotiating, especially when we are very angry, feel adamant about our position, consider the other side to be evil, or believe that our self-image is somehow at stake.

- *Negotiation is about giving up power.* Parents are often resistant to the idea of negotiating with their children, managers with their employees, or police with suspects because negotiation seems to imply giving away power. Ironically, parents negotiate with children, managers with employees, and police with suspects all the time, but without the negotiation label. Negotiation often involves applying power, recognizing someone else's power, or discussing arrangements that may realign power, but it does not necessarily imply giving away power. Negotiation is in fact often a way of exercising power more effectively.

- *Negotiation is about being nice.* Do we have to be friendly or deny our anger toward others when we negotiate? Do we have to treat others as if we approve of them in some way? Respect them? Want a relationship with them? Of course not. We have to be willing to communicate with the other parties, but we do not have to pretend that our feelings are anything other than what they are.

- *Negotiation is about being nasty.* Sometimes people assume that to negotiate you have to be belligerent, hard-nosed, and tough—in other words, the opposite of friendly. We may resist negotiation because we do not want to behave in these ways but we worry that the alternative to being nasty is being vulnerable.
- *Negotiation is a complex process.* The consequence of thinking of negotiation as a complex interaction is that we feel intimidated by it—we do not feel we can master it and therefore feel very vulnerable. Although negotiation has its complexities, its essence is fairly straightforward.
- *Negotiation is only okay when it is a win-win process.* Maybe in a perfect world all negotiations would be win-win processes, but in our world that is not possible or even desirable. Sometimes compromise is necessary. Sometimes one side really ought to lose. Sometimes the gist of a negotiation is about dividing up a limited resource. We do not encourage collaborative approaches to negotiation by being naïve about its win-lose aspects or by labeling suggestions for distributive solutions as violations of higher values concerning human interaction.
- *Negotiation is fundamentally a win-lose process (and if you don't recognize this you are naïve).* Although it may be naïve to think negotiation can always be win-win, it is equally misleading to think that negotiation necessarily involves winning and losing. If we think that our choice is to be a winner or a loser in a negotiation, then we face the dilemma of either being taken advantage of or trying to take advantage of others. Negotiation is in part about finding a successful way through unpalatable choices such as these.

The problem with these assumptions is not so much that we consciously ascribe to them. If asked directly, most of us would probably reject all of these in their most rigid or stark form. However, our culture is imbued with many of these attitudes. Consider how negotiation is portrayed in movies (Bruce Willis in *The Fifth Element,* 1997; John Travolta and Robert Duval in *A Civil Action,* 1998; Danny DeVito, Michael Douglas, and Kathleen Turner in *The War of the Roses,* 1989; or Jesse Eisenberg and Justin Timberlake in *The Social Network,* 2010, to name just a few).

Negotiation is frequently portrayed as a divisive power struggle in which the most devious, ruthless, or aggressive player will win. These attitudes are pervasive, and even if we consciously reject them they still have an impact on us. They each contain some truth, but as overarching approaches they are misleading and destructive because they encourage rigidity or resistance to engaging in a potentially advantageous process. So, if these assumptions do not define negotiation, what does?

WHAT IS NEGOTIATION? *Problem-Solving Decision-making*

Negotiation is an interaction in which people try to meet their needs or accomplish their goals by reaching an agreement with others who are trying to get their own needs met. Whether we call it problem solving, bargaining, cooperative decision making, or communicating, when two or more people try to reach a voluntary agreement about something, they are negotiating. They may be communicating directly, in writing, or through a third party. They may be friendly, hostile, positional, or open-minded; they may have good alternatives to negotiation or no acceptable choices. One of them may have a great deal of power and may not have to negotiate to meet his or her needs, or each may genuinely need the other to accomplish his or her goals. This interaction may be formally structured and labeled as a negotiation, or it may be informal and unstructured.

Does negotiation have to be voluntary? Participation in negotiation is not always voluntary. Labor and management are sometimes required to negotiate, as are people involved in grievances, civil suits, and divorces. Sometimes our alternatives to negotiation are not acceptable or desirable, and so we feel as if we have no choice but to negotiate. However, if we have no choice but to accept a particular outcome and no opportunity to advocate for our needs, then it is not negotiation. Sometimes a dictated or top-down decision is presented in the guise of negotiation, but this is not negotiation. Negotiation is also different from supplying information or a point of view to a decision maker. Unless we are involved in an effort to reach a mutual agreement or common plan of action, we are not engaged in negotiation. However, when we do make such an effort, even if the pressure is great, the power skewed, and the alternatives few, the process is some form of negotiation.

Negotiation implies advocacy. As negotiators, we advocate for our interests or the interests of those we represent. Although a negotiator is always an advocate, an advocate is not always a negotiator. Advocacy comes with its own set of assumptions. For example, we often think that the advocate's job is to claim as much as possible of a limited pie rather than to search for a mutually arrived-at outcome. We also advocate to others who are decision makers, such as judges, bosses, or legislative bodies. We often measure our competence as advocates (or the effectiveness of someone who is advocating for us) by how forceful we are or how much fervor we demonstrate. But often the most zealous advocate behaviors are not the most effective, even though they may allow us to trumpet how unwavering we have been in pursuit of our goals.

Sometimes an advocate or a system of advocacy (for example, the legal system, a trade union, an employee relations department) cultivates adversarial skills. At other times more collaborative or flexible skills are encouraged. Some of the resistance to collaborative strategies is based on concerns about their effectiveness, but often it is a product of an environment that does not encourage or reward cooperative approaches to advocacy or negotiation. And sometimes our approach to advocacy and to negotiation is determined by what we are more confident in and familiar with. When we are confident in our ability to advocate in an adversarial manner, that is the approach we will naturally rely on when the going gets tough and negotiations become tense. The decisive moment in the following labor-management negotiation occurred when a few key people made a courageous decision to try a less familiar and comfortable approach and to risk the displeasure of their allies.

The wounds from the last strike had not yet healed, but new contract negotiations were about to begin. The leadership and the union of a large corporation were determined to avoid a repetition of that last encounter, but their relationship remained very tense. They jointly hired three mediators (two from CDR Associates and one from a local conflict resolution organization) to work with them as they prepared for the negotiations. We were asked to train the two bargaining teams in collaborative negotiation procedures and to facilitate a discussion about how they might implement these procedures in the upcoming talks. We worked with about twenty people from each side at a four-day retreat, sometimes in their separate teams, sometimes together.

The training component was fascinating because everyone used the exercises to act out their fears and stereotypes about each other. At one point in a role play, a key (real-life) management negotiator made an agreement with the chief (real-life) union negotiator and then reneged on it. The people on the simulation team of the union negotiator were furious. As it happened, however, the management negotiator was prompted to do this (in the spirit of "let's have some fun with this role play") by one of the other members of his simulation team, who was in actuality a union negotiator. The debriefing for this simulation was an eye-opener for everyone. Union members realized how angry they were when they thought this was the action of a manager and how ready they were to see this as an example of management's nefarious values and manipulative behavior. When they realized it was one of their own leaders who had promoted this behavior, they were called on to face their own stereotypes and attributions. Despite the fact that it was just an exercise, in many ways this was the real beginning of the negotiations.

After this simulation, when the actual union and management teams began to discuss how to conduct the upcoming collective bargaining talks, several interesting parallels in the internal dynamics of the two groups became evident. Some in each group wanted to take a more collaborative approach and to end the personal attacks that had characterized previous negotiations, but there were also those who were convinced that under the guise of collaboration they were going to be manipulated by the other side. For individuals in either team to be too outspoken in advocating a collaborative approach was risky because by doing so they made themselves vulnerable to accusations of naïveté and weakness.

People struggled with this dilemma until they reached a crisis point. This occurred after one group had taken a chance and offered some important procedural and psychological concessions. The initial reaction of the other team was negative. Team members discounted the meaning and sincerity of the concessions and responded by once again venting their anger about the previous contract negotiations. The first team was very discouraged and was about to abandon the effort to design a new approach.

I met with the members of the second group at this point and said that they had reached crunch time. They had to decide whether to take a risk or to return to previous patterns of interacting. If they did not make a decisive conciliatory move now, it would be a while before they again had such an opportunity. I said that I could not evaluate what was the right decision for them to make, but I was convinced that this was the moment to either make a conciliatory response or pursue a different path. A tense debate followed during which one of the most respected negotiators in the group said that it was time to start doing things differently. In a subsequent joint meeting the second group expressed genuine appreciation for the concessions that the first group had made and reciprocated in a heartfelt and eloquent way. This really surprised the first group and went a long way toward alleviating the tension and suspicion in the room. During the final day of the retreat, both teams were productively engaged in setting up new procedures for negotiating and for union-management interactions in general.

Not everything went easily after this of course. Change is gradual and halting. But the negotiations did proceed much more smoothly, and in a relatively short amount of time a new contract was signed. Negotiators repeatedly referred to the discussions they had had during the retreat. Their willingness then to take some risks carried over to the actual negotiations.

Being an effective advocate is not equivalent to being either adversarial or collaborative. It means being competent at furthering the particular set of needs for which one is advocating. The strategic question that all advocates face is how to be credible as adversaries and at the same time be genuinely open to the potential that collaborative approaches offer. This dilemma is at the heart of most negotiations.

The Negotiator's Dilemma

How can negotiators protect their interests while developing cooperative relationships? This is the negotiator's dilemma. How do we enlarge the pie (create value, expand options, develop win-win outcomes) and also get as big a share of the pie as we want, deserve, or need (claim value, protect our interests)? Or, as I think we sometimes experience this dilemma, how can we avoid being either "jerks" or "suckers." This dilemma is one of the main challenges negotiators, and in fact all conflict interveners, must confront.

Approaches that may maximize our effectiveness along one dimension of negotiation often interfere with it in another. For example, to promote a cooperative negotiation it is important to share information, to be candid about fundamental interests, and to be honest about our alternatives. However, this can give valuable information to the other party should he or she decide to engage in hardball negotiations or to sue. Conversely, when we withhold this candor and proceed as if we are likely to end up in court, our chances of engaging in a collaborative negotiation process diminish. In this way we often create a self-fulfilling prophecy.

This dilemma is not hopeless. We do not have to choose one extreme or the other. But it is real and affects everyone's behavior in complex negotiations. Our effectiveness as negotiators is in part determined by how well we handle this dilemma. One way of understanding this challenge is to consider the dimensions of negotiation.

DIMENSIONS OF NEGOTIATION

Negotiators have two fundamental ways in which they can meet their needs in the face of limited resources and potentially competing interests. They can each try to claim as large a share of the available benefits for themselves (or the people they represent) as they need or want, or they can try to ensure that the total available benefits are sufficient to accommodate everyone's most important needs. Each of these approaches is present in almost all negotiations, and each tends to be associated with a particular set of strategies. (For other descriptions of these dimensions, see Lax and Sebenius, 1986, 2006; Mnookin, 1993; Thomas, 1983; Walton and McKersie, 1965.)

To the extent that a negotiation is about gaining as large a share of the available benefits as possible, it is distributive. That is, the negotiation is about dividing up or distributing the available benefits, value, goods, or services. When we operate along the distributive dimension, we are trying to get our needs met at others' expense, as they are trying to do at our expense. We are therefore in a structurally adversarial position (even if our behavior does not reflect this). This does not necessarily mean we are enemies or hostile toward each other. But we are still vying against each other in some sense. If I am selling you something, I am likely to want to get as much for it as I can, whereas you are likely to want to pay as little as possible. When most people think about negotiation, this distributive dimension (sometimes called the fixed-sum dimension) is what they have in mind.

most she it this way

Alternatively, we can try to meet our needs through increasing what is available for all and making sure everyone's needs are adequately addressed. To the degree that we are pursuing this integrative dimension, we have the common interest of "increasing the pie," and our needs are therefore integrated. In a negotiation over the sale of a house, for example, to the extent that a buyer and seller focus on minimizing taxes, third-party fees, and transaction costs as well as maintaining a good relationship with each other they are operating along the integrative dimension (also called the variable-sum dimension). Addressing the distributive realities while achieving the integrative potential is often the major challenge that negotiators face and is another aspect of the negotiator's dilemma. This was a significant challenge in a facilitated negotiation to decide how to deal with a highly contaminated site in Utah.

integrative

At one time the Murray Smelter in Murray, Utah, was the largest lead ore smelter in the world. It was operated by the ASARCO Corporation until it closed in 1949. The site was then sold in parcels, which were used for a concrete casting facility, an asphalt production plant, warehouses, trailer parks, and a variety of other light industrial or commercial purposes. It was eventually determined that this location contained some of the highest concentrations of arsenic and lead in the state and was therefore designated for possible listing as a Superfund priority site for environmental cleanup. The city of Murray viewed the site as having excellent potential for commercial development. It was located near a major interstate highway, on the route of a planned light rail system, and near the city's business district. City leaders wanted to avoid Superfund listing and to find a way to coordinate the cleanup and redevelopment.

The cost of the cleanup would be reduced significantly if the proposed roadway on the site could be constructed as a repository for low-level hazardous waste. The required levels of remediation would also be reduced if the site were covered with paving or other relatively impermeable barriers, and if it were not used for residences or for purposes that would require people to work outside. If a redevelopment plan could be worked out that would involve the sale of certain properties, a guarantee about future usage, ongoing monitoring of groundwater, and the construction of an appropriate roadway, everyone could achieve considerable benefits. The cleanup would be cheaper, quicker, and more effective; the city could develop this site into a prime commercial (and taxable) location; and the frequently contentious process of allocating responsibilities and agreeing on cleanup levels and technologies could be shortcut. However, this was a very big "if." Many pieces had to fall into place, each of which could have been subverted by any one of the many players involved. Much could be achieved for everyone, but only if no person or organization tried to claim too much of the benefit.

To work out the complex details of this plan, the Environmental Protection Agency (EPA) organized a roundtable process to discuss cleanup and redevelopment options. A CDR colleague and I served as facilitators. Participants included representatives from Murray, the EPA, the Utah Department of Environmental Quality, the state attorney general's office, the Utah Transportation Authority, ASARCO, all property owners and renters with long-term leases, the U.S. Department of Justice, and eventually the potential developer.

Many aspects of the negotiation were distributive. How much land would each property owner allocate for the roadway? What contribution would be made by those whose property did not abut the road? How much would different parties contribute to the cleanup? Many of these negotiations had to occur among people who had a history of conflict. If they had been too focused on meeting their needs at the expense of others, the whole process would have failed. A series of complicated distributive negotiations played out against the background of a powerful integrative potential. To attend solely to the integrative or win-win aspects was not realistic because significant distributive decisions had to be made. The parties were keenly aware of this. If any of these collateral negotiations had broken down or led to a court process, the whole opportunity could have collapsed. Naturally some parties acted as if they were perfectly willing for that to happen and even threatened it from time to time.

In the end, however, the integrative opportunity prevailed. An overall agreement was reached, which led to a consent decree. Cleanup procedures were implemented, the roadway was constructed as a repository for the on-site storage of low-level waste, and the property was developed for commercial purposes

can be there as either (or Not)

All negotiations have distributive and integrative aspects. No matter how committed negotiators are to a win-win approach, they are going to face some decisions about dividing up limited resources, and no matter how much a negotiation appears to be about trying to get the most of an available resource (say, money), there is always some potential for joint gain (future favors, emotional satisfaction, improved relationships). Sometimes one approach might dominate. Sometimes it is possible to incorporate both an integrative and distributive approach at the same time. Sometimes we cycle through different emphases in fairly rapid succession. And of course, different negotiators might focus on different dimensions at the same time. In fact, what makes negotiation so interesting is that no one side can solely determine which orientation will prevail. As in so many other areas of human interaction, negotiation is a jointly crafted experience. It is often very difficult to tell just how these dimensions are in play at any given time. We can get a clue, however, if we consider the basic characteristics of each approach and the underlying attitudes that define them.

DISTRIBUTIVE NEGOTIATION

How to get the most available

When we function primarily along the distributive dimension, we are focused on how to get the most of what is available for ourselves or the people we represent. As distributive negotiators, we may use a variety of tactics to convince others to agree to the allocation of benefits that we want. Several approaches are characteristic of the distributive dimension:

— in terms of questions

- *Issues tend to be framed in terms of how to compromise among conflicting needs or how to choose among mutually exclusive alternatives.* The distinguishing feature of distributive negotiation is not whether the issue is framed in harsh or gentle language. Distributive negotiation can be friendly, and integrative negotiation can be hostile. The key is that the issue is presented as a question about how to divide up a limited resource.

Ask as a question

- *Power is applied to wrest concessions out of other parties.* Rather than using power to develop creative options or to persuade others of the joint benefits to be accrued from a proposed solution, distributive negotiators apply power to convince others that they have no good alternative but to make concessions. In a distributive negotiation, we tend to focus on our "rights," on whether we are getting "the best deal," or on how well we are doing relative to others rather than on whether we are arriving at a wise solution that meets everyone's essential needs.

S)B about

- *Alternatives are used as leverage to convince others to compromise or to give up potential benefits.* Whereas in an integrative negotiation alternatives are used to enhance creativity and expand the options, in a distributive negotiation we are more likely to talk about how strong a court case we have and how willing we are to walk away from a negotiation. We may argue that we do not really need an agreement but that the other negotiators surely do. In short, we play the "alternatives game," attempting to manipulate others' perceptions about the alternatives (theirs and ours) to a negotiated settlement in order to leverage them into making concessions.

Distributive negotiators often refer to their "bottom line." They discuss this as if it were a definite location on the spectrum of possible outcomes: "Bottom line is I want the children to live with me during the school week"; "I am willing to sell this car for $7,500, but that is the bottom line." We generally use bottom line to mean the boundary between acceptable and unacceptable outcomes. But what determines this boundary, and how porous is it? Typically, when we view our BATNA, our best alternative to a negotiated agreement (Fisher and Ury, 1981), as better than the potential agreement, we have reached our bottom line. If I think I am better off refusing to make a deal than selling my car for less than $7,500, I have reached my bottom line. This is not, however, a simple cost-benefit consideration. We also think about whether we will lose face, about whether it is better to get nothing than to accept an unfair deal, about whether we would rather inflict pain on someone else than meet our own needs, about whether to consider the long-term ramifications of accepting an offer or to focus on the immediate consequences, and a host of other intangible and often unconscious considerations. A bottom line is at best a moving target, always subject to changing circumstances, new information, and evolving emotional stances.

Furthermore, we arrive at our bottom line through an interactive process that involves trying to influence each other's perceptions of the alternatives. If I am in a distributive negotiation with you, I may want you to believe that I have many viable alternatives and that you have none. In addition, I may try to convince you that I am near my bottom line so that you will make concessions to obtain an agreement. In evaluating whether I have reached a good agreement, I will try to figure out whether I have gotten the most I can out of you—that is, whether you are close to your bottom line.

- *Information is a key item in the negotiation.* Information is shared to the degree that it will convince others to compromise. Information that points out the weakness of others' position is helpful; information that points out the limits of our own alternatives is not. The way information is shared also reflects the dimension of the negotiation that is dominating the interaction. When information is presented as an argument for a particular outcome, that is usually a sign of a distributive approach. If it is presented as data to help everyone develop and evaluate alternatives, it is more likely that an integrative process is under way.
- *Agreement is reached when the parties accept a proposal they believe to be better than or at least as good as their realistic alternatives.* This is normally a very subjective determination. We often evaluate our alternatives unconsciously or at best impressionistically. We rely on emotional information as well as logical cost-benefit analysis, and what appears to be a good outcome one moment may seem like a terrible one the next.

Distributive negotiations are not necessarily adversarial. People can work together in a friendly and open manner to decide how to apportion a limited resource. Most purchase and sales negotiations are friendly, collaborative, and distributive. However, when negotiations are about resolving a significant conflict in which the stakes are high, relationships are poor, and emotions are raw, a distributive approach is likely to be contentious.

The most serious problem with a distributive approach is that it is not a very effective way of making sure that "value is not left on the table" or that the potential for joint gain has been adequately explored. For that to occur, work has to occur along the integrative dimension.

INTEGRATIVE NEGOTIATION

The more the integrative dimension of a negotiation can be maximized, the less extreme the negotiator's dilemma. (This dilemma never completely goes away, however.) As discussed earlier, to the degree that this dimension is present in a negotiation, we are oriented to "enlarging the pie"—that is, to maximizing the benefits available for distribution among all involved or to meeting each party's essential needs in some way.

Information is central to a successful integrative negotiation. Two approaches are essential to making progress along this dimension, and both require an open and thorough exchange of information. One is based on similarity of interests, the other on dissimilarity. Integrative solutions can be attained when people discover a common interest they can jointly pursue. Divorcing parents are both usually concerned about the well-being of their children. Environmentalists and industrialists often share a desire for predictability in governmental procedures for enforcing environmental regulations. Labor and management both care about the long-term viability of their organization. These joint interests can form the underpinning of an integrative negotiation.

But having different interests is another basis for an integrative outcome, as long as the interests are not in direct opposition to each other. If one parent wants to have particular influence over educational decisions for a child and the other wants to guide that child's religious upbringing, they have a basis for an integrative negotiation. Similarly, if one partner in a business dissolution cares about liquidity of assets and the other is concerned about long-term growth, they may have an opportunity for an integrative solution.

Realizing the integrative potential, however, requires the parties to share enough information to allow them to discover their common or complementary needs. Much of what characterizes effective integrative negotiation is therefore related to enabling a free flow of information and an open discussion of possible solutions.

Integrative negotiations tend to be characterized by the following principles: *Relationship centered*

- *Integrative negotiation is about building relationships.* Although most negotiations involve relationship-building activities, integrative negotiations are particularly dependent on them to be effective. This does not mean that people have to like, trust, admire, or enjoy each other. They do, however, have to be able to relate to each other well enough that they can work together to communicate their essential concerns and perspectives.

- *Integrative negotiation is about effective communication.* All negotiations of course involve communication, but specific attention to enhancing communication is essential to an integrative process. Negotiators develop a communication system. It may be carried over from previous interchanges, or it may be freshly created. The extent to which the integrative potential of a negotiation can be realized depends on the nature of the communication process that is built. Negotiators are seldom aware of this, but the creation of a communication system is often the result of a de facto negotiation within the primary negotiation. Sometimes it is essential to make this an overt and intentional focus as well.

- *Integrative negotiation is about education.* The more intense the integrative effort, the more energy needs to be devoted to mutual education. Participants have to educate each other about their concerns, the constraints under which they are operating, the choices they feel they have, and the relevant information they are bringing to the table. Normally this needs to take place before the parties focus on solutions or outcomes.

- *Integrative negotiation is a joint effort to address all parties' needs.* To the extent that a negotiation is integrative, it will take the form of a mutual problem-solving effort. This means that negotiators frame issues as mutual problems to be mutually solved and that they try to address each other's concerns, not just their own.

- *Integrative negotiation is a principled process.* There are three ways in which an integrative negotiation needs to be a principled process in order to promote the achievement of joint benefits.

  First, it is important that the negotiation be conducted in a way that meets the fundamental behavioral norms of the different participants. Although some individuals may feel that lying to people, misleading them, and intimidating them are acceptable behaviors in a negotiation, these behaviors do not promote mutual problem solving, effective communication, or rapport.

  Second, integrative negotiations are often characterized by agreements in principle that define the mutual gains being sought. This allows the distributive elements present in almost all negotiations to be addressed without threatening the overall integrative thrust. If parents agree in principle that their children should have full access to both of them, that full access means at least 40 percent of the time, and that each parent has a right to be involved in essential decisions about the children's education, religion, and geographical location, then the distributive discussions of holidays, specific schedules, and transition arrangements are less likely to undercut the overall integrative effort.

  Third, integrative negotiators try to distinguish between the basic principles or values they are promoting and the ways these can be realized. We can be very adamant about our essential concerns and values—and very insistent that these be addressed—but still remain open to a variety of ways this might occur.

- *Integrative negotiation is an interest-based process.* Interest-based negotiation and integrative negotiation are not identical (as I discuss in the next section). A distributive negotiation may be conducted through a careful consideration of each party's interests. But an effective integrative negotiation usually requires negotiators to have a clear view of both their own interests and those of the others involved. Moreover, an integrative approach deals not only with people's substantive issues but also with their procedural and psychological concerns. Usually the immediate focus of an integrative negotiation is at the level of interests, but sometimes it is necessary to address more fundamental concerns relating to identity or even survival. A successful integrative negotiation finds the optimal level of depth at which to pursue meaningful joint benefits. This is not a mechanistic process that rules out position taking or prescribes a particular set of steps that must be sequentially followed. Each negotiation is different, and there are multiple ways in which negotiation can be productively pursued. But unless a negotiation allows for a thorough exploration of the various needs and concerns parties may have, realizing its full integrative potential will be difficult.

- *Integrative negotiation encourages creativity in problem solving.* Developing mutually beneficial options can take considerable creativity. We usually find it easier to see how our needs can be met through others' concessions than to develop alternatives for joint gain. The challenge in an integrative negotiation is to develop an atmosphere that promotes this creativity. One of the main reasons to work on establishing rapport, reducing tension, and building trust is to promote a negotiation culture in which it is safe and beneficial to be creative. Often norms are embedded in negotiation that stifle creativity. For example, it can be hard to brainstorm a wide variety of potential outcomes if negotiators believe they cannot suggest an option for consideration unless they are willing to commit to it.

How open or closed a process is also affects how creative people can be. Too closed a process is likely to shut out inputs that might enhance creativity, but too open a process makes individuals much more careful about what they say. We have seen some interesting public debates in the recent past about these very questions. Should the negotiations to create the new

U.S. health care law have been open, as President Obama originally suggested? What is the impact of WikiLeaks on international negotiations, such as between the Palestinian Authority
and Israel? Too little openness undercuts accountability and
the capacity to bring key stakeholder groups into the problem-
solving process. Too much can stifle communication.

- *Integrative negotiation requires a genuine partnership among
the participants.* Unless negotiators become partners in the
pursuit and execution of mutually beneficial solutions, it is
hard for an integrative negotiation to take place. Partnership
does not imply being friendly or ignoring conflict. It does
mean that we must learn to work together to define issues;
develop suitable negotiation procedures; educate each other;
create a constructive negotiation culture; obtain important
information; develop options for consideration; evaluate,
modify, refine, and select options; and implement and
monitor agreements. Practically speaking, it means more of
this work is done jointly and less of it separately.

Integrative negotiation is not a panacea, nor is it always an
appropriate goal for negotiators. However, work along this dimension is often the most effective approach to addressing the negotiator's dilemma, particularly in the midst of high levels of conflict.
All negotiations have both distributive and integrative dimensions.
As important as it is to help people locked into a distributive process see the integrative potential, it is also essential that integrative
negotiators do not shy away from addressing the distributive elements of a problem.

The question arises as to what will occur when one negotiator is taking an integrative approach and another a distributive
approach. However, the question itself betrays a misunderstanding
of the interactive nature of negotiation. It may be that one party is
being more aggressive, adversarial, or hostile than the other, but
the degree to which a negotiation develops along the distributive
or integrative dimension is a product of the interaction among the
participants, not of the individual behavior of any one negotiator.
We behave in an integrative or distributive manner because the
situation calls for it or because in some way this meets our needs.

The interaction of different approaches, which is itself a sort of negotiation, determines the nature of the overall process.

The conflict intervener's challenge is to make sure that the integrative potential is maximized, to find a way of approaching the distributive elements without escalating a conflict, and to promote a negotiation culture that allows people to be effective advocates and effective partners at the same time. This is how we can help people address the negotiator's dilemma.

POSITIONAL AND INTEREST-BASED NEGOTIATION

Since the publication of *Getting to Yes* (Fisher and Ury, 1981), the concepts of positional and interest-based negotiation have become central to how many of us view the negotiation process. Positional negotiation is often equated with a distributive approach, and interest-based negotiation is associated with an integrative approach. But the concepts are not the same, and we miss the underlying dynamics in negotiation when we confuse them. The distributive and integrative dimensions of a negotiation are defined by the degree to which the emphasis of the negotiation process is on dividing up benefits among the parties or on maximizing benefits for all. Positional negotiation is differentiated from interest-based negotiation by the degree to which the process focuses on a proposed solution or an analysis of interests and needs. In positional negotiation, people focus on a series of proposed solutions (positions), which they defend or alter depending on the circumstances. In interest-based negotiation, people discuss their needs and concerns and look for options to address them. One set of concepts pertains to the basic structure of negotiation—how people define their purpose and their fundamental orientation toward accomplishing it—and the other is about tactics and motivation.

The distinction between positional and interest-based approaches can easily be overemphasized and misleading. A single-minded concentration on positions can quickly lead to adversarial and polarized interactions. So focusing, as a tactic, on a consideration of interests as opposed to debating proposed solutions can be very effective. As a conflict intervention trainer, I have found that the concepts of positions and interests are useful to people who want to learn new ways of approaching conflict. They provide a tangible way of distinguishing between cooperative and adversarial approaches and suggest useful tactics. But focusing on interests is not the same as engaging in an integrative approach to negotiation, and taking positions about the issues at hand does not necessarily obstruct engaging in collaborative problem solving. To understand this, it is important to consider the relationship between positions and interests and their role in negotiations.

All negotiations involve a focus on both interests and positions. Even the most adversarial bargainer will often express his or her interests and explore those of other parties. And even the most interest-based negotiator cannot and should not always shy away from presenting proposed solutions during a negotiation. It is naïve to think that a simple focus on interests will change the fundamental nature of negotiations or that an exchange of statements about positions is always a counterproductive activity. Such an exchange is often a useful and necessary step in an orderly and productive consideration of the nature of the conflict and the needs of the parties. Considering interests in the abstract is sometimes less effective than uncovering them through an analysis of the rationale behind the solutions negotiators propose, as was the case in this negotiation:

> In a negotiation about the location of a roadway through a community, early efforts to talk directly about stakeholders' interests elicited broad and somewhat bland statements about noise, accessibility, aesthetics, and safety. There was no new information here, and some people felt that they were going through an academic exercise. However, when particular proposals (positions) about roadway location were put forward, two things occurred. As people sought to understand the rationale for each proposal, people became more engaged and creative and a much richer discussion of interests ensued.

Although a focus on interests may lead to a more effective communication style, it is the change in how we communicate that is really important, and that change can occur in many ways.

As discussed previously, what usually needs to occur for a negotiation to be successful is for us to learn to communicate effectively with each other. If we really listen to each other and try to understand what is at stake for all participants in a negotiation, we will naturally focus on each other's needs.

Our basic attitude about what we are trying to accomplish is also more significant than whether we are focusing on positions or interests. Are we trying to win or to solve a problem? Do we see the other negotiators as enemies, adversaries, rivals, partners, or colleagues? Do we see the negotiation as a contest or a dialogue? Our attitudes may be reflected in how positional or interest based our negotiation style is, but it is the attitudes themselves that are usually the driving force.

Furthermore, positions and interests themselves are not as different as they might at first appear. The difference between positions and interests is usually a difference in depth of analysis and style of presentation. If I ask for custody of my children, that is a position. If instead I say it is important to me to be the primary parent and that I do not want to be obligated to negotiate essential parenting decisions, then I have presented my interests. But these interests can be presented as a new position. I can demand to be the primary parent with sole decision-making power. The interests behind this new position might be that I do not want to have to communicate on a regular basis with my ex-spouse and I want my children to attend the neighborhood school near my house. But these interests too can be put forward as positions.

What is important is whether negotiators have understood each other's needs at the appropriate level of depth. If the parties stay too shallow in their exploration of each other's concerns, they will find themselves bargaining without a clear picture of the real needs motivating the negotiation. If they go too deep, they will be trying to solve problems that may be unsolvable or at least beyond what is currently at stake. The problem with positional bargaining is not its focus on positions as opposed to interests but its potential to encourage an adversarial manner of presenting ideas, to discourage a thorough exploration of the major needs or concerns of disputants, and to make it more likely that parties will ignore the importance of establishing effective communication with each other.

STRATEGIC CHOICES IN NEGOTIATION

The decision as to whether to engage in a positional or interest-based approach is just one of several significant strategic choices that we make (or fall into) as we negotiate. None of these choices are absolute, irreversible, or exclusive, but taken as a whole they set the tone and direction for the entire process. These choices are essentially about how we think about and frame the purpose and process of negotiation:

- Will we focus more on working out an effective communication and problem-solving process or on achieving satisfactory outcomes?
- Will we focus on relationship building or on substantive deliberations?
- Will we make decisions based on likely alternatives ("the shadow of the law") or on how well we have addressed everyone's needs?
- Will this be a "rational discourse" or one that allows for the explicit expression of emotions?
- Will we try to follow a linear, step-by-step approach, or will we adopt a free-flowing, intuitive, or spontaneous style of interaction?
- Will we try to limit the negotiation to easily identifiable issues, or will we take on "wicked problems" (those with no clear definition or solution)?
- Will we take an inclusive approach to participation, or will we involve only those individuals with a direct capacity to make decisions relevant to the identified issues?
- Will we try to achieve our goals through the overt application of power, or will we try to engage others in a mutual problem-solving process?

This is by no means a comprehensive list of the strategic approaches we face, and the answers we collectively give to these questions will evolve significantly as negotiations proceed. Nonetheless, how we approach these choices is ultimately what determines the tenor and direction of the process. Of course, outside elements have a significant influence as well. No matter how integrative or relationally focused we and others may want a negotiation to be, time pressures, legal deadlines, constituent pressures, or intervening events will have a great impact on what happens at the negotiating table.

Analyzing negotiation in terms of these strategic choices or through the prism of the negotiator's dilemma can help clarify the choices negotiators face. But any linear or two-dimensional analysis also imposes conceptual limits on our understanding because negotiations take place in the midst of a constellation of forces that cannot be understood simply by analyzing what is going on among the parties at the table. Negotiation, and conflict more broadly, can often best be understood as complex adaptive systems of interaction (Coleman, Bui-Wrzosinska, Vallacher, and Nowak, 2006; Jones and Hughes, 2003; Mayer, 2004a).

Systems theory suggests language and concepts that are very different from the more linear analysis characteristic of discussions of integrative and distributive bargaining or positional and interest-based tactics. For example, a key question suggested by systems theory is how we can increase multidimensionality (the ability to view each other in complex terms so that one unwanted behavior does not define our entire view of the other person) and negative feedback loops (systems of communication that counteract the information, assumptions, or beliefs that reinforce conflict) (Coleman and others, 2006). Although systems language can seem foreign, the concepts are practical and increasingly familiar. A systems perspective might challenge us to consider, for example, how grievances between workers and first-level managers are reinforced by, and in turn reinforce, tension between top management and union leaders in a company or between labor and management in an entire industry? And systems concepts suggest a variety of tools for changing the nature of a conflict interaction that take us beyond a focus on individual motivations and strategic choices.

How Negotiators Reach Closure

Let's turn from how we approach the negotiation process to consider the endgame—how we reach closure in a negotiation. The process by which people agree to solutions in a negotiation is often subtle, although the final act may be quite straightforward. Several interrelated processes are usually in play.

THE CLOSING OF THE WAY

There is a Quaker saying that "progress occurs as the way closes behind." In a healthy negotiation, as more information is shared and more effective patterns of communication develop, options are identified and possible paths are opened. Equally important, however, is that potential approaches to resolution become narrower. Without such narrowing, closure is difficult. We may agree to rule out options because they are unacceptable to at least some of the participants. At other times, as more information is shared, it becomes clear that certain approaches will not work whereas others hold significant potential. There comes a point in many negotiations when the parameters within which a negotiated agreement is possible become clear. At this point participants have to decide whether an agreement within these parameters is better than no agreement at all. The course that many negotiations follow entails an effort to get to this point in a credible, constructive, and persuasive way.

CONVERGENCE OF INTEGRATIVE AND DISTRIBUTIVE NEGOTIATION

In most negotiations there are limits to the integrative potential of a resolution process, and there are also boundaries outside of which distributive agreements are not possible. An optimal solution to a negotiation may sometimes be thought of as one whereby no party can achieve any additional benefits except at the expense of another party. In other words, the full integrative potential of the situation has been achieved. Social scientists refer to this outcome as "Pareto optimality," because this phenomenon was analyzed by Italian social theorist Vilfredo Pareto (Lax and Sebenius, 1986).

The nearer we get to this point in a problem-solving process, the more difficult it becomes to find ways of achieving further mutual gains. As this happens, it is natural for us to begin thinking more distributively—that is, to focus on how to claim a greater share of the pie (the resources, value, or benefits desired by the negotiators). That is why, even in the most collaborative negotiations, there is often a lot of horse trading and increased tension at the end. Similarly, negotiations that have been primarily distributive often reach a point at which there does not appear to be enough of the pie left to meet the needs of each of the parties. As this occurs, our attention may well turn to whether there is a way to expand the pie. Thus integrative and distributive negotiations sometimes converge. How people bounce between these dimensions can sometimes look like this elaborate dance:

> Brenner Enterprises, a small exercise equipment manufacturer, had been renting space in a building owned by the Warren family. Brenner had three years left on its lease, but the Warrens wanted to terminate the lease early to take advantage of a lucrative offer by the XYZ supermarket chain to buy the property. The offer contained a considerable bonus if the property were free of tenants so that the chain could begin constructing a superstore immediately. Brenner was willing to consider moving, especially because its plans called for an expansion beyond the capacity of its current facility.
>
> On the surface a deal should have been easy to come by. However, both Brenner and the Warrens wanted to get the best deal for themselves that they could. Brenner wanted considerable compensation for moving early, and the Warrens wanted to make no concessions. According to Brenner, the Warrens were about to get a windfall, and it would be a serious inconvenience for Brenner to move earlier than it had planned to. The Warren family argued that Brenner would benefit greatly by getting out of its lease early and that if anything Brenner should pay some penalty. The following reconstructed interchanges were characteristic of how this negotiation played out:
>
> *Brenner:* We are willing to move early if that will help you, but it is inconvenient for us to do so, and we will incur significant additional expenses for which we expect to be compensated. If we cannot arrive at a fair compensation, we will be happy to stay.
>
> *Warren:* You *approached* us several months ago inquiring whether we would consider negotiating an early lease termination; so don't pretend that this is such a great sacrifice. We are willing to try to negotiate a reasonable deal, but if not, we will be happy to let you stay until your lease expires.
>
> [*Strategy note:* Both are playing the alternatives game here— Brenner says it is happy to stay. The Warren family dismisses

Brenner's concerns about leaving and say they are happy to have Brenner stay. Both are claiming that the alternative to negotiating an agreement is just fine for them.]

Warren: You were late with your rent twice last year, and you violated the lease provision about parking your vehicles. We think we have a case for terminating your lease. We would prefer to negotiate a friendly solution, and we are prepared to pay some small amount as an incentive to you to find a new location within three months.

Brenner: You failed to maintain the parking area in the condition the lease requires, and we have previously discussed the late payments. You have no case for termination. We are willing to move early if we receive adequate compensation for the inconvenience. We will probably have to go through a period of curtailed production while we move, and this will result in some significant losses. We are sure that any court would recognize this. Also, the soonest we could move would be in six months.

[*Strategy note:* Both are continuing to play the alternatives game—this time by arguing that each can force the other to comply. More important, however, is that they are indicating their willingness to deal and are beginning to reveal their interests, which have to do with timing, the amount of compensation, and the disruption of production. They are also suggesting principles that might be applied to a solution.]

Warren: So we have agreed that we will compensate you for the equivalent of four months rent if you move out within six months, and six months rent if you move out within four months, assuming our deal with XYZ Corporation goes through.

Brenner: We would also like you to share in our moving costs, and we need to be told for sure that this deal is on within the next two weeks or we will be unable to conduct essential planning for our business.

Warren: We cannot rush XYZ or it may back off the whole deal, which would hurt us both. Also, there is no way that we can assume part of your moving costs. You were going to have to incur those anyway—if not now, soon.

[*Strategy note:* They are working out a deal that is essentially integrative, although the discussion sure sounds like a distributive and positional negotiation. The closer they get to maximizing the integrative potential, the more they are trying to eke out some further distributive gains. When they run into a distributive roadblock, they naturally look for further integrative options.]

And so it went. While Brenner and the Warrens negotiated, the Warrens continued to talk with XYZ to try to get additional assistance in buying out Brenner's lease. In the end, as the deadline for closing a deal approached, Brenner and the Warrens worked out an agreement that included some assistance with moving, a six-month rent waiver, and a two-phased move in which Brenner would move its manufacturing operation in four months and its warehouse in six.

FRACTIONALIZATION

Another way negotiators reach agreement is by breaking a conflict down into smaller parts. This can make a negotiation more manageable and create opportunities for incremental successes. We can then gradually chip away at the larger conflict and develop an investment in preserving agreements that have already been reached. This approach, sometimes referred to as fractionalization (Fisher, 1964), can create opportunities for trade-offs and allows some issues to be settled and others to be deferred to a time when they are more amenable to resolution.

But fractionalization also carries dangers. Issues that are logically related can become more difficult to deal with separately (for example, seniority and affirmative action, spousal support and asset decisions). Sometimes reaching an agreement on the last remaining issue can be difficult because opportunities for trade-offs may have been diminished when earlier agreements were reached. Also, an issue that seems small and readily resolvable can become a real showstopper if it turns out to represent a fundamental underlying dispute that has not been addressed. The art of fractionalization is to divide a conflict into manageable chunks that are neither too large nor too small and that do not isolate any major issue in a way that makes creative problem solving more difficult.

AGREEMENTS IN PRINCIPLE

The flip side of fractionalization is generalization—that is, attacking a conflict at its most general level. General or in-principle agreements can often be reached on broad issues, and these can then be refined and specified until the parties reach concrete operational agreements. This approach can create a template and set of parameters for a final agreement. It can also help disputants get used to the very idea of agreeing and begin to build some momentum toward agreement before they have to commit themselves to specifics. But "the devil is in the details." People may feel they have an agreement only to see it fall apart when they attempt to negotiate the specifics. To see both the advantages and disadvantages of this approach, we can look at the history of attempts to implement the Oslo Accords, the Wye River Accords, or many other such efforts between the Israelis and the Palestinians. And sometimes it is easier to agree on the specifics than on the overall principle. Despite the pitfalls, starting negotiations by identifying potential agreements in principle can often pave the way for the rest of the discussion.

THE FRACTIONALIZATION-IN-PRINCIPLE LOOP

Most negotiations do not follow one or the other of the previous two strategies exclusively. Negotiators loop back and forth between fractionalizing issues and arriving at broader, more comprehensive agreements. Often we start with one approach, pursue it until we are no longer making progress, switch to the other approach, pursue that one as long as it is effective, then switch back to the first. I have frequently seen conflicted coworkers agree, sometimes almost too quickly, on general statements about respect, teamwork, and open communication. They then become stuck, however, when trying to make these agreements operational by specifying just how workload divisions, performance reviews, and decision making will work. The art of reaching closure often involves making wise decisions about when to go for more specific and detailed agreements, when to work on more general principles, and when to stop pursuing agreements for a time to delve more deeply into the needs of each party.

MATURATION OF A CONFLICT

In reaching closure, as in so many other steps in conflict engagement, timing is critical. We often have a pretty good idea from the outset of a negotiation about the kind of agreement we will reach, but until a conflict or issue has matured it is not possible to achieve closure. Brenner Enterprises and the Warren family probably could have predicted the outcome of their negotiations, but they still had to go through their dance. Trying to reach closure prematurely can harden resistance to a solution that might have been acceptable at a later time. Conversely, when we wait too long we may see a potential agreement unravel or fade in power.

When is a conflict mature? When participants have engaged in a mutual educational process; when emotions that have kept us from carefully considering our alternatives have subsided; when the issues have been effectively framed, essential information gathered and shared, and realistic alternatives identified and evaluated; and when the value of remaining in conflict has sufficiently diminished, a conflict has essentially matured. In other words, *complete* maturation of a complex conflict is a rare thing. The fact that a conflict is immature does not mean the resolution efforts are doomed. Immature conflicts can be resolved, but complete closure is likely to be an elusive goal.

William Zartman (2006) has proposed two conditions that make a conflict ripe for resolution, both largely matters of perception. One he calls the "push factor," the other the "pull factor." The push factor relates to whether parties have reached a "mutually hurting stalemate"—that is, they "find themselves locked in a conflict which they cannot escalate to victory and this deadlock is painful to both of them" (p. 144). The pull factor is a "way out," a "mutually enticing solution" (p. 146) that offers the prospect of a better future.

EMOTIONAL AND SUBSTANTIVE PROBLEM SOLVING

Because resolution requires that we deal with the feelings we have as well as the outcomes we are seeking, most closure requires some emotional discharge as well as problem solving. Often we think of these steps as sequential, but this can be misleading. We do not usually deal with our emotions first and our substantive concerns next; these two processes are intertwined. As discussed in Chapter Five, the cognitive, emotional, and behavioral dimensions of resolution tend to develop together and to reinforce one another. Frequently, as we approach closure in a negotiation we revisit each element of the conflict. We need to try on earlier perceptions of each other or of the dispute itself, and we need to again experience some of the feelings associated with the earlier stages of the process. As we face the reality of settling a conflict, many of our earlier fears and resentments are reawakened. Until we consider a potential agreement, we do not fully face the implications of a negotiated outcome, including the emotional ramifications.

That is why, at what appears to be the end of a negotiation process, we often encounter "doorknob issues" (issues that seem to arise as people have their hand on the doorknob on the way out of the room). These issues can be frustrating because they sometimes appear to threaten agreements that seemed almost complete, but they are the means by which we test whether we are really prepared to reach a deal. They can also be a mechanism for assuring ourselves that we really have gotten all we could reasonably expect out of a bargaining effort, and of course they are also often an attempt to secure a bit more at the end. If the structure of the agreement adequately addresses everyone's essential concerns, then it is unlikely that this last-minute testing will derail the process—but on occasion it does.

WHY WE REACH CLOSURE

Why we reach closure in a negotiation is a different question from how we do so. In many, perhaps most, negotiations, we reach a moment when we have to decide if we will accept an offer—or make an offer that we know is acceptable. We do so because our essential needs have been met and because we have achieved enough resolution on all three dimensions of conflict (cognitive, behavioral, and emotional) to take this step. But of course the process is far less rational than that. Sometimes we reach closure with enthusiasm, sometimes with trepidation, and sometimes with great regret. Often a symbolic act, a word of kindness, an acknowledgment, an apology, or a nonverbal gesture lets us feel sufficiently positive about what has happened or helps us to maintain our self-image well enough to allow us to enter into an agreement. A dramatic example of this occurred during the Camp David negotiations between President Anwar Sadat of Egypt and Prime

Minister Menachem Begin of Israel, which were conducted under the auspices of President Jimmy Carter in 1978:

> At the end of thirteen exhausting days of negotiations, when a final agreement had been drafted, Prime Minister Begin took exception to the wording of a side letter on the status of Jerusalem and threatened withdrawal from the negotiations and rejection of the entire agreement. The process seemed to be in an impasse. Rather than push him harder to cross the final bridge to settlement, which he felt would be counterproductive, President Carter instead gave Begin a set of autographed pictures of President and Mrs. Carter addressed to each of Begin's grandchildren. This gesture of personal consideration and commitment to the future moved Begin to accept a revised draft of the letter and to sign the agreement.

Not all negotiations succeed—or ought to. Those that do are unlikely to follow a simple, linear path. The process of reaching closure is full of setbacks, sidetracks, second-guessing, and false starts. Descriptions of negotiation as a linear, primarily rational process miss the complex and creative heart of the endeavor. When we are effective as negotiators, we remain clear about what is essential to us, flexible in our approach, and creative about how to accomplish our goals. But successful negotiation is always a joint enterprise, and the key challenge is finding a way to cocreate a constructive process in the face of divisive pressures, mistrust, and questionable behavior.

NEGOTIATING WITH UNETHICAL ADVERSARIES

We often are faced (or believe we are faced) with questions about the ethics of negotiating in the face of evil or highly unethical behavior. Should we try to reach an agreement with someone who has cheated us, abused us, or used highly unethical tactics? Should we negotiate in the face of threats or with people who want to use the negotiation process itself to compromise us? In the 2008 U.S. presidential campaign, John McCain and Barack Obama put forth very different views about negotiating with unscrupulous adversaries, such as Iran or North Korea.

Obama said: "Not talking doesn't make us look tough—it makes us look arrogant."

McCain countered: "I don't fear to negotiate. Instead, I have the knowledge and experience to understand the dangerous consequences of a naive approach to presidential summits based entirely on emotion." (Both statements were drawn from their respective campaign Web sites.)

Although the stakes may be a lot lower, in many negotiations we face analogous conflicting pulls, which relate to both our values and our self-image.

Robert Mnookin's recent book *Bargaining with the Devil: When to Negotiate, When to Fight* (2010) addresses this dilemma. He argues that we should approach this issue by evaluating what we stand to gain and lose by negotiating or not negotiating rather than by viewing it in strictly value-based terms. Mnookin cites the example of Nelson Mandela's decision to negotiate with F. W. de Klerk as an example in which negotiating with "evil" was the correct choice; he identifies the U.S. decision not to negotiate with the Taliban prior to the Afghanistan invasion in 2001 as also the right choice. Whether one agrees with Mnookin's assessment of these examples or not, his essential point is an important one. He argues that the wisdom and morality of negotiating in the face of evil have to be evaluated in terms of the specific alternatives in each case. He further argues that what feels like an ethical and emotional decision in fact has to be approached analytically and to some extent dispassionately—or the decision may not in fact end up being ethical or wise.

I think there is another way of looking at this issue that requires a broader view of what negotiation is. We often find ourselves in a de facto negotiation with those we consider evil or unethical, whether we label this as a negotiation or not. In fact, whether we sit down face-to-face, use intermediaries, negotiate through the media, or signal our intensions through indirection, we often have no choice but to negotiate. The fact that the United States said we were not negotiating with the Taliban did not mean that we were not engaged in a series of moves and countermoves that were in fact efforts to reach some meeting of the minds. We currently see a similar process occurring in the United States' dealings with North Korea and Iran. What we are really facing here are questions of framing and tactics: How overt should we be about what we are doing? How clearly should we frame an interaction as a negotiation? What strategies should we use to leverage the other party? How hard should we push? When should we agree to engage in face-to-face interchanges? From a tactical point of view, perhaps it is not always wise to label these interchanges as negotiations, but if we want to understand the dynamics of what is going on we should see them for what they are—forms of negotiation.

I think it is easy to overestimate the tactical utility of refusing to engage in direct communication. Sometimes refusing to talk may be the most effective alternative available to us, but that is usually because we are in a weak position and not a strong one. More often, direct communication provides us with an additional source of information and a wider set of options for how to pursue our goals and employ our power appropriately. It also can serve as a safeguard against destructive escalation.

Of course, direct communication is not always advisable. For example, if we are trying to deliver a clear and unambiguous message about unacceptable behavior, to rally our supporters for a potentially protracted struggle, or to insulate ourselves from tactics that are not easy for us to counter, then refusing to engage in direct negotiation may be wise. The refusal of the protestors in Egypt to negotiate directly with the government of Hosni Mubarak in February 2011 was probably a wise move. Negotiations at that time would have been likely to undercut the élan of the protests without the protesters' having accomplished their most important immediate goal, the end of his role. That did not mean, however, that a de facto negotiation of sorts was not going on, through intermediaries, through the press, and through the international community. It clearly was.

We all negotiate daily, and our success in our personal and professional lives is closely related to how effective we are as negotiators. Any effort to analyze the dynamics of negotiation, or of any complex human interaction, must inevitably run up against the reality that every person, situation, and system creates its own process. Furthermore, some of the most important occurrences in negotiation are unconscious, unintentional, or instinctive. People will not become better negotiators by trying to keep in mind at all times all of the dynamics described in this chapter. However, the more people understand the essential dimensions and dilemmas of the negotiation process, the better they will be at handling a wide variety of negotiation challenges. Becoming conscious of these dimensions and dilemmas does not require people to sacrifice their natural skills, their spontaneity, or their instinctive responses. But these skills and abilities need to be built on and refined, just as we work to improve our skills in music, sports, parenting, or any other endeavor that matters to us.

Chapter Nine

Working with Impasse

Conflicts sometime appear to lurch from impasse to impasse, and few disputes follow a straightforward path. Even the most skillful conflict interveners are sometimes at a loss for a way to move a conflict process forward in the face of what seems to be the unwillingness of some or all parties to engage in a constructive dialogue. Nothing we do can force someone else to be reasonable, flexible, or wise. Disputants can seem closed-minded, and conflicts can remain stuck in destructive patterns for extended periods. We can think of this as deadlock, impasse, breakdown, or failure, but each of these labels comes with judgments and assumptions about what people ought to do or how they ought to think. These judgments are sometimes the biggest obstacles we face in promoting a constructive approach to conflict.

In this chapter I use the term *impasse* because that is how it often feels—a point in a journey at which we are somehow blocked from moving forward. This is not necessarily a bad place to be or a sign of failure, poor decisions, or bad faith (although, of course, it may be). Sometimes impasse is where disputants need to be, and our task as interveners is to help them find a reasonable way of being there. What can appear as a hopeless dilemma when we take a short-term or time-limited view can often be understood as a natural and even productive part of a conflict process when we have a longer-range perspective. Let's start by considering the nature of impasse and the analytical tools that can help us make sense of it.

THE NATURE OF IMPASSE

When we experience an impasse in a conflict process, we feel unready or unable to move forward, or at least we do not believe we can do so using our current approach. Impasse is not necessarily destructive, although it can be, and it occurs because it in some way meets the needs of at least one of the parties involved in a dispute. We often think of impasse as being stuck, but this can be a misleading metaphor. Being stuck can imply that we would like to move forward or that it would be better for us to move forward if only our own inadequacies or the forces entrapping us were less severe. I do not think this is a helpful way of viewing impasse, even if it sometimes touches on the truth. Often we are in an impasse for very good reasons, and sometimes we are quite content to be there. The key to understanding impasse is to view it in terms of what it is accomplishing for those involved and what it means to them.

TACTICAL AND GENUINE IMPASSE

Impasses can be tactical, genuine, or both. Tactical impasses occur when disputants refuse to proceed with a dialogue, negotiation, or engagement effort in an attempt to increase their power, to put pressure on others to make concessions, or to enhance their negotiating position in some other way. In other words, tactical impasses occur when disputants intentionally use impasse as a means for gaining concessions in a negotiation or problem-solving process that they do not really wish to end. Tactical impasses usually result from a short-term calculation of costs and benefits and generally do not last very long. They are indicative of a distributive approach to negotiation. Employing them can be a high-risk strategy because they can escalate a conflict or backfire, but they can be effective (even if they seem unsavory at times). In high-stakes bargaining (for example, in the area of professional sports or in negotiations about the national debt) a key participant may either walk away from negotiations or threaten to end the discussion unless some "absolute" (and often unrealistic) condition is met. These tactics may leverage compromise and solidify support, and they may play well with constituents, but they also carry the risk of sabotaging what might otherwise be productive negotiations and make sound decision making more difficult. The paradox of tactical impasse is that for it to be credible it can't just be seen as tactical; it therefore has to plausibly carry the threat of genuine impasse.

One of the most dramatic examples of tactical impasse I have encountered as a mediator was also one of the least effective. In retrospect, it is not surprising that impasse was used so dramatically in this case because what was at issue was the future of a theater company.

> About forty members of a theater troupe were about to file a suit against the board of directors of a nonprofit performing arts center with which they were affiliated. For many years the actors, directors, and technical staff had accepted lower salaries and donated a great deal of time under the assumption that the money saved was being used to sustain and expand the theater facility and to build an endowment for a theatrical school. This arrangement came crashing down when the central figure in this organization, a well-known theater director and the CEO of the center, was suddenly fired because the board discovered that she had appropriated a great deal of money for her own purposes and that the building fund and endowment were basically nonexistent.
>
> Most of the theater troupe had looked to this director as a teacher, mentor, and friend. They felt personally betrayed and abused and wanted compensation for the money they had sacrificed. The board had acknowledged that some settlement was appropriate, but the board and the troupe members were far apart in their views of how big it should be. They asked a colleague and me to mediate this dispute.
>
> After several difficult and emotional meetings we were able to focus on a potential settlement formula. Important principles were agreed to and considerable progress was being made in arriving at specific terms when the attorney representing the members of the troupe suddenly announced that they were pulling out of the negotiations and proceeding with their suit in court. He indicated that his group had compromised as much as it possibly could; that he did not believe the board had taken any genuine responsibility for what had happened; and that unless the board was prepared to accept all the terms of the plaintiffs' "last and final" offer, they were going to court.

My co-mediator and I were surprised by the suddenness of this because we had thought that considerable progress was being made. We both suspected that this was primarily a tactic to wrest further concessions from the board, but we were not sure. When we met privately with the plaintiff group, the attorney was every bit as adamant but the plaintiffs seemed very uncomfortable. Clearly the attorney was trying to convince us that they were in fact ready to go to court, but by then we were quite sure this was a tactical move. Nevertheless, it was not an empty bluff. To pull this off, the attorney had to be willing to carry out the threat—even though my colleague and I thought this would eat up the resources the organization had to compensate the plaintiffs.

The board members were outraged. They felt they had been extremely generous. They also felt they had a fairly strong legal case themselves but that the process of taking the dispute to court would be detrimental to the organization. They now believed that the plaintiffs were not negotiating in good faith, and they were ready to "call their bluff"—which could have led to a genuine impasse. No one really wanted to go to court at this point, but there appeared to be no easy way to avoid the next step, which was to formally file a suit. This would almost certainly have led to considerable negative publicity for the organization, with serious financial consequences.

My colleague and I decided to do two things. First, we wrote up the agreements in principle and the range of outcomes that had been discussed so that they would not be lost and so that there would be tangible evidence of how far the discussions had come. Second, we redefined the impasse as an important time for each group to think through its choices and to see if any other approaches to a settlement might be developed. We did not try to get either group to make any further concessions.

Not surprisingly, the impasse did not last long. A key board member held a series of informal meetings with one of the plaintiffs to examine other options, and they were able to come up with a plan that was acceptable to the vast majority of the plaintiffs and to the board. It involved a few minor concessions to the plaintiffs, but, more important, it redefined the settlement offer in such a way that it was not the "take it or leave it" set of proposals previously identified but rather a new formula entirely. In the end it became the basis for settlement. Certain additional (although fairly small) gains were probably achieved through the use of this tactical impasse, but at a cost of considerably greater stress and anger than the parties might otherwise have experienced.

Genuine impasse occurs when we feel unable to move forward with an engagement effort without sacrificing something important. If, for example, the board members had felt that their only option besides impasse was to agree to terms that would bankrupt the center (which is in fact how they did feel at times), then they would have been at a genuine impasse. We usually experience this as beyond our control, and we feel we have no acceptable choice but to remain in an impasse. Of course disputants sometimes try to use a genuine impasse to their tactical advantage, and sometimes what starts out as a tactical impasse can become genuine. The tactical use of impasse by the theater troupe came very close to producing a genuine impasse, because what was tactical from the troupe's perspective was genuine from the board's.

Genuine impasse has both structural and personal aspects. That is, an impasse can be rooted in the structure of the conflict as well as in the emotions, values, communication skills, problem-solving capacities, or perceptions of the disputants.

DIMENSIONS OF IMPASSE

The dimensions of conflict and the wheel of conflict (see Chapter One) offer two frameworks for understanding the nature of an impasse. Impasses occur along the emotional, cognitive, or behavioral dimensions of conflict, and most play out on more than one of these dimensions.

When we cannot move forward because our feelings prevent such progress, we are in an emotional impasse. A divorcing couple so locked into their anger at each other that they cannot agree to anything, despite the potential for an agreement to meet important substantive needs, are in an emotional impasse. Sometimes arriving at a divorce agreement signifies an emotional acceptance of the end of the marriage for which people are not ready. Sometimes our level of anger is so great that the act of participating in a dialogue of any kind feels like a personal violation.

A cognitive impasse occurs when we cannot change our view of a conflict or the other parties and therefore remain locked into a destructive pattern of interaction. There was a very dramatic public example of a political leader struggling with this when Yasser Arafat and Yitzhak Rabin came together to conclude a peace agreement in the Rose Garden of the White House in 1993. With Bill Clinton standing in the background, clearly inviting them to shake hands with each other for the cameras, Arafat reached out a hand to Rabin. After pausing, and visibly struggling with this for a moment, Rabin reached over and shook the hand of the man he had long regarded as an enemy and a terrorist. To change his perception of Arafat and see him as a partner in peace was a major cognitive switch. Arafat had to overcome a similar cognitive obstacle. That they could make this attitudinal change was perhaps their major personal contribution to this effort. Achieving such a cognitive shift remains a major challenge for overcoming the obstacles to constructive engagement in the Middle East to this day. The struggle of Palestinians and Israelis to change their views of each other and to redefine the issues in their conflict so that they do not continue to vilify each other is critical to the achievement of peace in that region. Cognitive impasses are often the most difficult to overcome.

A behavioral impasse occurs when we cannot identify or agree on behaviors, or actions, to move an engagement effort forward or when behaviors continue to occur that keep a conflict process from progressing in a constructive way. Will a dam get built, or will it not? What pay raises or other benefits will we agree to in a contract negotiation? What level of emissions will become the legal limit for a certain chemical? This is the dimension on which people generally focus when they experience impasse, just as it is the dimension that most people think about when they consider conflict, but it is often derivative of the other two dimensions. When an impasse is genuinely based on the behavioral dimension, disputants feel that moving forward at that moment requires them either to do things that are not acceptable or to agree to others' doing something that is not acceptable.

SOURCES OF IMPASSE

We can also consider impasse in terms of the wheel of conflict. Impasse occurs because one or more of the disputants have needs that they believe or sense will not be adequately met by moving forward with an engagement effort. Sometimes the choice not to move forward is a very clear and deliberative decision; sometimes it is made instinctively or unconsciously. Often this decision involves choosing among competing needs. For example, if I have made a strong statement that I will not agree to something unless certain conditions are met (a commitment tactic), then I have created a need to maintain face by remaining true to this position even though I might meet other important needs by backing off. This was one of the ways in which the theater troupe nearly created a genuine impasse out of a tactical move. We dig this kind of hole for ourselves all the time. Resolving an impasse can be a matter of timing. Have I fought the good fight long enough that I can now gracefully accept a lesser agreement? Moving forward frequently means accepting that a perfect outcome is not possible, that not all of our needs can be completely met. This can be very hard to do, and sometimes it is easier to remain in an impasse than it is to face these choices.

Sometimes engagement efforts are ineffective because they address one level of need but the source of the impasse is at a different level. For example, if negotiations about situating a landfill in a community focus on traffic, aesthetics, emissions, discharges, and land use but fail to address how a community's image or sense of itself may be affected, then impasse is likely. Parents and adolescents often fail to work through their conflicts because, even though they can discuss concerns about dress, homework, curfews, and chores, they have no idea how to address issues of autonomy and dependence.

To understand an impasse and to address it, people have to focus on the real needs that are in play at the appropriate level of depth. Sometimes, as in Sheila's situation, that is almost impossible—and remaining in an impasse is really the best choice.

Sheila was a fifty-five-year-old production supervisor at an advertising agency. She had been overseeing the planning for a new set of commercials when her boss pulled her off the project and reassigned her. About six months earlier she had been passed over for a promotion that went to a younger man. When she inquired in a forceful and demanding way as to why she was being reassigned, she was told that her work was not of sufficient quality and that progress was not being made quickly enough. To add insult to injury, Roy, a younger male employee who had been reporting to her, was given the assignment. Sheila filed an age and gender discrimination suit.

In keeping with company policy, both sides were obligated to consider the possibility of mediation. This meant they had to meet with a "conflict resolution counselor" to discuss the advisability of mediating, although they were not bound to actually enter mediation. Of course, by meeting with a counselor they were in a way beginning a mediation process. I was asked to serve as the counselor. Normally this step would have been handled in-house, but the human resource director had been involved in a previous grievance filed by Sheila and felt that it would be advisable to bring in someone from the outside.

Jonathan, the department supervisor, felt that Sheila's work had long been substandard and that it was only because she was seen as "litigious" that she had not been demoted. He felt that he had taken a big risk by assigning her to the project in the first place. He had only done it, he said, because she had campaigned hard for a chance to prove herself after she was passed over for the promotion. In his view, she had been in totally over her head, and the only reason the project was not in big trouble was that Roy had been covering for her. He felt he would have been putting the company (and his own reputation) in jeopardy if he had not taken decisive action.

Sheila of course had a very different view. She felt that she was never given credit for what she had accomplished and that the agency was "an old boys' club with a glass ceiling." She felt that she had repeatedly "pulled Jonathan's chestnuts out of the fire" and that he was covering up his own incompetence by blaming her for problems for which she was not responsible. What was really interesting to me was that there was nothing Sheila really wanted out of the grievance procedure other than victory. She no longer wanted the project back. She was not interested in promotion, reassignment, or financial recognition of any kind. On the part of the grievance form that asked her to name the redress she was asking for, she had written some fairly confusing language about wanting "vindication" and a guarantee that "nothing like this will ever happen again." When the company suggested training programs to enhance her skills and other ways to support her in future projects, she dismissed those ideas out of hand.

Sheila confided to me that she thought things would change in the organization only if management were publicly humiliated in an arbitration or court proceeding. She was obviously very angry about what had happened, and beneath her anger was a significant injury to her pride and self-esteem. She was very clear that she would rather lose in an adversarial contest than work out an agreement, even though she realized that her job could be in jeopardy.

I filed a report in which I summarized and framed the issues and options as best I could, and I recommended that the parties not proceed with mediation. In fact, I was simply recognizing the decision Sheila had actually made. I could have tried harder to convince her to give it a try, but I did not think this would be fruitful given how clear she seemed to be. The case went to arbitration. Sheila lost and shortly afterward resigned.

I have often wondered what else might have been done to overcome this impasse. Could Sheila have received the recognition or acknowledgment she needed through mediation to allow her to discuss some realistic agreement? Was there some level at which I was not hearing her or understanding her feelings or needs? Probably, but I also believe that in a way she got just what she wanted. She stood up for herself. She did not compromise on what she felt was an assault on her dignity, and she tried very hard to get full vindication. When she did not, she gave herself an acceptable reason to leave what in some ways was a good job for her but in other ways was a dead end that was contributing to her deteriorating self-image.

As discussed in Chapter One, needs do not exist in a vacuum, and it is helpful to locate the impasse in other sections of the wheel of conflict as well. Are disputants unable to communicate effectively (or at all), and if not, why not? Have their emotions overwhelmed their ability to think clearly about ways to address their needs? Are historical forces hindering a resolution process, and are they too powerful for people to overcome? Is the immediate conflict part of a larger dispute from which it cannot be separated? Are structural factors impeding progress? Are people unable to move forward because they cannot overcome basic value differences or because it is more important for them to assert their values than to resolve the conflict?

A key to understanding impasse is to accept that from some vantage point it makes sense. We often look at impasse as a sign of failure, or we equate being in an impasse with taking a destructive or unreasonable approach to conflict. Often we use one of the three explanatory "crutches" described in Chapter Two. That is, we ascribe impasses to disputants' immoral or evil intention, to their irrational or crazy thinking, or to their overall stupidity. How else, we tell ourselves, can we explain Saddam Hussein, Muammar Gaddafi, Kim Jong-il, or Adolf Hitler? But these explanations merely end up begging the question of what is really going on.

The problem with these approaches is that they really explain nothing and they lead to inappropriate or rigid responses. If someone with power is really crazy or evil, then obviously the only way to change his or her behavior is by overwhelming force. Although it may be necessary at times to employ coercive power, it is much wiser to do this as a consequence of understanding the needs that are motivating disputants than as a consequence of a rationale that focuses on disputants' moral or mental deficiencies. There may be plenty of craziness and evil afoot, but they seldom explain why a certain approach to conflict predominates, particularly when we look beyond interpersonal disputes. Depicting impasse as stemming from insanity, stupidity, or immorality is often an excuse, a means for avoiding serious consideration of the essential needs that are at stake and the real sources of the problem.

Cocreating Impasse

Impasse is an interactional phenomenon. Although one party may be the immediate source of an impasse or may be in the more powerful position in an interchange, impasse is best understood as a system dynamic, as an obstacle to the free flow of energy in an interactional system. In conflict this flow of energy is largely expressed as communication and decision-making fluidity. This way of looking at impasse suggests that all parts of the system have a role in the way an impasse plays out or is expressed. Consider three possible responses to a negotiator who is adamantly refusing to consider a proposal that we think is reasonable. We can ignore this stance and move on to a different issue; we can turn on the pressure by threatening, cajoling, or persuading; or we can bring a new party into the discussion in the hope that this will change the nature of the interaction (and there are of course many other responses we might make as well). Which approach will be more effective depends on the circumstances, but clearly we have a role in crafting the nature of the impasse and determining how it unfolds. This does not mean we are necessarily equally responsible for the impasse, but it does suggest that in most circumstances we can have some impact on how it plays out. Of course, in conditions of significant power differentials, the less powerful party may have more limited choices and may be very vulnerable.

By considering impasse as a systems phenomenon, we can begin to consider a wider range of responses. For example, when we find ourselves stuck on a difficult issue, sometimes the best question to ask is not, How can we move past this impasse? but rather, Who is not talking (and should he or she be)?

MOVING THROUGH IMPASSE

As with so many aspects of effective conflict intervention, moving through impasse is usually more a matter of attitude than of tool or technique. Seldom will we break through a significant impasse simply by using a clever intervention strategy—unless that strategy addresses the fundamental cause of the impasse or the needs of the participants. Interveners and disputants are more likely to be effective in dealing with impasse if they operate with certain attitudes and outlooks.

- *Impasse is OK.* It is easy to feel that there is something wrong with people who are not ready to act constructively. But this attitude is seldom helpful. It leads to a focus on disputants' behaviors or personality rather than to an understanding of the nature of the conflicts that need to be addressed, and it can easily cause people to respond to an impasse by turning up the pressure to unproductive levels. The consequences of an impasse can be serious, but it is important not to proceed as if the problem were the impasse itself. It is better to have the attitude that impasses are acceptable in disputes.
- *People have good reasons for being in an impasse.* Disputants who choose not to move toward resolution are doing so for a good

reason from their own point of view. Sometimes remaining in an impasse is the only choice they feel they have. Sometimes what is important to others may be hidden or seem strange or unreasonable to conflict interveners, but it's not for us to decide what is important to them. Accepting that people are trying to accomplish something—from their own point of view, consciously or consciously, effectively or ineffectively—is necessary if we are going to take a constructive approach to impasse.

- *Disputants have to find their own way through an impasse.* Third parties can help, but if we take it upon ourselves to "solve a conflict," "fix a problem," or "break a deadlock" we are missing the point. We may be attracted to the dramatic image of a third party intervening in a powerful, creative, and dramatic way, and thereby ending an impasse, but that is seldom what happens and is more a reflection of our own needs than those of the disputants. We can help by working with disputants to address the source of the impasse or to find a creative way through it. But it is the disputants themselves who have to move through the impasse when and if they are ready. As interveners, when we take too much responsibility for overcoming an impasse, we can actually make things worse by allowing the parties individually and collectively to avoid responsibility for looking at their own situation clearly and courageously.

- *Anxiety and fear are not helpful.* Anxiety is often the biggest problem we face in an impasse. Anxiety and fear breed rigidity and shut down communication and creativity. Therefore it is usually important to avoid the temptation to try to move past impasse by increasing people's fear and anxiety. If the situation is really dangerous or the stakes are extremely high, then anxiety can be a natural response and perhaps a useful warning sign, but it is not normally a helpful tool for overcoming impasse.

- *Impasse is a natural and frequently helpful part of the conflict process.* Often disputants do not confront their choices in a realistic way until they find themselves in an impasse. Impasse helps people separate essential from less essential needs, and it can be an impetus for their achieving a better understanding of each other's perspective. If anxiety is not too high or anger too great, impasse can also be a great spur to creativity and risk taking. Sometimes resolutely remaining in an impasse is the only way a disputant can feel any sort of power. And sometimes people recognize that a conflict exists only after they find themselves in some kind of impasse.

- *An impasse may not have an immediate solution, but people can usually find a constructive next step.* It is often more useful to think through a helpful next step than to struggle with finding ways to "overcome" an impasse or "break" a deadlock. Not every problem has an immediate solution. At times the best thing to do is nothing. People occasionally need to be given permission to stay in an impasse. Regardless, it is often better to ask, What is the best thing that can be done now? rather than, How can this impasse be overcome?

- *In an impasse, slower is usually faster.* We often want to respond to impasse by turning on the pressure and by imposing deadlines. This does not usually help. Of course deadlines are sometimes genuine, and people will not always make a choice among unpleasant alternatives until the way closes behind and forces a decision. Sometimes there really is a golden opportunity to make progress, and efforts will unravel if an agreement is not reached in a timely manner. More frequently, however, the best approach is to provide more time rather than to impose deadlines. When people can take the time to think through their choices, revisit their concerns, and come to their own conclusions, they usually become more flexible, imaginative, and realistic. Under the pressure of deadlines, for example, a compromise often feels like capitulation, but given a little time to consider their choices, disputants are more likely to see compromise as a reasonable, conciliatory move. Therefore, providing more time and space often shortens the overall process considerably.

When people are faced with a genuine impasse and with significant time pressures, it is very hard to act on the basis of these principles. Yet they are usually our best hope for moving through an impasse. It was very hard for me not to take on Paul's panic in the following case, for example, but it was essential.

The creditors were breathing down Paul and Sharon's necks—
something had to be done right away, which meant it was time to
slow things down. Paul and Sharon had been married for twenty-
five years when they separated. Their children were grown, and
the major issue they needed to negotiate was the disposal of their
ranch in western Colorado. Paul had moved to Denver, where he
worked as a ranching supply salesman; Sharon continued to live in
the family home on the ranch. During the previous two years the
ranch had not been worked.

Sharon wanted to continue to live in the house and had some
general ideas about continuing to ranch. She felt that Paul should
assume the debts and she should take over the ranch. Paul wanted to
sell everything, pay off the debts, and divide up the remaining assets.
He argued that Sharon's proposal was a sure road to bankruptcy and
that the creditors would never agree to separate responsibility for
the debt from ownership of the ranch. Sharon had no faith in Paul's
ability to maintain a job and felt that keeping the ranch was the only
way she had any hope of achieving financial stability. This standoff had
been going on for about nine months when they began mediation.

Paul was extremely anxious about the time it was taking to
conclude a deal. He reiterated, almost as a mantra, that every day
they waited they were pouring money down the drain and getting
closer to financial ruin. If they sold the ranch and the equipment
soon, there would be some assets left to divide up; if they waited
too long, there would be nothing. He insisted that a decision had
to be made immediately. Even waiting until their next meeting
in two weeks would be too long (meetings were hard to schedule
because Sharon lived several hours away). Sharon responded to this
pressure by disengaging, canceling meetings, and blaming Paul for
poor management.

There was clearly a time factor that needed to be kept in mind,
but the effort to break the impasse by applying this kind of pressure
was counterproductive. Faster was slower in this case. So I decided
to slow things down to speed them up. I said that regardless of
the time pressure, they each needed to be assured that they were
making the right decision, and this meant obtaining financial and
legal advice and costing out different options. I suggested that
they also needed to meet with their creditors and that they needed
to assess how they might refinance and whether there were any
potential buyers available (Paul was sure there were).

Paul and I had a frank discussion about the problems involved
with this approach. Although acknowledging his predicament,

I said that there might be no way to avoid bankruptcy—but if there were, it would involve taking the time to assess the alternatives without feeling pressured. I also told him that he could not force Sharon to "face reality," as he put it, but he could help her look at options.

I asked Sharon whether she believed they were under the time pressure Paul had described. She thought Paul was exaggerating, but she did acknowledge that the longer they waited the more debts they amassed. What did she think needed to happen? She wanted Paul to negotiate a new financial arrangement that would keep her on the ranch. She was not ready to concede that any of the ranch had to be sold, although she understood that this might become necessary. "How would you know?" I asked. This question made her think, but she had no answer. I told her to take the time that she needed to think about these issues and to call me when she felt ready to discuss them further.

After about six weeks, Sharon called and said she wanted to discuss dividing the ranch and selling some of it. In the end they worked out an arrangement that left Sharon with the house, a few acres immediately around the house, and some equipment. The rest was sold. The debt was considerably reduced, and the threat of bankruptcy receded. I suspect a better financial outcome would have been possible six to eight months earlier. And probably they lost some additional assets during the time that the mediation process was on hold. But this was the price they had to pay to work their way through the impasse.

General Questions for Addressing Impasse

When we face an impasse, six questions can help us as we try to move forward, whether we are third parties or disputants:

- *Am I breathing (metaphorically speaking)?* The first thing to do in almost all intense interactions is to try to get as centered, focused, and relaxed as possible. All of us deal with impasses and other crises better if we contain our own anxiety and if we do not internalize the tension of others. Sometimes this literally means concentrating on our own breathing. Usually it means taking the time we need to think through a situation and our possible response to it. When faced with very tense and difficult circumstances, we often feel we must respond instantaneously, but we almost always have a moment to calm ourselves down and think about how to respond.

This lesson was forced on me early in my career when I was confronted with what was perhaps the most difficult interchange I have ever had to deal with in a family mediation.

I was working with a family on a revision of a parenting schedule for Stephanie, a teenage girl who had been living primarily with her father (Joe) and stepmother (Janice) while her mother (Phyllis) completed a technical training program. Now that Phyllis had finished this program, both she and Stephanie wanted to change the living arrangements. Although Joe was amenable to a change, he expressed concern that Phyllis was manipulating Stephanie, and he wanted to schedule a meeting with his daughter, Janice, and me to talk to Stephanie about what she really wanted. With Phyllis and Stephanie's consent, I arranged for this.

It quickly became apparent to me that there was another purpose for this meeting that had to do with Joe's relationship with Janice. He had been unable to articulate to her the reasons for the change, and there clearly was a great deal of tension between Stephanie and her stepmother. Joe wanted help in getting his daughter and wife to talk to each other. Janice was extremely angry at Phyllis for reasons that were not entirely clear to me, and she was unable to contain herself in front of Stephanie. Seemingly out of nowhere, Janice started telling Stephanie that Phyllis was a "slut" and a "whore." I was flabbergasted and for a moment speechless. Stephanie was crying, Joe was acting as if nothing unusual were happening, and Janice actually seemed to be enjoying herself. Something had to happen, but what?

I did breathe for a second, in effect giving myself permission not to do anything for a moment, and then decided that I had to do two things quickly—put a limit on Janice's behavior and remove Stephanie from this interaction. I was by no means clear about how to pull this off within the mediator's role, but I knew I had to try. So first I said that I would not allow that kind of talk in this session. Next I excused Stephanie and suggested she take a walk and that we talk a little later. When I met alone with Joe and Janice, I expressed concern about what had happened and asked what was going on.

Evidently Janice had been waiting for an "appropriate" setting to tell her stepdaughter just what she thought of Phyllis. We had an intense discussion about this, during which I asked Joe what he thought about what had taken place. He said, rather timidly, that he did not want his daughter to hear that kind of talk about her mother either and that he would talk to Janice about this. Janice fulminated somewhat further about Phyllis but then did agree not to criticize her in front of Stephanie in the future. I reinforced that commitment as best I could and indicated that I did not think calling Phyllis names was going to change Stephanie's opinion of her mother or discourage her from wanting to spend more time with her. I also said that I did not think it was good for children to hear their parent figures attack each other in this way.

Later I talked with Stephanie, who was extremely thankful that I had gotten her out of the room. She discussed how hard it was to relate to her stepmother, although she said that the behavior I had seen was extreme and unusual. I tried to give her some suggestions for dealing with the situation should it occur again, although I had no magic up my sleeve to offer her. Eventually a very different kind of parenting plan was settled on, which made Phyllis's home the primary residence for Stephanie. In the end, my most powerful impression was that some significant work needed to occur between Joe and Janice and that this parenting issue was to a large extent a smokescreen for problems in their relationship.

I still look back at that situation and wish there were something I could have done to prevent the attack from happening or to deal with the interaction more effectively. Perhaps the most important thing I did was to break the interaction and give everyone, myself included, more time.

- *What is the nature of the impasse?* Impasses sometimes look to be simply intransigence, stubbornness, or malevolence, but they are almost always much more complex than that. It is helpful to figure out what is blocking people from moving forward. Whether we rely on the wheel of conflict or on some other analytical approach, putting words to what we think is causing the impasse is often helpful. It is also useful to ask how the impasse is manifesting itself. For example, are people actively refusing to communicate or avoiding all interactions? Is behavior occurring that is bringing progress to a halt? Are people stubbornly holding on to an unworkable proposal?

- *What are people accomplishing and risking by remaining in an impasse?* From their point of view, people are accomplishing something by being in an impasse. Gaining some clarity about what that is can be enormously useful in trying to work out a way to move forward. At the same time, there are almost always risks or costs involved in remaining in an impasse. Both the benefits and the costs are often sensed by disputants but not necessarily articulated. Getting them out in the open can help people consider their choices more realistically and creatively.

- *Can disputants meet their needs in some other way than through remaining in an impasse?* Often the only way people can easily see to meet their needs or to protect themselves is to bring about an impasse. But other ways often exist, and it is helpful to at least consider what these might be.

- *Is it better for the parties to remain in an impasse?* The preceding questions lead to this key question, which we might not want to face but occasionally must. Sometimes it is better for people to stay in an impasse. This is usually a matter of timing. There are few conflicts in which a long-term impasse is the best place for disputants to be. For short periods, however, people may be making the very best choice possible for themselves by remaining in an impasse or by forcing an issue into a more adversarial or politicized arena, as in the following situation:

> When a colleague and I were asked to conduct a public dialogue about policies concerning the hunting and trapping of fur-bearing animals, we knew we were heading into some troubled waters— particularly given the wide-open format of the discussion. Everyone was welcome, and the meetings were attended by a broad variety of groups and individuals representing ranchers, trappers, biologists, regulators, environmentalists, and animal rights activists. Within each group there was a broad range of opinions and negotiating styles. Many of the people in attendance had a long history of litigation and political struggle with each other.
>
> The process was complicated and intense, leading to a broad consensus on how to approach these policies among the vast majority of the participants but not among representatives of some of the more fervent animal rights organizations or the trappers. Each of these two groups held out for its particular position on almost every issue.

Although this was frustrating for many of the participants who had worked hard to find an acceptable middle ground, my colleague and I quickly realized that these groups, from their own point of view, were doing exactly the right thing. The trappers believed they could override any consensus achieved in this process by appealing directly to the state legislature and that holding out was the best way to continue to receive the support of their associates, all of whom were firmly against any governmental regulation. To agree to significant limits on their trapping activities would brand them as traitors. For them it was better to go down as heroes to their peers than to agree to a compromise.

For the animal rights activists the prospect of achieving their goals through a ballot initiative was far more appealing than accepting the results of a policy negotiation. Future administrations or legislatures cannot easily overturn policies resulting from initiatives, and public campaigns could generate support for some of their broader concerns. They believed they could win with a properly worded initiative, and they wanted to try. A negotiated agreement would undercut the appeal of their proposal to the voters.

Both groups proved to be right about their alternatives. Although a broad consensus was reached and much of it was adopted by the relevant administrative agency, the legislature did intervene to weaken the proposed restrictions, thereby justifying the trappers' intransigence. A ballot initiative was then proposed and ultimately passed that codified many aspects of the consensus achieved in the group. Interestingly, neither of these two groups ended up with a significantly worse outcome than they would have achieved had they participated in the consensus process, and in many respects their needs were better served by remaining in an impasse.

My colleague and I had come to the conclusion fairly early in the process that there was no very cogent reason for some of the people to get past impasse. We therefore encouraged all those attending the meeting to focus on achieving the broadest consensus they could, but we also encouraged each group to develop its own policy alternatives if it wished to, all of which would be presented to the regulating body. In this way, the concerns of all groups were articulated but a broad consensus was also achieved. This was not as satisfying to most participants and certainly not to the government officials that convened the process as achieving a complete consensus would have been, but it was a realistic outcome in view of the genuine needs of the different participants.

- *Are we as conflict interveners working harder than those more directly affected?* If we are working harder and devoting more energy to moving a conflict process forward than are the disputants themselves, we are probably taking on too much responsibility for the outcome. Our work can be very demanding and energy intensive, but in most circumstances we need to be working in partnership with the disputants to be genuinely effective. If we are putting out all the effort while disputants remain passive, something is amiss.

SPECIFIC QUESTIONS FOR ADDRESSING IMPASSE

Once we have assessed the costs and benefits of an impasse and the alternatives to it, we can consider specific questions that may suggest an approach for helping disputants move forward:

- *Who needs to be involved to move through the impasse?* Changing the way a conflict between groups is being conducted often involves changing the people involved, so it is helpful to consider whether the right people are participating. Are people whose input is necessary missing? Are people involved whose participation is neither helpful nor necessary? Are people trying to solve a problem when they do not really have the power to do so? Sometimes simply altering slightly who is participating in the process can significantly change the dynamics that are contributing to an impasse.
- *What time frame should the parties be considering?* By either expanding or narrowing the time frame under consideration, many impasses can be either avoided or at least viewed from a more constructive perspective. Parents who cannot agree on a long-term parenting plan, for example, can sometimes agree on what to do during the next six months. Worker and management representatives who are totally stuck about how to handle an immediate decision can often profit from looking at the issue from a longer-term perspective. What is an impasse in one time frame is simply a phase of an ongoing interaction in another.

- *Are the parties considering the issue at an appropriate level of generality or specificity?* The preceding question about the time frame is one example of the larger question of generality and specificity. One of the ways of helping disputants move through impasses is to either generalize or specify the discussion. For example, during the dialogue about policies toward fur-bearing animals, finding the right level of generality was critical. The parties could easily have bogged down if they had engaged in philosophical discussions about life or nature, but they could also have been thrown off track by focusing too narrowly on the mechanisms of specific traps. Progress could be made, however, at the level of policy principles.

- *Are disputants' needs being addressed at the appropriate level of depth?* By probing people's needs or interests further and achieving a deeper understanding of them, new approaches to resolution can often be identified. Occasionally, however, it is necessary to pull back to a simpler and less far-reaching view of people's needs to have hope of making progress.

- *Do the parties have any uncertainty?* Progress is sometimes possible only when people have some doubt about their position or options. I often experience the urge to tell disputants (and sometimes myself), "Be less certain!" Where uncertainty exists, there is room for movement. Under stress we often do not like to exhibit uncertainty, and we adopt overly firm positions to reduce our anxiety or enhance our power. This makes it all the more important to listen carefully for signs of uncertainty.

- *How can commitment tactics be avoided or circumvented?* Commitment tactics are one of the greatest sources of rigidity and impasse in conflict. Disputants using these tactics lock themselves into a position or demand in an attempt to force others to compromise. When a faction in Congress says it will refuse to extend the government's capacity to borrow money unless significant cuts in spending are agreed to (which is occurring in the United States as I write this and which also occurred in 1995), we see an effort to use commitment tactics both to posture for constituents and to stake out a powerful but rigid negotiating position. If disputants can avoid commitment tactics, their flexibility increases; once commitment tactics have been employed, however, the challenge interveners face is how to help parties soften or circumvent their demands without a loss of face. Sometimes this can be done through a reframing process, sometimes through a reinterpretation of the meaning of a position or demand, and sometimes through enlarging the scope of the discussion. Occasionally, however, conflict interveners have to help people find a way of totally abandoning a previously strongly held position without a loss of dignity. This may require working with the other parties so they accept this change gracefully and tactfully.

- *Has the integrative potential been adequately considered?* Have disputants made any real effort to consider their potential for joint gain? Even when there is little likelihood of an integrative solution, the process of considering it can sometimes lead to a more productive negotiation process.

- *Is there a productive way to discuss distributive issues?* Often the key to moving through an impasse is to acknowledge the distributive elements of conflict and to find a nonconfrontational and matter-of-fact way to discuss them. One approach is to look for principles that might govern a reasonable distribution of benefits. Another is to look for agreements about the boundaries within which a distributive decision will be made. In a personal injury negotiation, for example, it is sometimes helpful to agree on an upper and lower limit for a settlement before trying to arrive at a particular agreement.

- *Have people faced their actual choices and taken responsibility for making them?* Disputants often need help in accepting that they have a decision to make and that the need to make this decision will not disappear. At the same time as they are asked to face this reality, it is often important to decrease any pressure on them to make the decision quickly or in a particular manner. In the dispute about the family ranch described earlier, this was in essence the tactic I used. I indicated that a decision would have to be made and got both parties to agree on the nature of the decision, but at the same time I worked to decrease the pressure on the wife to make the decision more quickly than she was prepared to.

- *Is the right question being asked?* Has the issue been framed appropriately, or has it been posed in a way that makes progress very hard to come by? When we see people struggling with an issue that they genuinely want to resolve, it is often helpful to ask whether an alternative question or framing would offer a more constructive focus.

- *What is the best next step the parties can take?* As noted earlier in this chapter, it is frequently more helpful to identify a constructive next step than to try to delineate a path through the entire conflict. I find it is often useful to point out to disputants that there is no guarantee that any one action or communication will lead to resolution but that if nothing is done the conflict will almost surely continue. Once disputants and third parties focus on a constructive next step, conflicts can seem less overwhelming.

CONFLICT WITHIN CONFLICT

An impasse may be viewed as a conflict within a conflict. Thus the same approaches we might employ to understand the overall conflict can help us work through an impasse. It has the same three dimensions—cognitive, emotional, and behavioral—as the larger conflict. The same range of needs drives it, and the elements described in the wheel of conflict also apply to it.

Often an impasse comes to symbolize the overall conflict. This can make the impasse harder to deal with because any discussion of the specific problem becomes a surrogate for discussing the more far-reaching issue on which disputants may not be ready to move. The most fundamental conflict between Israel and the Palestinians is not about settlements on the West Bank, appropriate responses to terrorism, or the status of Jerusalem, although each of these issues is important to the parties. It is about the identity, security, and economic integrity of the Israelis and the Palestinians. The most genuine conflict between divorcing parents is seldom about how many nights a child will spend in each home; it is about what kind of relationship each parent will have with the child and how the parents will now relate to each other as parents but no longer as spouses. On the one hand, if we confuse an impasse on a particular issue with the overall conflict, we can close some important doors. On the other hand, by keeping the larger and more enduring elements of a conflict in perspective, the particular impasse we are facing may seem less problematic or daunting.

CHAPTER TEN

MEDIATION

We often equate mediation with conflict intervention. That is, when we think of how to intervene in conflict, how to help move people through a conflict process, how to build a conflict intervention practice, and how to market ourselves, we start with mediation. Over time we may expand our vision of what other roles we might take in a conflict, but for most conflict professionals and for the general public as well, mediation is still viewed as the central tool and primary professional expression of conflict intervention. As discussed in Chapter Six, this view is limiting, both for the field of conflict intervention as a whole and for mediators in particular, but it is also understandable. Mediation is a particularly visible manifestation of the work that conflict interveners do. Under its banner, clients can be solicited, training protocols can be established, and practice standards can be set. Although the larger field of conflict engagement, intervention, and resolution provides the professional and intellectual foundation for mediation, mediation as a practice can be presented in a much more concrete way to the public.

Contemplate these three (actual) conversations from a high school reunion I attended a number of years ago:

Person A: Bernie, what are you doing with your life?

Me: I work in the field of conflict intervention. I live in Boulder, Colorado . . .

Person A: I hear Boulder is a terrific place.

Person B:	Bernie, so what's happening with you?
Me:	I'm a partner in a conflict resolution organization in Boulder . . .
Person B:	Boulder is supposed to be really beautiful.

Person C:	Bernie, tell me about yourself.
Me:	I have a practice as a mediator, and I live in Boulder . . .
Person C:	I'll bet you get some really interesting work. Let me tell you about this conflict I have . . .

Although the tendency to equate mediation (and sometimes arbitration) with conflict intervention is natural, I believe we need to define our field more broadly. Mediation is a role, a skill, an approach, and a practice specialty. I don't think it is useful to view it as a professional discipline. Mediation, like negotiation, advocacy, or communication, is a life skill that everyone must occasionally employ. It is a powerful intervention tool. But it does not stand well on its own as a profession. That does not mean that the practice of mediation cannot be professionalized. It can be.

Those of us who make our living by offering our services as mediators need to be grounded in a broader and more developed professional framework. Like most new fields of practice, mediation is derivative of existing disciplines and should borrow from them as extensively as is helpful. But unless the practice of mediation is thoroughly anchored in a professional discipline that is based on more foundational goals, values, and intellectual requirements than mediation alone can offer, its growth will be limited, its independence constrained, and its conceptual framework simplistic. I believe we should think of mediation as one approach within the broader field of conflict intervention. That is where mediation's future intellectual and professional development lies. This is also the best long-term answer to the efforts of other professions (law in particular) to place mediation under their auspices.

This does not mean that every mediator has to have a degree in conflict studies any more than he or she needs a degree in mediation. There should always be a place for people to function as mediators without making a full-time commitment to mediation as a field of practice. But those who present themselves as

professional mediators need to acquaint themselves with the fundamental concepts of conflict and conflict engagement. As important
as it is for mediators to understand the mediation process, unless
they are grounded in a thorough understanding of the dynamics of
conflict, they will tend to view their work as a series of intervention
strategies and not as an application of a rich and growing body of
knowledge about the various ways individuals and systems engage
in conflict.

Having said this, it is important to look at what mediators
in particular offer to the promotion of constructive conflict
engagement.

What Mediators Bring to the Table

Mediation can be defined as the intervention of a third party to
help disputants communicate with each other about how best
to deal with a conflict. A mediator does not make a decision or
impose a solution but rather assists the disputants as they attempt
to find their own way through the conflict. Sometimes mediation
is defined as the intervention of a neutral third party, but not all
mediators are neutral (some might argue that none are). The
essence of mediation, as I see it, is neither its focus on a negotiated solution nor the neutrality of the mediator. Although many
mediators aspire to be neutral or define their purpose as achieving the resolution of conflict, the essence of mediation seems to
me to be its focus on helping facilitate an effective communication process. The practice of mediation varies greatly, and some
mediation can be so focused on hammering out an agreement
that the mediator can in fact appear to be imposing a solution.
But the heart of the process is the work a mediator does to help
people in conflict communicate about the conflict in a constructive way.

Mediation works. Under the right circumstances, it makes
a big difference in how well people handle conflict. This seems
clear from the many studies of mediation that have reviewed
the impact of mediation in a variety of settings (see, for example, Kressel, Pruitt, and Assoc., 1989; Orr, Emerson, and Keyes,
2008; Pearson, 1982; Thoennes, 2009). But why? There have been

mediators or mediating structures in almost all societies. These people and institutions have sometimes been presented as formalized, neutral, and process focused interveners, but more often they have played a less formal and also less neutral role. Religious and political leaders, elders, and influential community members have been important sources of mediation services.

With increasing social and geographical mobility and the greater institutionalization of community life, however, these informal mechanisms of community-based conflict intervention have become less prominent or effective. As a result, more formal systems have evolved. The most developed of these formal conflict intervention systems have been the courts and such political institutions as town councils and planning boards. But these have normally been better suited for making decisions than for building consensus or encouraging dialogue among those in conflict. So it is natural that the use of formal mediation processes and related approaches is on the rise. They are fulfilling a need that has always existed. But what exactly is this need, and how do mediators fill it?

An enormous gap exists between dealing with our conflicts on our own and seeking the help of others. Avoidance is often our first response to conflict. And if we cannot avoid a conflict, we want to minimize it. Turning to others for help, particularly professionals, requires us to face a conflict more directly and openly. When we do seek outside help, our inclination is often to turn the conflict entirely over to others to manage, negotiate, resolve, or pursue. We delay getting legal assistance, but when we do we may want our lawyers to "take care of the problem." Or we may try our very best to handle a conflict with a coworker, but when we finally go to our employer we want them to fix it. Of course, sometimes we have no choice but to involve others or an outside system because of the nature of the conflict or our role in it. But the tendency to waiver between avoiding a conflict, dealing with it on our own, or turning it over entirely to others seems very widespread.

Yet despite this desire to get rid of the problem, we usually still want some say in how a conflict is pursued and what kind of outcome is achieved. Most of us are more inclined to commit to a decision and more apt to experience psychological closure if we feel involved in a significant way in the process. Moreover, our participation is essential to crafting effective solutions or to dealing with the relational and attitudinal aspects of conflict. The power of mediation is the potential it has to bridge the gap between dealing with conflicts on our own and surrendering that power to others. Mediation can help us maintain our power over important issues in our lives, as it assists us in moving through a difficult conflict process in a constructive way. The need for this kind of assistance seems almost universal—and so does resistance to asking for it.

What do mediators bring to a conflict that helps bridge this gap? Mediators alter a conflict dynamic in five significant ways:

- *They change the structure of the interaction.* Often the mere presence of a third party changes the course of a conflict, regardless of any specific intervention. Disputants have to adjust their approach to the conflict simply to accommodate the participation of someone with whom they are not in conflict. They change the way they present issues, communicate, and express their emotions. This usually means that people will tone down their most adversarial behavior when a mediator is around, but the opposite may happen too. That is, sometimes the presence of a third party provides the additional security people need to unleash their more negative behaviors or feelings. Also, the mediator often arranges for new systems of interaction, new types of meetings, new participants, altered time frames, modified agendas, and other structural alterations to the interaction process.
- *They bring an approach to mediation.* Mediators operate from a wide variety of backgrounds and philosophies (many of which I discuss later in this chapter), and in many different institutional contexts, so the particular approach or process they use varies tremendously. What is important, however, is that they have an approach, ideally a flexible one, that guides their work. For example, they might have a particular sequence of stages they try to take parties through; a characteristic way of using caucuses; a set of ground rules; a specific approach to identifying issues, interests, options, and relevant information; and a definition of their own purpose and role. The very existence of a clear approach is comforting to many disputants and adds a certain predictability and

definition to the interaction process. It also adds to the mediator's influence over the interaction.

- *They bring a set of skills in communication, negotiation, and problem solving.* Mediators bring skills that may be natural to them, but they also bring skills they have learned, practiced, and refined, such as deep listening, reframing, analyzing conflict, delivering difficult messages, encouraging creativity, managing the use of power, identifying areas of potential agreement, managing crises, maintaining neutrality, and understanding cultural differences.

- *They bring their personal commitment, vision, and humanity to the interaction.* Mediators enter a dispute with a set of beliefs about the potential of mediation to assist disputants, a commitment to contribute to the resolution process, and a vision of how to proceed. The energy and optimism of a mediator are extremely important assets that can have a major influence on how a mediation effort unfolds. Mediators also bring who they are as human beings. A mediator's warmth, sense of humor, commitment to the disputants, and ability to establish rapport with them are critical to his or her effectiveness. Of course, this is also about connecting with the humanity of disputants and engaging their capacity to connect as well. Sometimes mediators just "click" with the parties, and at other times, despite their best efforts, that connection does not develop, in which case they are likely to be less effective.

- *They bring a set of values and ethics.* Maybe the most important things mediators bring to a conflict are their values and ethical standards. These define mediators' most important commitments to their clients, and they profoundly affect the resolution process. Disputants do not necessarily adopt these values, but by entering into mediation they implicitly acknowledge them and therefore cannot help but buy into them to some extent. For example, a mediator is generally committed to helping parties find a way of communicating honestly and openly with each other about difficult issues and to allowing parties to express the concerns that are most important to them. By entering into mediation, disputants implicitly commit themselves to at least trying to communicate in this way. This does not mean that they necessarily follow this commitment, but a tacit expectation is usually there. These ethical commitments are a foundation on which parties can develop trust, respect, and comfort with the mediation process.

Of course, how mediators bring these elements to the process varies widely. They affect the interaction structure in many different ways. They bring diverse personal styles, skills, and procedures, and there are certainly many variations among mediators in their values and ethical principles. Specific procedures and tactics are easier to teach and to develop than are personal characteristics, but the more intangible personal traits are often the most important. The commitment of mediators; their ability to connect with each of the disputants; their optimism, integrity, and openness; and their clarity about their values are often the most powerful contributions they have to make. (For a discussion of mediators' different approaches, see Kolb, 1983; Kolb and Assoc., 1994; Riskin, 1996, 2003.)

What mediators do not normally bring to the process (although many think they do) is the best solution, the power to make people reasonable, the ability to change the genuine alternatives people face, or additional resources. In my mediation practice, when I have thought that I had arrived at a brilliant solution to a conflict, it was never brilliant and usually not a solution. Mediators may occasionally be able to see some alternatives that are not immediately clear to parties because of access to confidential information on both sides, because they are not as emotionally caught up in a dispute as the parties, or because of previous experience and substantive knowledge. But most often it is not that the solution is lacking but that the road to getting there is difficult. Parties have almost always lived with the conflict a lot longer and more intensively than the mediator has, and if what was missing were simply a creative solution it probably would have occurred to them. What we can do is help parties engage in a different kind of communication, begin to see the conflict in a different way, and consider the broad range of needs that they and the other parties are experiencing. In this way we can set the stage for them to find their own way, brilliant or otherwise, through a conflict.

Of course, if we are talking about a presidential envoy mediating an agreement in Northern Ireland, a president mediating between Israelis and Palestinians, or a city manager mediating a dispute between two city departments, then the mediator does bring significant power and resources. But these are not pure mediation processes, and the mediator's power places its own set of limitations on the mediator's role.

Mostly it is in the limitation of what we can do as mediators that our most important resource for contributing to a constructive engagement process lies. Because we cannot provide additional resources or alter the fundamental approaches and behavior of individual disputants, disputants can more readily turn to us in a confidential and forthright manner. As mediators, we are easier to trust when we have less power over the outcomes. When we have greater power over substantive outcomes (say, in a mediation-arbitration situation or in advisory mediation), disputants will naturally treat us as decision makers and approach us with more caution or with a different purpose.

CONSTELLATION OF APPROACHES TO MEDIATION

When we look at the variety of approaches third parties bring to mediation, it can seem as if we are viewing fundamentally different approaches to conflict. And in many respects we are. The differences between a settlement-oriented evaluative mediator and an empowerment-oriented transformative mediator are significant. Evaluative mediators focus on the strengths and weaknesses of disputants' legal case, on the outcome they are likely to face if they take their dispute to trial, and on the settlement range they should therefore consider. Transformative mediators do not focus on outcomes at all, and look instead for opportunities for empowerment and recognition. They do not suggest a particular agenda or propose a constructive framing of the issues because they believe this imposes the mediator's goals and outlook on the parties (Bush and Folger, 2005). The only common thread between these approaches seems to be the desire to help parties, from an impartial stance, to find a way through their conflict.

One problem with this wide range of approaches is determining how to categorize or conceptualize them. The most common taxonomy characterizes mediation along a spectrum with evaluative styles at one end, transformative mediation at the other, and facilitative approaches occupying the broad middle. There are several problems with categorizing mediation in this way. For one, there are no clear criteria that define this spectrum, and it is not evident, at least to me, why a facilitative approach is viewed as a middle ground between an evaluative and transformative approach. Furthermore, many approaches to mediation do not easily fit into this spectrum.

Another problem is that no one quite knows what is meant by facilitative mediation. I tried to define this a number of years ago (Mayer, 2004b) in a chapter for a book on divorce mediation (Folberg, Milne, and Salem, 2004). This book contains clear descriptions of transformative, evaluative, and hybrid processes as well. In it I suggested four hallmarks of facilitative mediation—that it is oriented toward process (as opposed to substance); centered on clients (they do the work of negotiating, problem solving, and identifying issues); focused on communication; and based on interests (as opposed to positions). But others may understand the facilitative approach differently. Transformative mediators may think that a facilitative approach inevitably leads to a focus on outcomes and agreements. Evaluative mediators may think that facilitative mediators do not provide significant structure or assistance to parties who want an immediate solution. I believe that the facilitative approach does not imply a focus on outcomes and can provide considerable structure and assistance to parties. But because there is such a broad range of styles that fall under the facilitative rubric, it is not surprising that facilitative mediation is characterized in so many different ways. Most effective approaches to mediation require good facilitative skills, and most mediators can be viewed as operating from within the facilitator role.

Len Riskin proposed a "grid for the perplexed" to characterize different styles of mediation (1996). Riskin created a matrix based on two variables: where the mediator stands on the evaluative-facilitative continuum and whether he or she takes a broad or a narrow view of problem definition (for example, What should the divorce agreement say about which nights the child will be in each home? versus What approach do the parents want to take to rearing their child?). This grid has been widely used to characterize mediation styles, but Riskin himself felt it was time to "retire" the grid because it was confusing in some ways and did not adequately characterize the range of approaches mediators actually take (Riskin, 2003).

So we are left with a constellation of approaches to mediation that have not been clearly categorized. I am not going to attempt a categorization. Instead I suggest we think about several questions that can help define a mediator's approach:

- To what degree does a mediator focus on achieving a settlement to defined issues versus attending to how he or she can help promote a constructive communication process?
- Does the mediator believe that solutions will emerge from the parties' interchange with each other, or does the mediator see himself or herself as the primary intermediary for communication and solution generation?
- Does the mediator focus primarily on one dimension of conflict (behavioral, emotional, or cognitive), on a combination of two dimensions, or on all three?
- How much emphasis does the mediator place on exploring underlying needs and concerns?
- Does the mediator devote considerable effort to identifying alternatives to a negotiated deal (for example, what will happen in court)?
- Does the mediator see the purpose of mediation as solving problems, transforming relationships, or encouraging a constructive communication process?
- Does the mediator attend to the enduring elements of a conflict, or does he or she focus primarily on the issues that lend themselves to immediate solutions?
- How much attention does the mediator pay to the discourse and narrative framework of a dispute?
- How flexible is the mediator in his or her approach? Does the mediator see the disputants as having an important role in determining the approach he or she will take?

This is by no means a comprehensive list, but taken together these questions can provide a pretty rich picture of a mediator's orientation. Perhaps the most important people to be asking these questions are mediators seeking to evaluate their own outlook. Whatever our approach, it is important for all of us who mediate to remember that in the end this is not about us but about the parties. If promoting a particular approach overtakes our focus on addressing the needs of the disputants, then we have lost sight of our most important commitment.

WHEN MEDIATORS FIGHT

As mediators, we are no different from anyone else; we don't always walk our talk, practice what we preach, or model good conflict behavior. And over the years there have been some interesting battles (OK, maybe not battles—conflicts) about how to practice mediation. The most prominent of these in recent years have been among proponents of transformative mediation and those skeptical of this approach. I discussed some of the arguments of proponents and critics of this and other approaches in Chapter Six. This has been a mostly enlightening debate about the ways in which mediator presumptions govern practice, even when we are not aware of them; about how focused we should be on resolving disputes; and about the importance of clarity of purpose versus flexibility of practice. But at times we have fallen into what we can call a fundamental attribution error—attributing our differences and some of the problems we may see with each other's approaches to the character and motives of the people involved. Nonetheless, I think the debate about these conflicting views has been healthy.

Another important difference of opinion among mediators has come to be known as the Susskind-Stulberg debate (Stulberg, 1981; Susskind, 1981). In a series of exchanges in the *Vermont Law Review*, Larry Susskind and Josh Stulberg, mediation pioneers, debated the responsibility of the mediator for ensuring that the outcome of a mediation process is not socially harmful or unethical. The question at the heart of this debate is, How much responsibility does the mediator have to make sure weaker parties are not overwhelmed in mediation, unrepresented parties are not damaged, and social interests are not undermined?

Perhaps the most durable and contentious debate has been over whether and how to mediate in cases in which there has been a history of family violence. For many years women's advocates argued that mediation could endanger victims, is a threatening forum, and could perpetuate a pattern of intimidation and control. Many family mediators argued that this was too sweeping a statement and that sometimes mediation is the safest and quickest way to end a destructive relationship. They also raised the issue of victim autonomy—What if the victim wanted to mediate? In more recent years there have been a number of very useful dialogues among victims' advocates, mediators, and domestic violence experts, and the discussion has become much more nuanced (Ver Steegh and Dalton, 2008).

Other debates—some contentious, some less so—have occurred over the use of the caucus (always, never, sometimes, extensively, sparsely, maintaining confidentiality, disclosing relevant information, and so forth); the cultural presumptions of mediators; the professionalization of mediation (for example, training requirements, certification, and substantive specialization); collaborative practice and mediation; screening cases for mediation; and the list goes on. These debates have, by and large, been valuable, even when they have not been carried out in the best of all possible ways. As with all areas of human endeavor, constructive engagement over difficult issues is essential to move our field forward.

WHAT DISPUTANTS WANT FROM A MEDIATOR

What mediators offer and what disputants want from mediation are sometimes at odds and always different. Disputants want mediators to help them get their needs met, to assist them in maintaining their self-image ("saving face"), to conduct a fair process, and to keep them safe. Disputants often want or think they want mediators to figure out a good solution, to put pressure on each of the parties (but mostly the others) to accept a compromise, and to hammer out an agreement. As mediation goes forward, parties often get in touch with a different set of needs—to receive validation, to have a powerful voice, to be understood (and to understand), and to have their psychological and procedural interests respected. But these needs are often latent, unexpressed, or not clearly understood. They are variants of what people want more generally in conflict (see Chapter Six).

As mediators, most of us will at times focus on helping disputants achieve an acceptable outcome and on hammering out a workable compromise, and this is an important part of what we offer and what people want from us. But I do not believe that this is the essence of our most important challenge or potential contribution. In serious conflict, it is not the absence of an effective solution that perpetuates a destructive interaction but the lack of an effective process or structure for communication and engagement. Unless we can somehow bring about a change in how people interact, our capacity to make a genuine difference will be limited. As a result there is often a tension between what we believe our function to be and what clients or their representatives specifically request. Consider the following thoughts written to me by an attorney who is very experienced at representing clients in mediation:

> Most lawyers prefer active directive mediators—mediators whose mission is arriving at a settlement, who urge the parties to settle, who cajole, who plead, who persuade. We bring our clients to mediation because we want to find a settlement. When a mediator spends the day simply communicating positions back and forth, and then at the end announces, "Jeepers, you guys are too far apart," then we feel that we've wasted our money. Lawyers are smart enough to communicate each other's position back and forth. We are looking for an active ingredient, who can give us more than we already have.

Of course, nobody wants to waste a day in a process that accomplishes nothing, but what is interesting in this statement is its description of the ways many attorneys believe mediators can be helpful. The alternatives posed here are "cajoling, pleading, persuading," and "simply communicating positions back and forth." According to this lawyer, attorneys want mediators to be outcome focused and to commit to arriving at a settlement. They perceive mediators who do not do this as ineffective, patronizing, and naïve. The idea of mediators assisting by delving deeper and helping parties look more broadly at a conflict, for example, is dismissed as "fluff," or as not real. Yet the deeper the conflict, the more necessary such "fluff" is.

Simply put, disputants often want mediators to hear their point of view and then convince everyone else involved that they are right and should get their way. More sophisticated clients understand that some compromise is necessary and that part of negotiation involves looking at new approaches to a problem, but they still want the mediator to help them advocate their interests.

If mediators are to be effective, therefore, they have to help parties do just that. They have to listen to all of the parties carefully and give each disputant an opportunity to present his or her most powerful argument in an effective way. Here is where the real skill and art of the mediator becomes evident, and where the approach of the mediator and the desires of the parties can converge. If the mediator is focused not on "cajoling, pleading, and persuading" but on helping each disputant present his or her views in a cogent manner and on working to ensure that everyone's ideas and needs have been taken seriously, then the disputants and the mediator are working together. Furthermore, if the mediator helps each disputant carefully and realistically think through his or her choices at various points in the process, they are all likely to be working from a complementary set of goals. The mediator must start "where the clients are at" and travel in partnership with them from there.

Our purposes as mediators do not have to be identical to those of our clients, but we should not be working at cross-purposes either. We would do well to listen when our clients express not only their goals for mediation but also their ideas about what role they want us to play. Inherent in those ideas will be very significant concerns that need to be addressed. This does not mean that we have to be cajolers or arm-twisters, or that we have to focus exclusively on finding a solution. It does, however, mean that we need to be very sensitive to the challenge posed by the differences between our sense of how to accomplish the purposes of mediation and our clients' expectations. In effective processes, mediators and the parties to the conflict are constantly reevaluating and negotiating exactly what they are trying to accomplish in mediation and how. Mediation, as other conflict engagement efforts, requires ongoing attention to defining the purpose and nature of the endeavor and the expectations of all participants.

Of course, some mediators view their role exactly as described by my attorney friend. They believe that their job is to get an agreement and that the best way to do this is to confront parties with the weaknesses of their respective positions, the necessity of compromise, and the merits of the offers that have been made. There is nothing intrinsically wrong with this approach, and in many situations it is more likely than alternative methods to lead to an agreement. However, it is unlikely to achieve a deep level of resolution. For arriving at a dollar amount in a personal injury or patent infringement case, it may be appropriate. For helping people repair a work relationship, achieve a broadly accepted consensus about how to approach a public policy question, or learn how to be effective coparents, such an approach may be not only ineffective but also harmful.

Things get really interesting for mediators when the clients themselves have very different ideas concerning what mediation should be about. Several years ago I was involved in a case in which the clients tried to bridge their different views about mediation by hiring two mediators who had never worked together, but I was not cooperating:

> Two different municipalities jointly owned and managed the same water treatment facility. When one of them wanted to expand the facility, years of tense relationships boiled over. So they decided to mediate. The problem was that they had very different views about how and with whom they should do this. The municipality wishing to expand was interested in a mediation that focused on the financial and contractual issues. They proposed a retired judge as a mediator. The other municipality felt that issues related to management practices, communication, and respect also needed to be raised. They proposed that I mediate. They resolved this issue, or so they thought, by asking us to co-mediate. I frequently co-mediate, but not with someone I have never met or worked with. In this case, I also gathered that our styles would be very different and perhaps our basic approaches to mediation would differ as well.
>
> I raised my reservations with the representatives of the municipalities, saying I did not want to work out my co-mediation

relationship on their dime. They put considerable pressure on me to change my mind because they felt this was their only way forward, and I did agree to consult with the retired judge. I had a very amicable phone call with him, but it was clear to me that our respective approaches were in fact very different. So I told the representatives that I thought either of us might work as their mediator but that I did not think they should hire us both. I would completely understand if they wanted to hire the other mediator, but I asked them to make a choice. In the end (and I was never clear how they came to this decision), they hired me.

I had to do a bit of fence mending with the expanding municipality's representative, but this actually proved very fruitful because by opening up the issue of what their concerns were about my approach, we uncovered some of their underlying interests. In the mediation, we discussed financial issues, communication, management approaches, and how they might handle conflicts in the future. They reached an agreement that seemed to work for them. I am quite sure that the retired judge would, in his own way, have helped them to that point as well, but he would have taken a very different route. We could each be effective separately, but not together.

PREMISES OF MEDIATION

Regardless of the approach taken, certain implied assumptions tend to govern how a mediation process unfolds. These premises exist because of the structure of mediation, and they define some of its greatest strengths and limitations.

- *Disputants need help (and can benefit from it).* A conflict goes to mediation because parties need help to interact effectively. They may have failed in their independent efforts to work on their dispute, or they may recognize that without mediation the conflict is likely to escalate or be prolonged. The acceptance by disputants that they need help is an important source of mediator power and legitimacy. When parties do not believe they need help (in a mandatory process, for example), the mediator's job becomes much more difficult.
- *There is an advantage to disputants' entering into a voluntary process.* Why not go straight to a third-party decision maker

where at least some substantive outcome is guaranteed? There are certain tactical reasons not to do this—uncertainty about the outcome or the time and transaction costs of going to trial or arbitration, for example. But beyond this is the notion that people are likely to take more ownership over the interaction and reach better, more carefully crafted, and more durable solutions if their participation is voluntary and if they are the primary architects of those solutions. It is therefore worthwhile for them to try to work with a mediator before turning the decision over to an external decision maker.

- *Mediators help people communicate more effectively and work on their conflicts more constructively, even though they do not have the power to impose an outcome.* Participating in mediation usually implies that there is at least a possibility that a third party with no power over the outcome can make a difference. More than that, mediators' lack of decision-making power is part of what allows disputants to engage in the process. The deal disputants make with a mediator is, in essence, "I'll give you power to run an interaction (up to a point), and I will reveal things to you and listen to your ideas about how to proceed, but in the end I get to decide."

- *Process is important.* For the most part, participation in mediation suggests that it is not just the elusive solution that is missing when parties are in conflict—something about the process of the interaction needs work. How negotiations are conducted and how communication occurs are important. Mediators are called in to alter the process.

- *Third parties can be attentive to potentially competing interests and stories.* People do not necessarily have to believe a mediator can be neutral, impartial, or even fair. But by entering into mediation they accept the possibility that a third party can at least understand competing needs and views and can conduct a process without exclusively promoting the position of one side. Moreover, disputants often have to accept that mediators can listen to entirely different stories without having to choose one of them as the only reality. This implies the possibility (although parties usually do not explicitly accept this) that apparently contradictory narratives can be legitimate.

These assumptions exist regardless of the approach of the mediator. Other assumptions are dependent on the particular approach taken or are rooted in the system or culture within which the mediation occurs. For example, there is no automatic assumption that direct communication among the parties is beneficial, and mediators vary widely on how they handle such communication. Many believe that direct communication is critical to an effective resolution process, although it may not always be possible. But other mediators, often those specializing in commercial cases, do not believe in bringing the parties together until the basis of an agreement has been crafted. The implication of the first approach is that people in conflict, even if they are very upset with each other, are capable of and can benefit from direct communication with effective third-party assistance. The implication of the second belief is that progress is easier to make if a consideration of the issues occurs without the additional stress of face-to-face contact among contesting disputants.

Mediators also have different approaches to confidentiality. There is significant legal protection for the confidentiality of mediation in most parts of the United States and Canada, and most mediators use confidentiality as an important tool when trying to change the dynamics of a negotiation. However, not all mediation is confidential—public policy mediation in particular often has to occur in public. Mediators differ in opinion and practice about the confidentiality of private communication—for example, in regard to whether they will reveal what occurred in mediation if the parties give them a release to do so and what confidentiality restrictions parties must agree to when they enter into mediation. Furthermore, court practices, statutory frameworks, and interpretations of professional obligations vary considerably from jurisdiction to jurisdiction in their interpretation of the parameters around confidentiality in mediation. Confidentiality is a strategic and legal consideration, but not one that is necessarily built into the structure of mediation itself. What is always necessary for the credibility of the process is that the ground rules around confidentiality be clear from the beginning.

Impartiality and *neutrality* (terms interpreted in many different ways) are usually associated with mediation but are not implicit in the fundamental structure of the mediator's role. Without getting into a discussion of whether it is even feasible for third parties to be completely neutral or impartial, it is clear that most mediators put themselves forward as having no interest in any particular outcome, no special relationship with any of the parties, and no intention of advocating for any one disputant at the expense of another. In this sense they indicate that they are neutral, unbiased, and impartial and offer that as part of what they bring to the process.

But mediation does not demand neutrality or impartiality. In many settings the mediator is not neutral and may have a special connection to one of the parties. In-house mediators in organizations, village elders in mediative roles, and family members who try to reconcile differences among other family members may not be neutral or impartial. What is required is for the mediator to try to help the parties interact with each other more effectively and to not take the side of one of the parties in the mediation.

The mediator's credibility is established in different ways depending on the values and needs of the people involved and the cultural context in which mediation occurs. In the middle-class professional world in which most of us operate, the promise of impartiality, neutrality, and confidentiality is usually essential for establishing the credibility and safety of mediation. But in other settings the community standing and personal status of the mediator may be far more important.

WHAT MEDIATORS ACTUALLY DO

What is it mediators actually do to influence a conflict? Mediators work in many ways, and each has an assortment of approaches. There is probably no single activity that all mediators would agree is part of their standard practice. Some evaluative mediators might not take any steps to promote direct communication among disputants. Transformative mediators might not take on the task of building an agenda or framing issues. Within the broad scope of what most mediators do, however, there are certain characteristic activities or tasks. (For the most comprehensive discussion of the processes and interventions mediators use, see Moore, 2003. For additional perspectives, see Folberg and Taylor, 1984;

Friedman and Himmelstein, 2009; Haynes, 1981, 1994; Rubin, 1981; Saposnek, 1998; Williams, 1998.) Following are some of the key activities in which mediators engage:

In the Beginning
- Assess whether and how to intervene in a conflict
- Create or redesign an arena for communication and negotiation
- Assist parties in their consideration of whether to participate
- Negotiate the purpose, structure, and guidelines of mediation with the parties

Throughout the Process
- Help each party to feel heard and to hear others
- Identify the key issues that parties need to address and the needs driving these issues
- Frame and reframe issues, suggestions, and concerns
- Work to create an atmosphere of safety
- Manage emotions and communication
- Explore needs at a useful level of depth
- Deal with unproductive power dynamics
- Help disputants work across cultural, gender, class, and other differences
- Encourage incremental and reciprocal risk taking
- Facilitate an effective negotiation process
- Deal with impasse

During the Problem-Solving Phase
- Encourage creativity
- Help parties develop and discuss options with each other
- Help people think through their choices
- Apply appropriate amounts of pressure
- Articulate and solidify potential agreements
- Discuss implementation of agreements

After Problem Solving (or When the Focus Is Not on Problem Solving)
- Help disputants build durable systems of communication
- Consider the ongoing elements of the conflict and how best to address them

- Discuss ongoing monitoring
- Discuss ways to anticipate and manage new conflicts
- Work with disputants on developing sources of support for implementing agreements or dealing with continued conflict
- Evaluate the effectiveness of the mediation process

This is by no means a complete list. For example, I have not mentioned drafting agreements; dealing with intraparty conflicts; communicating with others, such as lawyers, judges, and substantive experts; or teaching communication or negotiation skills, all of which are common activities of mediators. But the interventions listed here are, in my view, at the core of what mediators generally do to promote constructive interaction.

Most mediators will at some point engage in almost all of these activities. The most effective mediators are those who can approach each dispute strategically and flexibly. That is, they have a variety of approaches to each of these tasks and can choose among these approaches based on their assessment of the needs of the particular situation. This does not mean that they are always aware of doing this. Like any other skilled practitioners, the most accomplished mediators make many of their choices without consciously thinking them through. But I believe that effective mediators, if asked, can nevertheless articulate the thinking behind these decisions.

Let's consider several of these intervention activities further:

MEDIATORS ASSESS WHETHER AND HOW TO INTERVENE IN A CONFLICT

Just because mediation is requested does not mean it is appropriate, and even when it is appropriate there are many different ways of proceeding. The first step in most interventions, therefore, is some assessment of the appropriateness of mediation. Often this assessment is rapid and sometimes interspersed with other activities, such as data gathering and contracting. At other times it requires an extensive and focused effort. This process may be completely separate from the mediation itself. In many environmental disputes this is referred to as a "situation assessment," and it is not always conducted by the ultimate mediators. In some court-based or community mediation programs, an intake worker will make an initial assessment before referring the case to mediation. Of course, the mediator still has the responsibility for determining how and ultimately whether to proceed.

The decision to not mediate or to suggest some other form of intervention is in itself an important contribution to promoting a constructive process. One of the worst situations in which mediators can find themselves is in the middle of a dispute that is not appropriate for mediation but in which all the key parties are committed to going through with it. Mediators sometimes find themselves "holding a tiger by its tail"—realizing that mediation is not appropriate or even ethical for a specific dispute but not knowing how to let go safely. Several years ago a colleague and I found ourselves literally wanting to get out of town but not quite knowing how:

> Two teachers at a private school had filed a complaint against the acting headmaster and his assistant alleging intimidation and hostility in the workplace. The headmaster claimed that the teachers were refusing to accept the legitimate decisions of the board and the leaders of the institution and were fomenting "chaos and anarchy," and he threatened "significant disciplinary action." This standoff had found its way to the front page of the local newspaper. Subsequent to the appearance of that article, a large number of teachers and parents signed a letter requesting that a mediator be brought in, which the administration readily agreed to, and my colleague and I were contacted.
>
> We drove several hours to the small town in which the school was located for two days of meetings. During the first day we conducted individual interviews with all the primary parties and with others who had knowledge of the situation. On the second day we were planning to hold joint conversations with the people who were in conflict. However, after a few meetings on the first day, including several with the headmaster and his associate, my colleague and I both sensed that there was more going on than we were being told . . . a lot more. The headmaster was uncomfortable with any questions about what would have to happen to improve working relations but very eagerly told us just how "crazy" the teachers were. What was really telling, however, was the headmaster's response to our questions about what he hoped to get out of mediation. There was nothing he could articulate

except a desire to show the staff and parents that he had followed through on their request.

Finally, we bluntly asked him whether he had already decided to take personnel action against the teachers and whether this was subject to discussion. After obtaining a reassurance about the confidentiality of our discussions, he said that the board, on his recommendation, had already decided to fire the two teachers and that a letter of dismissal had been prepared and approved by the board and the board's attorney. He and the board members all felt, however, that they had to go through with the mediation because they had promised the rest of the staff that they would do so. He was sure that mediation would fail and that the letter of dismissal could then be delivered.

What really convinced us that this was a hopeless situation was that letter. It was over one hundred pages long! Hours or maybe days of devoted effort had been put into its creation. The commitment of the headmaster and his assistant to this course of action was obvious. We probed for any sign of flexibility from the headmaster and from some of the board members we met with later that evening, but there was none that we could discern. So we stated that it was inappropriate to proceed with mediation.

But there was a problem. How could we stop the process at this point, given that everyone else was expecting and preparing for a joint discussion the next day? We could not break confidentiality, but we also could not proceed with an illegitimate process. We asked the directors whether they were willing to indicate that they had in fact already made a decision. They were not, feeling this would imply (accurately) that their offer to mediate had been misleading if not dishonest. As mediators, we felt stuck. But it was clear to us that proceeding with the mediation would be unethical and destructive. We could see considerable potential for how we might help after the announcement was made, but not before.

Early the next morning we met with the different parties before the scheduled joint session and told each that we did not believe the situation was amenable to mediation at this time, but we were unable to give very satisfactory reasons why. We did our best to finesse the issue, but it was probably obvious to many that we were doing this because the die was cast. I think they understood where we were coming from and did not blame us, but it certainly did not help to ease the conflict. We suggested to the headmaster, his assistant, and the board that there might be a need for mediation after some of the dust settled from the dismissal. They seemed to feel that they just needed to tough out the next step and everything would work out. It didn't, at least not in the way they anticipated.

The letter was delivered, the teachers dismissed. They filed a suit. Eventually the headmaster and his assistant were dismissed, and the teachers were offered their jobs back. Instead they arrived at a monetary agreement with the board and took jobs elsewhere.

My colleague and I had planned on using our first day of interviews for assessing the situation and planning our intervention. In retrospect we both wished we had done more of this before we ever arrived on-site. But at least we did not jump into the actual mediation without doing any assessment. Perhaps if we had all of this would have come out anyway, and in the end maybe something positive might have occurred. More likely, however, we would have been conducting a sham process used for purposes of manipulation rather than for genuine discussion of the conflict.

MEDIATORS ASSIST PARTIES IN THEIR CONSIDERATION OF WHETHER TO PARTICIPATE

Often not all parties to a conflict have agreed to participate in mediation (or even an assessment of the situation). How mediators obtain not only consent but also commitment to mediation is very indicative of their overall approach. Some rely heavily on persuasion, guilt, or a hard sell about the advantages of mediation and the consequences of nonparticipation. I believe that these approaches can easily become counterproductive because they turn mediators into salespersons for the process and open the door for them to take on too much responsibility for the outcome. How we obtain agreement to participate has to be congruent with how we want people to engage with the process.

I have found it more effective to approach resistant parties by offering to help them think through the pros and cons of mediation for their circumstances rather than by trying to convince them to participate. I almost always tell people who are wavering about whether to participate that I don't know if it is wise for them to enter into mediation. That's a decision clients must make, because I can't know all of their considerations or concerns and I am not the one who will have to live with the consequences of entering into mediation. What I can do is help them understand what might occur in mediation and how particular concerns might be addressed. One of the greatest services mediators provide is not just getting people to participate but doing so in a way that builds momentum for a collaborative process. Another important service is helping people decide not to mediate when that is the best decision for them.

MEDIATORS MANAGE EMOTIONS AND COMMUNICATION

This is a primary tool of the trade. Mediators help people express their emotions or feelings as necessary and appropriate, and they manage the flow of communication. This may be the area characterized by the greatest variation in mediator style. Some mediators place a heavy focus on helping people express their feelings, whereas others shy away from this in the name of avoiding therapy and concentrating on helping people reach an agreement. Some mediators are very relaxed and easy about letting parties communicate directly from the outset. Others conduct the process so that almost all communication goes through the mediator—sometimes to the extreme of never bringing the parties together. Perhaps this is related to mediator self-confidence. That is, the more secure mediators are in their ability to manage emotions and communication, the fewer restrictions on direct interaction they are likely to impose.

MEDIATORS EXPLORE NEEDS AT A USEFUL LEVEL OF DEPTH

As discussed in Chapter Five, the art of creative conflict engagement involves finding the right level of depth for exploring people's needs, interests, hopes, and fears. This requires a discussion at a deep enough level so that the most significant forces driving the conflict can be addressed. Mediators help each person explore the conflict at the level of depth that is relevant to him or her, and then they try to find a way of discussing everyone's needs that encompasses the different levels that apply to each disputant.

MEDIATORS ENCOURAGE INCREMENTAL AND RECIPROCAL RISK TAKING

Negotiating difficult issues when a lot is at stake takes courage. Disputants make themselves vulnerable when they raise a conflict, reveal their concerns, provide information, agree to negotiate, express their feelings, take responsibility for their part of the problems, suggest ways forward, or commit to agreements. If they take too large a risk, they may encourage an adversary to try to exploit a perceived advantage, and this may ultimately lead to an escalation of the conflict. But unless some risks are taken, progress is hard to come by. This is a version of the negotiator's dilemma discussed in Chapter Eight. Trust is built by incremental and reciprocal risk taking. As people make tentative concessions or share important data and receive reciprocal concessions and information, confidence is built and resolution promoted. For this process to work, the risk must be large enough to be meaningful but not so enormous that the party taking the risk is made disproportionately vulnerable.

Mediators work with parties to encourage some risk taking, help them think through just how large a risk is advisable, and nudge them to reciprocate when others have shown a willingness to take a risk. People are usually much more aware of their own concessions and the risks they have taken than those of others, so mediators have to help them recognize others' concessions and risk taking as well. When mediators talk about orchestrating compromises or trade-offs among parties, in essence what they are doing is arranging for an exchange of risks.

MEDIATORS ENCOURAGE CREATIVITY

When conflict is intense and emotions are rampant, creativity can suffer. One way mediators deal with this is by working to create a comfortable, relaxed atmosphere in which different ideas can be put forward and discussed without people being exposed to personal attack. They also try to ensure that people feel they can suggest ideas without having to immediately defend them or commit to them. Mediators often focus parties on integrative or joint-gain possibilities that they have not adequately explored, and in general mediators try to get people to look at a dispute from a new perspective that will open up more creative ways of thinking.

What may be less effective is to substitute the mediator's creativity for that of the disputants. Mediators sometimes believe they can find the solution to a problem because of their experience, their communication with the different parties, or their own creative abilities. Although I have occasionally identified a potential solution of which nobody else seemed aware, usually because of the confidential access I had to different parties, the real challenge is to encourage disputants to identify potential new approaches themselves. There is an art to putting forward ideas at the right time and with the right amount of tentativeness to help prime the pump of others' creativity or get an option on the table that would be tainted if it were suggested by one of the parties to the conflict. But it is important for mediators to avoid becoming personally committed to a particular approach, especially to the point where they start trying to convince the parties of its merits. And the best source of creativity is almost always the parties themselves. The mediator's highest value is not in figuring out creative solutions but in promoting an open, relaxed atmosphere and an effective communication and problem-solving process that elicits the creativity of all the parties. Mediators also need to be alert to the possibility that creative solutions will come from unexpected sources.

> Charlie and David taught everyone involved in their parents' divorce a lesson in creativity and flexibility. The parents of these two preadolescent boys had already overcome a lot of animosity as they tried to work out parenting arrangements in mediation. The mother was about to graduate from a professional school and wanted to take on a greater parenting role. Her class schedule had limited her flexibility, but now she had a job with regular hours. The father had resented her entering this program to begin with and blamed it for their divorce. He had been resistant to making any change in the arrangements before issues about decision making, church, and education were settled.
>
> These parents were beginning to work with each other in a more constructive way, but scheduling Monday nights became a major obstacle. The boys were active in a Boy Scout troop that met near the father's home. For the parents' tentative schedule to work,

however, the boys would need to be at the mother's house, forty miles away, on Mondays. This was too great a distance to manage on a school night. We discussed all sorts of different ideas in our sessions, but nothing seemed to work.

I decided to talk about this directly with Charlie and David, because each parent was worried that the other would manipulate the children in any discussion of living arrangements. The boys came in together, and when I got around to asking about Boy Scouts, they both said how important that activity was to them. But almost immediately they also mentioned a troop some of their friends belonged to near the mother's house that was doing "cool" things. End of problem. I really wondered why neither of the parents nor I had thought about the possibility of a different troop, but we hadn't. It took the wisdom of the boys to identify a creative solution to the parents' impasse.

MEDIATORS HELP PEOPLE THINK THROUGH THEIR CHOICES

Mediators sometimes work to nail down potential agreements when the parties are ready to commit to them. At other times they need to slow down the process so that parties can make a deliberate and nonpressured choice among what are often less-than-ideal options. Mediators may have to do a little bit of both things at once. Typically, when an agreement seems possible, mediators will articulate it, trying to frame it in a balanced and clear way; ask people whether they are ready to commit to it; and, if they are, write it down. But there is often an important pause at this point, during which people have second thoughts, doubts, or premonitions of "buyer's remorse." When this pause happens, mediators can experience an impulse to turn on the pressure. However, what is often the most useful thing to do is the opposite, to decrease the pressure and give people more time or emotional space for considering their choices.

This is often a difficult point in a conflict, one at which potential agreements can fall apart. Seldom, however, have I seen a mediation fail because people took the time to think through their alternatives at this stage. More often I have seen agreements unravel because people were uncomfortable with commitments that they had made under pressure.

MEDIATORS APPLY APPROPRIATE AMOUNTS OF PRESSURE

Even in a very facilitative mediation, mediators apply pressure in some form to the parties to encourage them to take a step forward. They may or may not be aware of or comfortable with this aspect of their work, but it goes with their role. When mediators encourage disputants to make an offer, to respond to concessions, to acknowledge what they have heard, to share their own concerns, or to think through their real options, there is almost always some degree of pressure involved. Sometimes mediators put time limits on the process, and this too amounts to pressure on the parties. The mediator may not be intending to put pressure on the parties, but the mediator has a great deal of psychological and procedural power. Experienced mediators are aware of this inherent power and will use it intentionally and sensitively.

There is a fundamental difference, however, between putting pressure on someone to agree to a particular outcome and encouraging him or her to take a conciliatory step. If mediators believe their role is to identify a reasonable solution and "cajole, plead, and persuade" parties toward that outcome, then the pressure they put on can become quite intense. If mediators see their role as one of helping the parties engage in a collaborative process, they are more likely to use their power to assist and encourage parties to communicate and negotiate constructively.

WHEN MEDIATION WORKS, AND WHEN IT FAILS

Assisting Harvey and Laura with their divorce negotiations resulted in probably the most successful failure I have had as a mediator. Harvey and Laura had left the mediation hopelessly deadlocked and had taken their case to court. In the mediation they had fought bitterly about everything, but they did reach tentative agreement on most of the issues in their complex divorce. I had drafted a comprehensive memorandum of understanding, but as we were reviewing it they had several disagreements about its specifics and broke off mediation, indicating that they would prefer to take their chances in court.

At the time I viewed this as a failed mediation. But about three years later one of their attorneys called me to say they had some new issues and wanted to return to mediation to "update their agreement." "What agreement?" I asked, and pointed out that they had not reached any agreement. The lawyer told me I was wrong. In court they had each presented their copy of the memorandum. Although they had some minor additional requests, the judge basically entered the draft agreement as the court order. The couple referred to this as "the bible," and it had become the cornerstone of their postdivorce parenting and financial relations. When I met with them, each had a well-worn copy of the draft agreement, with highlighting, annotating, and underlining.

As it turned out, they had been able to use mediation to negotiate the terms of an agreement, but they had been too angry with each other to voluntarily close the deal. They needed an outside authority to impose it on them. In considering their request for a return to mediation, I felt concerned that they might feel that mediation had manipulated them into an outcome they did not really want but were stuck with anyway. But they seemed perfectly happy with the way their original mediation had played out. There may have been aspects of the agreement that each would have preferred to change, but they felt that it was as good a solution as they could expect. They had just needed someone else to finalize it.

This case pointed out for me the elusive nature of what mediation really accomplishes and the difficulty in clearly identifying when it has genuinely worked or what we mean by success and by failure. I believe that successful mediations do not necessarily end in agreements and that failed mediations sometimes do. People usually come to mediators because they want help in reaching an agreement. So achieving movement in that direction is one measure of how well a mediation process has worked in meeting the goals of the parties. But equating success with reaching an agreement and failure with not achieving one is very limiting, particularly in complex disputes. The longer, more involved, and more intense a conflict, the less useful it is to see reaching an agreement as equivalent to having a successful process. Agreements are often just steps along the way. Mediators can be particularly helpful by assisting disputants in taking those steps, but their larger purpose is to help people engage in the conflict in a constructive way.

Mediation has been successful when the addition of a third party has helped people proceed with an engagement effort appropriate to their particular circumstances. It is not successful if it does not help promote such an effort. Sometimes the true measure of whether a successful engagement process has occurred is whether or not an agreement has been reached. In many commercial mediations, for example, agreement and successful engagement go together. But in many public policy, workplace, and interpersonal conflicts, reaching a consensus— especially one that is premature or overly general—may be less valuable than helping people confront their differences, articulate their beliefs, and develop constructive frameworks for ongoing communication.

Mediation is a powerful intervention. Societies need mediators, and in almost all cultures there are people who act in a mediative way. All of us take on this role from time to time. Similarly, we all sometimes need someone to assist us in working on our differences rather than imposing an outcome on us. But just like any other approach to human interaction, mediation has its limits and is not always appropriate.

Even though the mediator role is a basic element in human interaction, it is probably an inadequately developed or institutionalized function in much of the world. Historically most mediation has been provided in the context of less mobile and complex societies. Where community structures were strong, extended family systems powerful, and social networks durable, there were many effective, informal mediative roles. But fewer such structures exist now, and the need for formal mediation services has grown.

Something is gained and something is lost whenever formal processes with trained personnel are substituted for informal processes, whether we are talking about counseling, advocacy, education, medical care, or conflict intervention. When people bemoan the loss of community, part of what they miss is the more personal, familiar, and accessible approaches of smaller and less institutionalized processes. There is a built-in contradiction here that defines mediation's greatest challenge: mediators are trying to provide a formal and professional intervention to help people handle their conflicts in an informal way and without giving up power to other formal and professionalized procedures. The tension created by this contradiction gives a creative impulse to mediation, but it also explains much of the resistance to mediation's more extensive use.

Chapter Eleven

Other Approaches to Conflict Intervention

As the field of conflict intervention has developed, how practitioners define their role and conceptualize their work has evolved and diversified. Although mediation continues to be an essential component of the work we do, we also offer a much broader range of approaches to conflict, as we must if we are to meet the needs of people in conflict. In Chapter Six I discussed how we can conceptualize our purpose and our role in a broader way that is more in keeping with the realities of how conflict is experienced and the help that disputants want and need. I also discussed the three fundamental roles conflict specialists play—third party, ally, and system intervener. I focus in this chapter on the range of approaches to conflict that are needed to offer disputants and potential disputants a comprehensive array of services.

Conflict Intervention as a Continuum of Services

As conflict specialists, the more we can view our field in its broadest dimensions, the better able we will be to make a differential assessment of each conflict situation. That is, the initial question conflict specialists ought to ask is not whether or how to mediate a dispute but what kind of approach is needed at any given time to help a conflict progress in a constructive way (and how that approach can be provided).

An ongoing challenge we face as a field and as individuals working in different areas of conflict is how to develop an effective *continuum of conflict intervention services* and to identify the essential elements of this continuum. In many of the contexts within which we work, such as corporations, court programs, government agencies, or communities, conflict intervention services tend to be developed on an ad hoc basis in response to particular disputes or problems. This is often inevitable, natural, and, frequently healthy because it is difficult and perhaps unwise to build a whole range of new services in these arenas from scratch. But as we develop new services, whether on an ad hoc or systemic basis, we need to be aware of the range of services that constitute a healthy system and how these can be provided in a coherent way.

Over the past decade there has been an encouraging amount of innovation and diversification in the services we offer. Currently the conflict intervention field encompasses people who provide mediation, arbitration, research, evaluation, training, facilitation, coaching, collaborative practice, dispute system design, restorative justice, parenting coordination, and settlement conferencing, among other services. But we still struggle at times with figuring out how best to link these services; what a continuum of services, or interventions, might look like; and how this continuum might be applied to different conflicts.

To clarify the elements of this continuum, it is important that we consider the types of assistance people in conflict need. In Chapter Ten I discussed what mediators offer to a conflict resolution process. However, we also should consider the limitations of mediation and specifically what needs it does not address. This can help identify the characteristics that a continuum of services should possess.

LIMITS OF MEDIATION

As versatile and useful as mediation is, there are significant limits on what it can provide to people in conflict. These limits are not problems to be rectified. In fact, they are essential to what mediation offers to people in conflict. Mediation's power derives in part from what it does not attempt to do. For example, mediators do not generally make decisions about who is right or push for specific outcomes. This is one reason disputants will often share confidential information with a mediator. However, third-party evaluations or recommendations are sometimes useful to disputants. Mediators do not generally advocate for one side, and this too is an important source of the mediator's ability to have a constructive impact on a conflict, but effective advocates are also essential to many conflict interventions.

The major limits of mediation are identified in the paragraphs that follow. In introducing each limit, I suggest conflict intervention approaches that can do what mediation does not do and that are therefore important potential elements in an effective continuum of services. Neither mediation nor any of the other approaches discussed in this chapter are by themselves the key to helping people in conflict. Taken together, they offer a powerful set of intervention tools to promote a more constructive approach to conflict.

- *Mediation is primarily used to intervene in conflict rather than to prevent it.* To be sure, mediation can be used to negotiate an agreement before a conflict has developed, but that is not its primary application. People for the most part employ mediation when a conflict has already arisen and they feel they need help in managing or resolving it. Approaches such as partnering, team building, and dispute system design are often more useful for preventing conflict and are designed to forestall the need for conflict intervention.
- *Mediation by definition involves a third party who is directly involved in the communication or problem-solving process.* Even though we may, as mediators, seek to empower disputants and leave them with the primary responsibility for how a conflict is handled, our presence at the table changes the disputants' role. People are frequently reluctant to give up even procedural power to a mediator or to reveal their circumstances or concerns to any outsider. As useful as mediation can be, most disputes will be resolved by those involved, without direct outside assistance. Thus there is a need for interventions that are designed to help people solve their own disputes without the direct participation of any third party. Training is one example of

such an intervention, as are coaching, dispute system design, and strategic consultation. Working with groups to help them prepare for a negotiation can be a powerful intervention.

Several years ago a state agency and all the county service-providing agencies it funded were sued by a national advocacy group in a class action to force the provision of additional services to the agencies' clients. The advocacy group presented the action as a "friendly suit" on the grounds that it was actually trying to force the state legislature to provide more money for the agencies' programs. But the agencies felt that the suit could easily lead to their losing control over their programs and to a serious increase in the "bureaucracy of accountability." A colleague and I were asked to assist the state and county agencies in preparing for the settlement negotiations that were about to take place.

We worked with the agencies in three ways. We facilitated a set of planning sessions during which agency representatives discussed their objectives, their strategy, and the structure of their negotiating team. This included devising a plan for communicating effectively with each other and for making decisions during the negotiation process. We also conducted a training program in collaborative negotiation procedures for the negotiation team, and we provided consultation to the team as the talks proceeded.

Our hope had been to involve both sides in a facilitated planning session to discuss how to conduct the negotiations, and we had invited the negotiators from the advocacy group to participate in the training sessions. They politely declined, feeling comfortable in their own ability to negotiate and probably wanting to maintain some personal distance at this stage of the process given the likelihood of litigation. We felt, however, that the offer to participate was critical in setting up a positive and open tone for the negotiations. Furthermore, they said they were very pleased that the agency negotiators were getting this training.

We took no direct role in the negotiations, which were complex and at times difficult. However, an agreement was eventually negotiated that was approved by the governor, the legislature, and the courts. It became the basis of some significant changes in the process by which services were delivered. Although the negotiations were tough, relationships among the key players were for the most part constructive.

How much did our work contribute to this outcome? Despite the favorable comments of the agencies' negotiating team, it is hard to know what impact our efforts had. Whatever influence we had resulted from our roles as the team's advisers, trainers, and coaches. Our ability to fulfill these roles would have been seriously curtailed if we had served as mediators because we would have had to maintain a degree of impartiality that would not have allowed us to give the same kind of advice and feedback. Also, I doubt that the team members would have been quite as forthcoming about their internal differences and their concerns about the weakness of their case if we had been working equally with both sides.

- *Mediation is usually focused on helping people with a negotiation—that is, on helping them arrive at a mutually acceptable outcome concerning an identified set of issues.* Mediation may of course be focused on communication, reconciliation, public participation, and related interpersonal processes, but it is most clearly designed and most frequently employed for assisting with negotiations. Most of the procedures, guidelines, confidentiality protocols, training, and marketing associated with mediation are oriented toward negotiation assistance. Although many of us who work as conflict interveners have critiqued the domination of this view of mediation (Bush and Folger, 2005; Mayer, 2004a), it continues to be the most prevalent approach.

  Sometimes people start mediation believing that negotiation assistance is needed, only to discover that they have hardly any issues to negotiate. Instead they may need assistance with reconciliation or healing, or simply with communicating. Up to a point mediators can help with these needs, but such approaches as reconciliation, counseling, facilitating dialogue processes, and initiating comprehensive programmatic interventions are often more suitable.

- *Mediation does not necessarily lead to an agreement.* It is a premise of mediation that people have the right to decide whether to accept or reject any tentative outcomes developed in the mediation process. Mediation is consensus oriented. It therefore does not automatically produce an outcome. When mediation processes have integrity—that is, when the principles of voluntariness and consensus are genuinely adhered to—a certain percentage of cases will not result in agreement. I am always suspicious of mediators who claim they achieve an extremely high rate of agreements. Too high a success rate could well be a sign of overly coercive practice (or of statistical manipulation). A certain percentage of cases ought not to reach agreement because the basis for a sound agreement has not yet been achieved.

Yet sometimes the guarantee of a decisive outcome is important, either because the situation demands it or because the parties to a conflict want it. For example, organizations often want an alternative to litigation to settle grievances that have not been resolved in mediation. A highly contentious divorced couple may want or at least need an effective method for making ongoing parenting decisions that they are incapable of agreeing on themselves. Arbitration, private judging, parenting coordination, and mediation-arbitration are some of the approaches used when people want a guaranteed outcome.

- *Mediation is process focused.* Mediators are not normally contracted to provide substantive expertise, and when they are hired for that reason, their process role can be detrimentally affected. Mediators generally need some substantive expertise in, or at least familiarity with, the kinds of issues with which they are working. But this is to ensure that they understand those issues, can help parties evaluate their alternatives, can detect important unspoken issues, and can understand the implications of different options under consideration.

Often, however, the parties themselves have a need for substantive information and technical assistance. Mediators can offer small amounts of such information on occasion without diluting their role as impartial facilitators. For example, a mediator might explain the steps in a grievance system, the formulas involved in child support calculations, or the time schedule for putting together an environmental impact statement. But the more mediators make the provision of substantive information or advice the centerpiece of their work, the harder it will be for them to focus on promoting effective communication, negotiation, and decision making.

Disputants often receive all their substantive assistance from people who are highly partisan, such as their lawyers or technical experts committed to a particular cause. As a result the various parties often operate on the basis of different, inconsistent, and sometimes biased information. In many environmental disputes, for example, the battle of experts is a serious obstacle to a constructive dialogue. Alternative and less biased approaches to collecting, analyzing, and interpreting information are often essential to the success of a conflict intervention effort. This has led to an increased use of fact finders, child development experts, financial specialists, neutral evaluators, evaluative mediators, technical panels, and other resources for obtaining balanced or impartial substantive information.

- *Mediation naturally operates at the level of interests.* Although mediators sometimes explore the deeper levels of needs, their natural focus is on interests. The mediation process is generally structured to push people to move beyond their focus on what it is they want to a somewhat deeper consideration of why they want it. But mediation is not generally set up to push people to consider their identity needs or to explore deeper psychological and interpersonal processes. To get to this level, it is usually necessary to develop a deeper rapport, spend more time, and work at a greater distance from the immediate conflict than most forms of mediation allow. Furthermore, although mediators have been used to defuse tense situations in which lives are at stake, the more common types of mediation are not designed to address immediate survival needs either.

  For example, divorce mediation is seldom the best place to deal with an immediate crisis in which the physical safety and well-being of children are at issue. Similarly, the fundamental concerns individuals who are divorcing may have about the meaning of their lives and their ability to sustain an intimate relationship are not best dealt with by most mediation processes. There are conflict intervention approaches that are more oriented toward dealing with issues of identity. Reconciliation processes, counseling, longer-term dialogues, and programmatic approaches to building relationships are better suited to dealing with conflict at this level. Survival issues usually require crisis intervention and tangible resources of some kind.

- Mediation is a short-term intervention. Mediation is normally structured as a time-limited intervention with a particular focus, and that focus is usually the attainment of some specific and immediate goal. But many serious conflicts require long-term, systemic, and multifaceted interventions. The process of building peace in Northern Ireland, Nepal, or Rwanda, for example, has required multiple mediations, but it has also required many other processes as well, such as economic development, grassroots peace building, initiating institutionalized communication structures, and multiyear strategic planning.

These limitations do not mean that mediators cannot or do not adapt to particular conflicts by altering the structure of what they do and the roles they play. Mediators have to be flexible, adaptable, and creative. Many creative new conflict intervention strategies have arisen when mediators or other conflict interveners have found themselves facing a situation calling for a significantly altered approach, and many new interventions first appear as hybrids constructed from the particular roles a specific situation demands.

On several occasions I have found myself developing what felt to me to be entirely new and unfamiliar roles in response to very specific requests from clients.

> Helping siblings permanently sever their relationship was not the business I thought I was in, but that was what I found myself doing. Two adult brothers came to me as a result of a dispute about an inheritance. The terms of their mother's will specified that they should consult a "third party" before taking legal action. The older brother, who had experienced a series of business failures, had received a significantly greater part of the estate, and his younger sibling felt manipulated and cheated. He confided in me that he did not have the money, the legal case, or the resilience to take this to court but wanted a chance to state his views in a way that his older brother would have to listen to. After that, he wanted help in saying "goodbye forever." Perhaps it is not surprising that this exactly mirrored the desire of his brother. He wanted to make his case and then "wish his brother well."
>
> They both felt there was nothing to negotiate. The basic damage had already been done to their relationship, and they

now wanted help in achieving closure—but not under the guise of therapy. To them, therapy implied a desire to heal the relationship and reestablish better communication.

Probably more to satisfy my needs than theirs I explored with them individually whether there was anything that might be said or agreed to that could prompt them to reconsider their decision to sever their relationship. Although the younger brother would have liked a more equal division of the estate, he believed that this was not going to occur in mediation, and he was right. There really was no outcome that either of them wanted other than this facilitated "siblingectomy." In individual sessions I listened to the worst feelings each had about the other, and I explored with them what they wanted to say and what they were likely to hear. We discussed how they might present their views and feelings and respond to what they heard with dignity, honesty, and sensitivity.

The joint meeting, in a weird sort of way, was extremely moving. Each brother talked about feeling that the other was the "favored child" and about how much he thought he had sacrificed for the other. Each described how he thought the other had manipulated their mother. Most important, both talked about their need to "end the relationship." They did remember better times between them, and although skeptical, neither ruled out the possibility of contact at some point in the future. Then they both thanked me and with tears in their eyes said goodbye. I checked in with each of them shortly thereafter, and they both said that the meeting had accomplished exactly what they wanted.

Was this some sort of reverse conciliation process? A kind of antimediation? Whatever its label, I felt this hybrid of counseling, mediation, and facilitation had somehow accomplished an important purpose that would allow healing for each of them. They seemed to feel freer to go on with the rest of their lives after this encounter. Maybe they will reconnect someday, and perhaps having been through this process will make that easier, but there is no way of knowing this. I have since encountered a number of situations in which facilitated leave-taking might have been useful—relinquishment of children to adoption, divorce where no ongoing contact is expected, and dissolution of long-term business partnerships, to name a few. A number of religious traditions provide for ceremonies of separation. There is probably a much greater need for a secular version of this kind of service than we realize.

There are many similar examples of new approaches developing in response to the particular challenges of individual conflicts. Mediation-arbitration, sometimes called med/arb, arose when clients who could not settle a case in mediation but had invested time in the process and developed a good rapport with the mediator wanted that mediator to render a decision. Sometimes people (or their lawyers) who have an ongoing but hostile relationship (such as divorced parents or antagonistic but successful business partners) contract with a third party to be available to make immediate decisions, often by phone, as conflicts arise. The use of parent coordinators to deal with high-conflict divorce cases (and to prevent repeated trips to court to resolve parenting disputes) is increasingly common (Barris and others, 2001). Lawyers and other professionals who want to provide effective legal and problem-solving assistance to parents but who do not want to become embroiled in litigation have developed the concept of collaborative practice, used primarily (but not only) with divorcing couples. There are many interesting elements to this approach, but three key features set it apart from the more standard approach to representation: a commitment to a cooperative approach to negotiation, the participation of multidisciplinary teams, and the use of a disqualification agreement whereby all parties agree that their lawyers will be representing them for settlement purposes only and that they will retain new lawyers if their case goes to trial (Cameron, 2004; Tessler, 2001; Webb and Ousky, 2006). This is a version of what Forrest Mosten has called the "unbundling" of legal services (Mosten, 1997).

New approaches to conflict intervention are designed constantly, although not always intentionally. Some of them are essentially variations on how a particular service is delivered, but often an entirely new role emerges from the demands of a particular situation. Great care must be taken to clarify exactly what this role is. One sure way to create distrust and suspicion of a conflict specialist is for a disputant to have one understanding of the nature of the process and the role of the professional and the intervener to operate on a different assumption. And of course, not all innovations end up being constructive, workable, or even ethical:

Liz and Rich had been married for about ten years when they approached me to mediate their divorce. With some difficulty they succeeded in reaching a comprehensive divorce settlement that became the basis for their legal divorce. In those early years of my work in the conflict field I still maintained a practice as a family therapist, and about eighteen months later they approached me with an interesting request—they were planning on getting back together and wanted me to act as a marriage counselor.

At first I refused on the grounds that I had worked with them in an entirely different capacity and that this would blur my role in a way that I was not comfortable with. I instead referred them to a couple of other marriage counselors. After several weeks they returned, more adamant this time, saying they were comfortable with me and the referrals had not really worked for them. So, with some misgivings, I agreed to work with them in this capacity, but I told them I would not be willing to serve again as their mediator should that need arise. After several weeks of working together in therapy, they decided to go forward with their marriage.

Not surprisingly, several years later they separated once again, and despite our earlier agreement they again approached me for mediation, but this time I stuck to my decision not to revert to the role of mediator. I do not, in retrospect, think there was any real problem with my having switched roles in their case, other than that I was no longer available as a mediator. But when they returned again, I did not think that switching between these functions added a significant additional benefit, and given the potential ethical and practical problems with combining the role of mediator and marital counselor I never again agreed to a transition of this nature.

COMPONENTS OF AN INTERVENTION CONTINUUM

An effective continuum of services can include a broad variety of specific components depending on the type of conflict and the setting to which they are targeted. What is needed for any particular conflict will vary at different stages in the conflict process, and no one system is likely to offer all the components a particular conflict might require. But there are certain generic types of assistance that disputants need. It is useful to keep these in mind as we build systems of conflict intervention, knowing that how these are specifically created and offered will vary tremendously and that no individual practitioner will offer all of these services. Figure 11.1 presents six generic types of dispute intervention activities that together form a comprehensive continuum of services. Lets consider each of these further.

PREVENTION

Prevention activities may be geared toward making sure that a conflict does not arise to begin with, or they may focus on preventing a destructive escalation of a conflict that has already developed. In either case we can consider two broad approaches—substantive and procedural. People can anticipate the substantive concerns that may cause or escalate a conflict and deal with them before they become problematic, or they can agree on procedures for communication and problem solving to forestall conflict or prevent it from escalating should it arise.

FIGURE 11.1 CONFLICT INTERVENTION SYSTEM

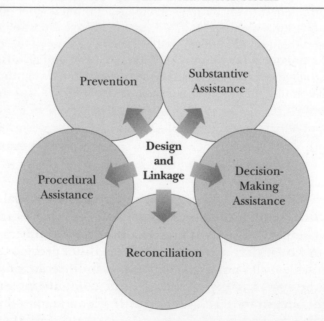

Anticipating and dealing with issues that have not yet caused overt conflict but might do so later can be a very effective and powerful approach to intervention. A prenuptial agreement, a partnership buyout provision, an agreement about what will happen if a contract is not executed in a timely way, and a decision on land use made before there are development pressures are examples of a substantive approach to prevention. A procedural approach could involve opening more effective channels of communication or decision making, such as by arranging for regular meetings between contractors and their clients to review the progress of a project or establishing an employee council, a citizen's advisory group, or effective public participation processes.

The potential for a conflict to escalate in a destructive way can be mitigated by early detection and rapid response systems and by the establishment of ongoing structures to monitor and address conflicts as they arise. One way in which citizen advisory councils have been effective resources for government agencies and industrial facilities is by helping them identify conflicts with the community at an early stage and by acting as a communication link among the parties involved before these situations have a chance to escalate (Mayer, Ghais, and McKay, 1999). Sometimes, however, to make sure an issue is addressed or the concerns of certain disputants are taken seriously, escalation is essential. As I write this, the Middle East is awash in protests seeking fundamental political and social changes. Several authoritarian governments have already fallen, and still more may do so as a result of these activities. Preventing escalation under these circumstances would be neither possible nor desirable. What makes sense instead is to focus on how to minimize the destructive or violent nature of the escalation. In this respect, the training that many of the leaders in Egypt, Jordan, Tunisia, and elsewhere received from the Center for Nonviolent Conflict in nonviolent approaches to social change can be viewed as a sort of anticipatory effort to guide escalation in a constructive and yet very powerful direction (Stolberg, 2011).

Prevention processes are often outgrowths of previous conflict intervention efforts. Difficult negotiations or interactions in particular may result in the establishment of preventive measures for the future. Prevention, then, should not be seen as something that necessarily precedes conflict. Instead it is often a link that builds on the lessons and momentum from past conflict to redefine how future interactions will take place. The institutionalization of conflict intervention activities is itself a prevention effort. Prevention should not be seen as a form of avoidance. Effective prevention is about dealing with important concerns that people have before they erupt into conflict, not about avoiding or minimizing an existing conflict. In fact, effective prevention generally encourages people to face potential problems that they might rather avoid.

Conflict practitioners play a variety of roles in prevention. They point out the need for prevention, help parties agree on preventive measures, consult on the design of prevention systems, coach people in how to use prevention procedures, and facilitate or organize the operation of prevention activities. They also provide training in communication, teamwork, nonviolence, conflict management, and related topics.

The line between prevention and intervention is a thin one. Often the effort to put preventive processes into place starts by revisiting a previous conflict and dealing with unresolved issues. Escalated conflicts are often addressed from the point of view of prevention as well. I have on occasion been asked to help prepare labor and management negotiating teams for the next round of bargaining. These ostensibly preventive activities almost always begin with an intense discussion of what happened in the last round of negotiations. Before people can focus on the future, they almost always have to revisit their lingering feelings from the past. After processing some of these issues, some genuine preventive planning can take place. This is just one way in which conflict is not a linear process with a clear beginning and end. Prevention, reconciliation, negotiation, escalation, de-escalation, and resolution all have a way of melding into each other.

Procedural Assistance

Systems of conflict resolution have usually been built around the provision of procedural assistance, which frequently takes the form of mediation or facilitation. Process is in many ways the conflict intervener's specialty. The acceptance and growth of the conflict field have been fueled by the increasing awareness that trained third parties can significantly assist people in conflict by focusing on the process of how people communicate and interact as well as by a growing understanding of the difference between procedural assistance and decision making.

Although mediation may be the most established form of procedural assistance, it is not the only type. Other procedural roles are being developed or formalized all the time. Some of these are aspects of mediation (for example, situation assessment) that are developing into independent intervention services. Others (for example, training) are not generally part of the mediation process. Allies and system interveners as well as third parties offer procedural assistance. Coaches may help prepare disputants to be effective in a conflict engagement effort. Advocates sometimes view their role primarily in terms of process assistance. And system managers play important roles in developing and maintaining intervention approaches that are primarily procedural in nature. Approaches to process assistance in addition to mediation include the following:

Assessment

When organizations or public agencies are involved in complex disputes, they often find it useful to hire a conflict specialist at the outset to assess the situation and recommend what, if any, type of procedural assistance or other approach to intervention might be useful. Although the assessor sometimes later serves as the mediator or facilitator, there is a potential conflict of interest in combining these roles. Sometimes, therefore, the person doing the assessment is contracted for that task alone.

Convening

Conveners help start a process but do not necessarily assume responsibility for conducting it. They identify potential participants, discuss their concerns about participation, identify an overall set of issues to be addressed, develop a preliminary formulation of the purpose and design of the process, and arrange for the initial gathering of the parties in a suitable forum. The participants may then run the process themselves, or a different third party may be brought in as a facilitator or mediator. Sometimes the convener has an ongoing role during a process, but at other times his or her purpose is served once the dialogue or negotiation begins. Often the functions of situation assessment and convening are combined, and one person or team does both.

Facilitation

Facilitation seems to have widely different meanings to different people, implying everything from chairing meetings to conducting group therapy. In the conflict field, a facilitator usually is someone who is conducting an interaction of some kind and whose focus is on guiding and improving the process of the interaction. Facilitators are not generally substantive experts or decision makers and are usually not stakeholders themselves (but sometimes they are). Their function is to help a group accomplish its goals or purposes. Mediation is in essence a form of facilitation in which the focus is on helping people to communicate about an identified conflict or to engage in a negotiation process. Facilitators are often used to help people arrive at a consensus-based decision, an agreement that all participants can accept, but facilitators are also used to conduct interactions in which no decision or agreements are sought—such as public input meetings, focus groups, or brainstorming sessions. The role of the facilitator is in essence to guide a group process and, where decision making is involved, to orchestrate a consensus-building effort. (For an extensive discussion of the consensus process, see Susskind and Cruikshank, 2006; Susskind, McKearnan, and Thomas-Larner, 1999.)

The concept of facilitation is broad and somewhat fuzzy, however, and a great many activities are labeled as facilitation. Mediators are sometimes called facilitators, as are trainers, counselors, organizational consultants, team leaders, and therapists. I have sometimes been hired as a facilitator because people did not want a mediator and at other times as a mediator because people did not want a facilitator, and in both instances I had to do essentially the same work—that is, help a group communicate about a conflict and arrive at some common understanding of how to proceed.

To some people, facilitation sounds less controlling or intrusive than mediation but also less powerful. I see facilitation as encompassing a broad category of activities for guiding a group process. Facilitation may help in many different aspects of an interaction, not just in conflict intervention or decision making. Any time a person has the task of focusing on the process of an interaction as opposed to the substantive issues themselves, he or she is taking the facilitator's role. (For three different approaches to facilitation, see Doyle and Strauss, 1976; Ghais, 2005; Schwarz, 2002.)

Training

Conflict training is about helping people develop a set of skills or learn a new way of understanding conflict and communication. Training is not generally designed to help people work on a specific conflict, but it can play a major role in helping people conduct or participate in a conflict intervention effort. The line between training and intervention can be fuzzy or nonexistent, especially when people or teams who are in conflict participate in joint training. Some of the most powerful steps I have seen people take to break an unproductive pattern of interaction have come during such trainings. As important as the substantive purpose of a training can be, it is often secondary to the personal rapport that can be built and the understanding of different perspectives that can develop as a result of bringing people together in an educational forum.

It is not unusual for an organization to ask for training in conflict resolution when what it needs is help in dealing with a conflict. This can be frustrating for participants because real issues might be hovering over an educational experience without being directly addressed, or it can be an opening for them to begin to tackle these underlying issues.

Sometimes training is intentionally built into a broader conflict intervention effort to provide a forum for people to come together—to provide a common vocabulary, set of principles, and skills that participants can use in other elements of the process. As with so much of what we do, the key here is transparency. We can use training in many different ways, but we need to be clear about its purpose and intent or we can easily generate distrust and resistance.

Coaching

Coaching or consulting with disputants about engaging in conflict is an increasingly popular approach to conflict intervention. But it remains underused as a systematic approach to helping people deal with conflict. I have worked with many organizations that have grievance procedures calling for direct meetings between the grievant and a manager as a first or second step. Seldom, however, is there a provision for advice, consultation, coaching, or any other assistance to help make these direct meetings productive. Too often the assistance that is available is either adversarial or focused on the substance rather than the process of the negotiation. An effective mechanism for coaching employees or managers involved in a grievance, parents going through a divorce, families involved in the child protection system, or parties to a community dispute, to name a few examples, can make an enormous difference in how a conflict process unfolds. In many circumstances lawyers provide de facto conflict coaching; sometimes they do this very effectively, but lawyers also play an important substantive role and are more oriented to representing people in negotiations than to preparing their clients to engage in conflict themselves.

Coaches help parties think through their own key concerns and goals as well as those of others. They work with clients to consider their alternatives, plan how to frame their concerns and suggestions, and think about how to listen to and acknowledge other parties even as they disagree with them. Coaches can also prepare people to deal with aggressive behaviors and to find a way to be both powerful and collaborative in their approach to conflict. A coach's focus often goes beyond addressing a particular conflict to a more generalized effort to develop a client's ability to handle conflict effectively. (For further discussion of the coaching role, see Jones and Brinkert, 2008; Mayer, 2004a; Noble, 2012.)

SUBSTANTIVE ASSISTANCE

Credible and impartial sources of legal, technical, financial, scientific, or other kinds of information can be very hard to come by. I have often wished there were a way for a divorcing couple, early in their decision-making process, to hear the same legal opinions at the same time. Some attorneys are willing to sit down with a couple, especially if they have no attorney-client relationship, and discuss these matters. Some mediators will attempt to provide this information. And the growth of collaborative practice provides a model of negotiation that can allow both attorneys to provide legal information to their clients in a joint session. But by and large the only real opportunity that couples have to hear impartial legal analysis together is during a settlement conference with a judge or settlement officer.

Developing approaches to constructively provide substantive information to disputants is an important element of the services we can offer people in conflict. This can be accomplished in many ways.

Providing Technical Advice and Fact Finding

Technical experts tend to view themselves as objective and unbiased, but usually whoever they report to or receive their payment from must ultimately be pleased by the overall pattern of their findings if they are to continue to work for that person. Thus over time there is pressure for them to emphasize findings that are favorable to their employer. It is no accident, for example, that studies on the impact of smoking generated by the tobacco industry have produced very different results from studies produced by health advocacy groups. Even when information is genuinely unbiased and independent, the perception of the parties about the reliability of the information is also important. We see this, for example, in the widespread suspicion of the results of scientific research into global climate change. Finding ways to bring technical information to the table in a credible and accessible manner is therefore vital in many conflicts.

Conflict specialists have attempted to meet this need in different ways. They have acted as fact finders, with the mission of producing an objective and unbiased analysis of a conflict and its potential solutions. Technical consultants have worked for a dialogue group as a whole or have been hired by a convener or facilitator rather than by one of the parties. Sometimes, in anticipation of possible conflicts (particularly in large construction projects), potential disputants have put together a panel of substantive experts or have agreed on a consultant who will make technical recommendations or rule on technical issues. Mini-trials have been used in large contractual disputes to lay out both technical and legal information for negotiators. A mini-trial is a sort of mock trial in which lawyers put on their best case in front of the key decision makers prior to settlement negotiations.

Data Gathering

Conflict interveners often work with disputants to create meaningful ways for them to gain access to information. In a public policy negotiation that involves significant data issues, for example, it is generally important for participants to help formulate the key questions that need to be answered and to review the methodology for obtaining information. Sometimes the data generated by one party to a dispute are accepted as credible if everyone has had a chance to review the methodology and if the parties feel that the technical experts have been open and straightforward in discussing their findings. Sometimes it is essential that the technical expert be an independent consultant. And at other times the input of credible and independent technical advisers is disregarded because they did not work effectively with the group to whom they were reporting.

Often the issue that conflict interveners face is an imbalance in access to technical information. When one party, perhaps an industry group, has access to a great deal of technical expertise and support and another party, maybe a community group, has none, providing a neutral expert may not be enough. It is sometimes necessary to find a way for the community group to gain access to technical or other consultants who will be their confidential advisers.

Coaching Substantive Experts

Conflict specialists sometimes help substantive experts fulfill what for them can be an unfamiliar role as participants in a negotiation or consensus-building process. Financial planners, business evaluators, health care professionals, environmental scientists, and child development experts, for example, are increasingly called on to act not only as expert witnesses in litigation but also as participants in collaborative conflict engagement processes. Conflict specialists can offer coaching about how to present information or respond to skeptics, provide experts with an opportunity to rehearse presentations, and give ongoing feedback. Sometimes conflict interveners find themselves mediating between a technical expert and a group of disputants. Fortunately, a growing number of independent individuals and organizations are becoming experienced in providing impartial, substantive input into conflict intervention processes. The role of these experts can be critical to the success of a consensus-building effort, as it was in this dialogue on waste-management policy.

I received my first exposure to the concept of "Gucci garbage" when I worked with two adjoining municipalities after they had received federal funds to investigate alternative approaches to solid waste management. One of the conditions of the grant was that the municipalities convene an advisory group composed of representatives of the waste-management industry, recycling organizations, the communities involved, and relevant public interest and environmental organizations. A colleague and I were hired to facilitate the meetings of this group, and several technical consulting firms were contracted to provide substantive input.

Although its members encompassed many different points of view, the group developed a good internal communication and decision-making process. But it faced complex issues about which there was very inconsistent information. The initial question laid out by the municipalities was, Should a plant that incinerates waste and generates energy be built in this area? This issue raised all sorts of questions about environmental, economic, and health impacts. The group redefined this question as, What should be the strategy for managing waste in this region to minimize negative environmental, economic, and health impacts, and is there a role for a waste-to-energy facility within this strategy?

The technical consultants were a critical part of these discussions, but the group had very different reactions to the economic specialists and the engineering consultant. On the one hand, the economic experts never established a strong personal rapport with the group, and, despite receiving suggestions from the group, from the other technical consultants, and from my colleague and me, they were never able to structure a presentation that seemed accessible and relevant to the participants. As a result the group members never believed that they were receiving reliable economic data, and this inhibited their confidence about making bold recommendations.

On the other hand, the engineering consultant was extremely well liked, personable, and responsive to group dynamics. Participants trusted the information he presented and felt that he was not pushing a particular point of view. One day he showed up with a sack full of typical garbage and laid it on a table in front of the group. He then proceeded to tell a story about what would happen under different scenarios with the different contents of the sack. It was useful, funny, enjoyable, and relevant (even if a little smelly). The group felt a great deal of confidence in using the information he provided in their considerations.

The recommendations of the group reflected their different responses to the experts. They believed the primary tasks to be accomplished in solid waste management were to create a regional waste-management strategy, to maximize the reuse and recycling programs, and to make existing facilities more efficient. They recommended against constructing a large energy-generating waste incinerator because they did not think it was needed, did not believe its economic benefits had been established, and were concerned that it would draw resources away from reuse or recycling efforts. They did believe that a smaller and more targeted facility to process a more refined set of waste (thus *Gucci garbage*—the term the engineering consultant used) was appropriate. Such a plant might be acceptable, for example, as a means to handle waste at a new airport. Most of this group's recommendations were accepted. The nature of those recommendations was a direct reflection of the quality of the input from the various experts and of the relationships group members had with them.

RECONCILIATION

A comprehensive system of conflict services requires approaches that focus not only on the issues involved but also on the relationships among the parties. Building peace requires a deeper focus, one that is sometimes called conflict transformation (Lederach, 1995); peacemaking (Curle, 1971); or reconciliation. In Chapter Five I discussed the three dimensions (emotional, cognitive, and behavioral) of resolution. Often conflict intervention processes focus on the behavioral dimension and do not address the emotional or cognitive dimensions. Yet unless there is progress on these dimensions as well, it is unlikely that fundamental changes in the relationships among disputants will occur.

Multiple efforts over time and at many different levels are usually necessary to address deeply rooted conflicts and to promote genuine reconciliation. This is true whether we are talking about violent ethnic conflicts, such as those in Rwanda, Iraq, or Kashmir, or bitter interpersonal disputes, such as those between deeply conflicted divorcing couples. But progress can be made even on the most difficult and bitter disputes, and for every story of an intractable conflict that has gone on for years there is a story of how former enemies have made peace. We are witnessing some amazing transformations in the world—in Northern Ireland, Rwanda, and South Africa, for example. Optimism mixed with realism and hopefulness mixed with watchfulness are extremely important traits for conflict specialists.

Conflict interveners have been central to many reconciliation activities. Sometimes they have functioned through the more established roles, acting, for example, as mediators or facilitators. Victim-offender mediation has proven to be an effective means for bringing a level of reconciliation and a deeper learning to perpetrators and victims in certain kinds of cases (Umbreit, 1994). Victim-offender mediation is one example of a broader movement that seeks to respond to violence with efforts at "restoration" rather than retribution (Dussich and Schellenberg, 2010). Restorative justice programs have been used with youth, with adult offenders, to address ethnic violence, and in international conflicts. Perhaps the most famous example of this is the Truth and Reconciliation Commission in South Africa (Tutu, 1999). Similar efforts have been used in Rwanda, Sierre Leone, Chile, and many other places that have experienced serious violence. Truth and reconciliation processes have also been implemented where there has been a long history of exploitation or personal violence, such as in Canada in regard to the Indian Residential School Agreement that sought to deal with years of exploitation of First Canadian youth in government-operated residential schools.

Reconciliation processes require approaches that go beyond immediate conflict resolution efforts. We can identify four basic approaches to reconciliation. One approach helps people go through their own individual healing process. For example, groups that help victims of violence confront and share their experiences or that help perpetrators face their own demons can be vital to reconciliation efforts. A second approach involves the development of safe forums for communication and interaction that allow people to get to know each other as human beings. Camps that bring youths from conflicting regions together or programs that encourage different ethnic groups to work together on common problems are examples of this approach. Sometimes the best way to accomplish this is indirectly, through projects that are not explicitly aimed at bringing disputants together or helping them work through their experiences in conflict but that address other interests they have.

> One of the most impressive reconciliation efforts I have seen was at a community center in Banja Luka, which is situated in the heart of the Serbian section of Bosnia and which was the site of some horrible ethnic violence during the Bosnian civil war. At this center there were many reconciliation efforts under way—a variety of classes, recreational activities, and discussion groups. But the most interesting to me was a radio station. It only broadcast over a two-square-mile area, but teenagers and young adults from all ethnic groups eagerly worked together to run the station. Most of them had suffered terribly during the fighting, but at the station they worked together, had fun together, got to know each other, and occasionally shared their personal experiences of war with each other.

A third approach brings people together for a direct, in-depth dialogue about a conflict and all the feelings and pain that have gone with it. Sometimes this process encourages people both to take responsibility for their own actions and to forgive others for theirs. The Truth and Reconciliation Commission in South Africa mentioned earlier, and similar programs elsewhere, are examples of this kind of effort. The fourth strategy is to address directly the serious substantive problems that make reconciliation difficult (for example, inadequate housing, unemployment, or fears for personal safety). Unless the ongoing sources of stress that keep people from feeling safe and secure are addressed, reconciliation efforts won't work. In other words, for reconciliation to take root, people's survival and security needs must be dealt with.

Decision-Making Assistance

Consensus-based decision-making processes are sometimes inappropriate or ineffective. People may be unwilling or unable to reach an agreement. An immediate decision may be essential even though disputants are not ready or able to agree on one. Some decisions may not be important enough to merit the time and resources required to achieve consensus. On other occasions a decision must be made so quickly that there is no time to implement a consensus-based approach. For these and other reasons, people often need an alternative to voluntary, or consensus-based, approaches to decision making.

Traditional governmental or organizational mechanisms for making decisions in the face of conflict (courts, legislative bodies, executive fiat, management hierarchies, quasi-judicial panels, and so on) are often too cumbersome or too toxic to be practical or constructive. Moreover, their very structure may polarize a conflict. Conflict resolution structures therefore need to provide access to effective and efficient means of decision making for parties when consensus-based approaches won't work.

Two fundamental types of decision-making services are needed—advisory and binding. Giving an advisory opinion can be a bit like supplying substantive information, but it is an important option because it can offer people a relatively cheap and quick foretaste of what might occur in a more expensive, lengthier, and possibly more toxic binding process. Advisory or evaluative mediation, nonbinding arbitration, advisory dispute panels, and certain types of fact finding are all examples of advisory approaches. Binding approaches, such as formal arbitration, med/arb, binding dispute panels, or parenting coordination, commit parties to the outcome, either through contractual mechanisms, by court order, or through statutory frameworks.

Advisory Mediation

Advisory mediation is often used in grievances. In advisory mediation, mediators first attempt to facilitate an agreement, but if that fails they render an advisory opinion, stating how they would rule were they to arbitrate the case. In one study the bulk of cases settled during the mediation phase, and of those that did not settle, the majority settled subsequent to the announcement of the advisory opinion but before going to arbitration (Ury, Brett, and Goldberg, 1988). Evaluative mediators may offer their sense of what the parameters of a legal outcome are likely to be, and this can help move a decision-making process along.

Arbitration

Binding alternatives to court-based decision making are perhaps the most prevalent formal conflict intervention approach in labor-management, corporate, and consumer disputes. Arbitrators approach their work in many different ways. For example, they may take a rights-based or an interest-based approach. A rights-based arbitrator will try to decide how a dispute would be dealt with if it were a legal case or how to apply a set of legal principles or contractual obligations to a dispute, and will consider the parties' interests only secondarily or tangentially. An interest-based arbitrator will try to sort through the key concerns of the parties and determine a way of addressing these within the framework of the law. It is of course important that arbitrators be clear with their clients about the basis on which they make decisions. Rights-based approaches are more likely to be used to resolve contractual disputes. Interest-based arbitration may be more characteristic of family intervention processes, such as in the work of parenting coordinators who are assigned to make decisions about day-to-day parenting questions that highly conflicted parents are unable to handle (Barris and others, 2001).

Mediation-Arbitration

Many other varieties of decision making can be brought to bear in different circumstances. Mediation-arbitration (in which the same person acts as mediator and arbitrator) and mediation then arbitration (in which disputants are automatically referred from a mediator to an arbitrator if mediation is inconclusive) are two alternative ways of providing both procedural and decision-making assistance.

Expert Decision Making

Sometimes people in high-conflict relationships contract with substantive experts to be available over a specified period to render rapid and binding decisions about issues in their area of expertise. Divorced parents may use child development experts; construction contracts may provide for decision making from a designated engineer; business partners may use financial management experts.

DESIGN AND LINKAGE

The continuum of available conflict intervention services is rapidly becoming more varied, sophisticated, and creative. However, for a constellation of services to constitute a system of intervention there has to be an effective means of coordinating and linking them with each other. In other words, there has to be an intentional approach to designing the dispute system itself. Dispute system design is an approach to conflict intervention that is both preventive and systemic. Conflict specialists often work with organizations or groups that are anticipating a set of conflicts they are likely to face over time, such as grievances, customer complaints, neighborhood conflicts, or citizen appeals of government actions. Together with representatives of the different groups involved, a designer may work out a system of linked conflict prevention and intervention steps to deal with the most commonly anticipated disputes. There are a number of principles that designers usually try to incorporate in such processes. (Some of these principles have been described elsewhere; see CDR Associates, 1996; Constantino and Merchant, 1995; Pearlstein and others, 2005; Slaikeu and Hasson, 1998; Ury and others, 1988.)

Dispute systems are most effective if they

- Emphasize mechanisms to assist disputants in making their own decisions (unless matters of overall organizational or public policy are involved)
- Encourage disputants to handle conflicts on the basis of their needs and interests rather than turning immediately to rights- or power-based approaches
- Provide mechanisms that help disputants not only settle differences but also repair relationships and restore effective communication
- Provide choices, giving disputants a variety of mechanisms for dealing with conflict depending on their needs and the circumstances of the conflict at hand
- Provide efficient and user-friendly rights-based alternatives when consensus-based approaches do not work
- Give disputants as many chances as possible to revert to a needs-based focus even after they have entered into a rights-based process

- Provide for the intervention of third-party decision makers to minimize stress, expense, and toxicity
- Make decision-making and conflict intervention procedures transparent, accessible, understandable, and easy to use
- Are developed with the active participation of potential users of the new system
- Provide an approach to implementation, monitoring, and evaluation that reflect the values and goals of the dispute system as a whole
- Ensure that the dispute system really is a system—that is, that the connections between its elements are well thought out and smooth in operation
- Are built on the strengths of existing conflict resolution mechanisms and with a careful consideration of the existing organizational structure or group norms

The last principle reflects an important lesson that dispute system designers have learned about working with organizations. Although there may occasionally be circumstances in which profound organizational change or systems breakdown requires and allows implementing a whole new system, it is important not to "build cathedrals." Ideal systems are seldom realistic systems. Often the most important question is, What are the key changes that can be made at a given time that will move a dispute system in a more collaborative direction?

Another challenge is to make the dispute system concept itself tangible and accessible to people who are trying to formulate a practical, day-to-day approach for dealing with conflict. The concept can seem abstract, theoretical, and ungrounded to practitioners if they cannot translate it into usable everyday actions.

Despite these challenges, the dispute systems approach is critical to effective conflict intervention. For the concept of a continuum of services to be more than an abstract idea there must be a linkage mechanism among its different components and a way of deciding which service is appropriate to a particular circumstance. Dispute system designers face this challenge constantly and are thus on the front line of the ongoing effort to implement an increasingly sophisticated approach to conflict.

NEW TECHNOLOGIES FOR DEALING WITH CONFLICT

In this chapter I have focused on the range of intervention strategies designed to provide the services people need in order to engage in conflict effectively. As the conflict field develops new approaches to conflict, such as coaching, collaborative practice, restorative justice, and dialogue processes, we are also developing new technologies for delivering these services. And disputants are creating their own technologies for obtaining the help they need, too. For example, legal information is increasingly available through Internet sources (try a Google search on almost any legal issue), but so is information about medical, financial, and technical issues, or for that matter about almost anything we can even imagine being in conflict over. This alone changes how dispute services, as well as medical, legal, financial, and other types of interventions, unfold and can be provided. Perhaps, in designing dispute systems, we can alter our focus on providing adequate substantive information accordingly. Instead of focusing primarily on individuals or experts who can provide information, we also need to emphasize the development of better, more objective, more accessible, and more salient technological resources.

The use of online dispute intervention technologies has been growing rapidly (Katsch and Rifkin, 2001; Rule, 2002). Although these technologies may not (yet) provide an effective freestanding mechanism for conflict intervention, they are increasingly important tools for conflict interveners. For example:

- Twitter, Facebook, electronic bulletin boards, and other online mechanisms can be used to supplement ongoing consensus-building efforts. They provide a mechanism to share information quickly, obtain input into documents, and schedule meetings; they allow for dialogue among multiple participants; and they enable participants to maintain a central repository for all relevant documents.
- A variety of dispute-intervention-oriented software programs can help parties organize their issues and consider their alternatives quickly.

- Some online mechanisms, such as those used by eBay and PayPal, actually allow for the resolution of disputes without direct contact with any third party or between the disputants. On eBay, for example, disputes about transactions can be handled through a service called "Square Trade," which allows for direct and free online negotiations, or through online mediated negotiations, which are available for a nominal fee ("Dispute Resolution Overview," n.d.).
- Skype and other online communication programs allow people at different locations to interact in a richer way.

Other technological innovations have changed how conflict intervention processes occur. For example, I have worked on a number of consensus-building processes in which proposals or draft documents were projected from a computer onto a screen viewable by all participants. As suggested changes were made, these could be quickly entered and viewed, and then as people were leaving the session the document could be either printed out and given to participants or instantly sent to an electronic mailing list or electronic bulletin board. Sometimes sitting at the computer and working on the wording of a proposed statement for everyone to view have seemed to me to be much more powerful and useful than standing up in front of the group and acting as a discussion facilitator. In working on divorce agreements, it is often helpful to use software to calculate child support obligations. When information about each party's income, relevant expenses, and parenting days are loaded in, the software can indicate child support obligations, and the implications of changing the assumptions about financial data or the proposed parenting arrangements can quickly be seen. And this is just the start. We can quickly assess the tax implications of different arrangements, different ways of amortizing debt, the present value of a future transaction, and so on. When used effectively, these programs can greatly assist people in considering their choices, and they allow the mediator to stay in a facilitative role at the same time as significant substantive information is made available.

Of course, there is always a danger that the mediator and the parties will become more focused on the technology than on the interpersonal or system dynamics that underlie a dispute, or that they will rely on the computer to provide the sort of nuanced information that requires input from and dialogue with a substantive expert. And technology is not a panacea. It can change our practice and provide us with significant additional tools, but it does not change the underlying needs people have, and is it not a substitute for effective relationship-building and communication skills.

THE COMMON PURPOSE OF CONFLICT INTERVENTION

With the proliferation of dispute intervention services, technologies, systems, and practitioners, it is easy to lose sight of what the common purpose of conflict intervention is. I have suggested as a generic purpose the goal of promoting a constructive approach to conflict engagement. This raises the question of what constitutes a constructive approach to conflict. Although we can emphasize many different aspects to this, there are four essential underlying assumptions or values about what makes for constructive engagement that seem characteristic, if not of every element in an effective conflict intervention system, at least of the system as a whole. (For a fuller discussion of the elements of constructive engagement, see Mayer, 2009b.) These four values are

- *A commitment to dialogue.* Dialogue involves more than just offering input or exchanging proposals and counterproposals. It requires genuine listening; inquiring; trying to understand the concerns, hopes, fears, and ideas of everyone; and trying to raise one's own concerns or views in a clear, respectful, and cogent way.
- *An emphasis on needs.* Constructive engagement is characterized by a focus on what is important to disputants, what they are trying to accomplish, and what their underlying concerns are, as opposed to what they have the power to impose or the legal basis to claim.
- *Empowerment.* Constructive engagement requires that all parties to a conflict are sufficiently empowered to articulate their concerns and needs and to evaluate their choices.

Empowerment also implies self-determination. To the extent feasible, effective conflict systems maximize the degree to which disputants maintain the ability to find their own way through conflict.

- *Respect.* Respect for individual autonomy and for diversity, and respect for the right of everyone to live free from fear and oppression, are at the heart of a constructive approach to conflict.

No matter what approach we take to conflict, our common commitment is to these values. This perhaps more than anything else is what ties us together as a field of practice.

Almost all of us who work as conflict interveners play several roles, but almost none of us can or should fulfill the whole gamut of roles that make up the system of conflict services. The more conscious we are about the range of interventions needed to develop a continuum that truly serves our client base, the more we will be able to make sophisticated judgments about exactly what services people need in any particular conflict. The more aware we are of what we can and cannot provide, the more responsible we will be in making referrals. The growing richness of the conflict field will enhance the work of each of us by providing links to a set of interventions more powerful than any of us can provide on our own.

CHAPTER TWELVE

WHY WE INTERVENE
IN CONFLICT

This book considers how we can think about conflict in a useful and productive way. It is not meant to sell conflict intervention as a field or to instruct people in how to practice mediation, negotiation, or facilitation. I believe that good practice comes from sound thinking as informed and refined by practice. Our growth as conflict interveners requires that we become increasingly sophisticated in our thinking, that we learn to apply our concepts and to test them in our practical efforts, and that we use these experiences to reevaluate our thinking. The ability to engage in this reflective process is a characteristic of an advanced practitioner (Lang and Taylor, 2000; Schön, 1983). A clear and accessible conceptual framework not only helps us deepen our work but also helps us learn from our experience.

Our values are even more important in guiding our work than is our thinking about conflict, however. A powerful commitment to the values that guide our work is the most important foundation on which we can operate. They are the source of our dedication to our work and the compass that guides us through our most difficult moments. They are also the essential glue that holds our field together and the fundamental reason why we have credibility with the public. Furthermore, if the concepts we use to understand what we do and our approach to implementing these concepts in practice are not grounded in our values or reflective of them, their power will be curtailed. To stay grounded in these values, we have to keep asking ourselves why we are doing this work—what is our core motivation for wanting to be conflict specialists. Each of us will, of course, have a different answer, but we can certainly learn from each other. In this spirit I offer the following reflection on my own motivations and journey into conflict work.

I enjoy working with people who are trying to make their way through conflict, finding it challenging, meaningful, and fun, and I almost always feel that I am connecting with people about something important to their lives and their world. My work has taken me to many interesting parts of the globe where profound change has been in the works, and I have had the opportunity to meet some amazing and wonderful individuals. My colleagues are interesting, warm people with values that I appreciate. Working with them has been a privilege. These are major benefits from working in this field. But none of them are at the core of what has motivated me to devote the last thirty-plus years to conflict work. At the core of my commitment lie three aspirations that I believe are shared by many conflict practitioners. I want to see conflicts handled more constructively; I want to be part, albeit in a small way, of making this a better world; and I want my work to challenge me to grow personally.

Finding a Better Way to Deal with Conflict

When people find themselves in conflict, the mechanisms available to assist them—in keeping with the way society responds to many other crises—tend to take power away from the disputants. Power is ceded to judges, lawyers, mental health professionals, government entities, child custody evaluators, technical experts, arbitrators, and so forth. I believe we need to find a way of helping people in conflict maintain as much power over their lives and their decisions as possible, both as a practical matter and as a core value. Sometimes in crisis situations, such as medical emergencies, or in high-conflict legal actions, people have no choice but to cede some power to others, but we should always try to make sure that the degree to which this happens is minimized and that power is returned to people as quickly as possible. Powerlessness does not promote a constructive approach to conflict.

For example, parents who neglect or abuse their children often do so in response to feeling overwhelmed and powerless. The response of the child protection system (to some extent inevitably) is often to further overwhelm and disempower them. We must find ways to protect children as we also empower parents to be parents and families to be families. That is the point of the increasingly widespread use of mediation and other conflict resolution mechanisms (family group conferences, for example) in child welfare (Mayer, 1985, 2009a). The challenge is how (when necessary) to take enough power away from parents to protect their children while helping them maintain or develop enough positive power to become more effective and humane parents.

The essence of what the conflict field has to offer to disputants is an empowering approach to dealing with serious conflict. The goal and the value is to help people in conflict maintain as much power as possible over their lives while ensuring that other people's rights and concerns are also respected and protected. Our understandable and fundamentally humane desire to fix things for disputants, to take over so that people can be protected from themselves, is at the heart of what disempowers people in conflict. Conflict specialists have to accept that sometimes people will make very bad choices for themselves, but that is their right. The consequence of our taking on the responsibility of preventing people from making poor decisions is that we also take away a significant degree of personal autonomy. It is therefore essential that conflict professionals trust people's ability to make good decisions for themselves and accept their right to make what may be poor decisions as well. This is a defining belief of effective conflict intervention practice.

Related to this is a creative dilemma that conflict specialists face—the question of whether they are in the business of trying to change people. Does profound engagement require personal change? Is conflict work about helping people grow as individuals, "transform," or in some way become better? And if it is, how do we reconcile this with the fact that people do not usually come to us for this purpose? How do we empower people if we also have an agenda to change them? The paradox is that much of what we do can and often does have the practical effect of changing people, but this result is also closely connected to the fact that it is not our major motive. I believe that conflict interveners often contribute to profound personal change, but in a way that is indirect and respectful of personal autonomy. As we help people work through conflict on as deep a level as is practical and necessary to accomplish their goals, personal change is a frequent by-product. But the fact that personal growth is a by-product rather than our central goal is critical to what makes our work powerful and empowering.

Another way we can make a constructive impact on how conflict is handled is by helping people think about disputes differently. When we can help people step outside of the negotiator's dilemma, of the choice of whether to act to preserve their relationships or to protect their interests, we have accomplished something significant. But to do this we have to genuinely believe that it is both important and possible to promote one's own views and concerns and to be respectful of others. Conflict interveners have to believe that people can be strong and kind, wise and compassionate, and nice and smart at the same time. Our confidence that disputants can both protect themselves and deal with others in a principled manner is one of the most important things we can transmit to our clients. For conflict specialists, realistic optimism is an ethical commitment.

All people have difficult choices to make in life, and no one can always get what he or she wants. Sometimes, in the name of peace, resolution, or progress, disputants have to give up something very important to them. But people can address their most important needs and protect their essential interests with dignity, compassion, and respect for those they are in conflict with, even when they don't like these other people or are very angry at them. People in conflict can get beyond their anger and fear as they strive to make wise choices, even when under great duress. By participating in this field, we help make these beliefs a practical reality in a complicated world.

CHANGING THE WORLD

For most of us, the purpose of our work goes beyond finding better ways of dealing with conflict. It involves a commitment to contribute to a better world. Of course finding better ways of handling conflict is part of making a better world, but I think there are other ways in which many of us see our work as contributing to fundamental and positive social change.

Violence and intolerance are problems virtually everywhere. Our ability to learn to engage in conflict without demonizing each other is a major challenge that will shape our future. As I have been preparing this new edition, Libyans are fighting and killing each other, Syrians and Yemenis protesting for a more democratic government are being gunned down, war continues in Afghanistan and Iraq, violence continues to plague the area we call the Holy Land, students are periodically attacked and killed by other students, and a congresswoman from Arizona struggles to recover from an attack on her at an event she held to reach out to her constituents. We all struggle to make sense out of these occurrences and wonder what we can do to respond to them. Clearly we have a great deal to learn about how to live with one another. Our work in conflict is in part an effort to further our understanding about how to live together peacefully in a world in which conflict is inevitable and often necessary.

Part of the peacemaker's challenge is to find ways of building more respect for diversity. Much of what conflict work is about is helping people respect differences and learn to see them as potential sources of strength rather than as threats. We are constantly in the forefront of helping people understand that diversity, for every challenge it poses, presents important opportunities as well. We do this not in an abstract way but rather by helping people deal practically with troubling problems they are having with those they view as different. When people experience success in finding a more constructive way through conflict, they begin to break down the walls that have separated them from each other.

Another way in which the conflict field promotes social change relates to the impact we as conflict specialists have on efforts to deepen democracy and promote social justice. When I was a college student in the 1960s, active in various social movements, we were often quite understandably taken to task for having a much clearer idea about what we were against than what we were for. Activists made many attempts at articulating the kind of society they were advocating, but the most durable concept that emerged was *participatory democracy* (Haydon, 2005). Underlying the almost visceral appeal of this term was the way it evoked a widely held desire to move away from the hierarchical and patriarchal structure of government and the major institutions of our society, such as corporations, universities, courts, families, and religions. The practical meaning of participatory democracy, however, was never clear to most of us, certainly not to me.

What was clear then and remains clear today is that the call for more meaningful participation in the institutions that we are part of touches on an important need all of us experience. On multiple fronts and for many years we have been asking for and at times demanding more direct input into the decisions that affect our lives. In communities throughout North America, for example, citizens have insisted on more meaningful input on land use decisions, transportation plans, police policies, fire station locations, the siting of almost any public facility, the allocation of public funds, and almost every other issue governments face. Schools have created school improvement teams, parent advisory groups, and other accountability and input structures. Employers have embraced many variations of employee input processes. They may be called flat organizational structures, team management, employee councils, quality circles, total quality management, or industrial democracy, but, whatever the label, they all involve attempts to give employees more participation in decision making and more accountability for those decisions. Corporations form citizen advisory groups and negotiate "good neighbor agreements" with the communities in which they are located. And of course there are all the consensus-building dialogues, town meetings, regulatory negotiations, and policy roundtables in which conflict specialists are so often involved. All of this points to our desire for more involvement in decision making. In fact, this is participatory democracy in action.

Some of these new structures for democracy are faddish. Others are more for show or for discouraging confrontational public protests than for encouraging genuine dialogue and problem solving. But those that lack real substance do not usually last. The reason many of these new mechanisms for participation have endured and grown is that they meet a genuine need for involvement and participation, for meaning and community, that we all have. They also provide an opportunity for people to build better relationships and to arrive at creative ways of dealing with difficult problems. The infrastructure of participation is growing and becoming more imbedded in our social institutions because it meets a fundamental need and, although its processes are sometimes muddled, it more often than not produces better results than do more politicized, hierarchical, or adversarial approaches.

However, there is a downside to all this participation. Decision making can become very time consuming and convoluted. Decision makers, managers, and the public often feel overwhelmed by process. On the one hand, for example, deciding where to locate a sanitary landfill was a relatively simple matter forty years ago. Now it involves many layers of often contentious public involvement. On the other hand, many of those older landfills were not safe or thoughtfully located. In order for participatory democracy to work, to provide meaningful opportunities for participation, to give people input over the critical decisions affecting their lives, and to assist them in dealing with the major public and organizational conflicts that affect them, the tools of the conflict field are critical. In order to allow democracy to deepen without overwhelming people with process, the contributions of this field are essential.

Furthermore, as important as participation and dialogue are, we are naturally cynical about processes that seem to be more about public relations than about genuine dialogue. There is a huge difference between forums that promote genuine engagement concerning difficult issues and ones that provide endless opportunities for one-way communication and grandstanding in the name of input but no real opportunity for dialogue. Government officials, corporate executives, and political leaders are often reluctant to engage in a genuine give-and-take about difficult issues with people who might hold very different points of view; unless they are willing to take part in and promote such engagement, however, the participatory urge of citizens, employees, or community members is likely to remain unfulfilled. One of the prime contributions of conflict practitioners is to help structure and conduct input processes so that they are genuine dialogues, so that real engagement with difficult issues occurs, and so that this engagement remains constructive.

Conflict intervention strategies are also essential if democracy is to take root in regions where it is still a new and untested system. Democracy is at a crossroads in numerous parts of the world. In many countries people are trying to embrace democratic principles and the freedoms that go along with them, but these efforts are also unleashing serious conflicts. Democracy is sometimes equated with instability, violence, and increasing inequality in the distribution of wealth. Democratic political and economic institutions are being attacked as the cause of personal insecurity and economic deterioration. Ethnic conflicts have occasionally increased as centralized and authoritarian governments have collapsed. These conflicts have been used by anti-democratic forces to try to maintain or reestablish dictatorial political structures. The first argument used by such authoritarian rulers as Saddam Hussein of Iraq, Hosni Mubarak of Egypt, or Kim Jong-il of North Korea has always been that the alternative to their rule is anarchy, violence, terrorism, and chaos. In effect, they echo the words attributed to Louis XV of France, fifteen years before the French Revolution: "Après moi le déluge" ("After me the deluge").

The need for effective consensus-building and conflict engagement processes that can have an impact on the lives of ordinary citizens in emerging democracies remains great. The obstacles to implementing them are sometimes daunting, but without these processes consolidating democratic gains and solidifying hard-won freedoms will remain an elusive goal. Democracy's strongest safeguard is ultimately the belief and expectation of citizens that they are entitled to participate in the decisions that govern their lives. This belief and expectation is reinforced by meaningful experiences in participatory governance. Effective conflict engagement procedures can therefore play an important role in helping emerging democracies become genuine democracies and arrive at a constructive way to deal with some of the divisive pressures they face.

This cannot be accomplished by simply exporting Western models of conflict resolution and decision making. But as we learn how to deepen democracy in existing democratic societies we can provide an example, a set of insights, a wealth of experience, and above all a sense of optimism for people elsewhere in the world. Others' efforts to create democracy will offer countless lessons and ideas to the more established democratic world as well.

At the heart of many of these struggles is the question of social justice. Can democratic approaches to governance enhance the struggle for social justice? Can democratic structures protect the weak, restrain the acquisitive impulses of the powerful, and balance the distribution of economic and other social benefits in a wise manner? I believe that establishing a democratic framework is ultimately the only way in which enduring social justice can be obtained. However, when we look at our seeming incapacity for addressing our most profound social problems, like global warming, the rising disparity between the rich and the poor, the energy crisis, our flagging economic well-being, health care, and nuclear proliferation, for example, it is easy to become skeptical. It's also easy to become skeptical about participatory approaches to conflict when we watch the nature of our discourse devolve into harsh rhetoric, polarization, and intolerance of differences. It's easy to think we need less conflict engagement rather than more. But I think the answer is more democracy; more deeply rooted public participation; and more forums for discussing, debating about, and struggling with our most important problems. The more people are empowered to make decisions for themselves and the more channels we create for people to engage with those they disagree with, the better we will be able to deal with the challenges that face us.

I find it both interesting and a bit disheartening that people so seldom talk to each other on a citizen-to-citizen level about significant issues about which they may disagree. Electoral candidates, abortion, religion, gun control, or military actions, for example, are often taboo topics. It's as if the choice is either to remain silent or to enter into an unpleasant and hostile interaction, possibly losing a friend, alienating a relative, or creating unnecessary conflict with a colleague in the process. But if we don't learn to talk with each other about important issues, we cede one of the most important avenues each of us has to participate in our civic life.

The opposite of hostile and divisive public discourse is not the absence of communication but rather the establishment of more powerful and constructive means of engaging with difficult issues. So we don't need less conflict, we need more—more genuine, heartfelt, powerful, and ethical conflict. Not the faux conflict served up by *Fox News* or *Crossfire,* but genuine conflict among real people about real issues. We need to remember that democracy is not ultimately bestowed from above but taken from below, and the best way we can make it come alive is to engage in the difficult but energizing exchanges that are its best and most lively expression.

Conflict work is in essence about helping all of us to find a better means of entering into dialogue with those we disagree with and thereby to have a greater say over our own lives, particularly (but not only) during times of crisis. That is why I believe the work of conflict specialists is key to deepening democracy and promoting social justice.

CHANGING THE CONFLICT PRACTITIONER

In conflict intervention, as in any intense field of work, practitioners as well as clients undergo change. If we are not involved in this business in part because of its personal growth potential for us, we are not fully involved. This is not about being unprofessional, putting our needs before those of our clients, or focusing narcissistically on our own development. It is about being fully engaged, present, and committed to what we are doing. Unless we see our engagement as offering something to us personally, helping us to be the kind of people we want to be and to play the role we want to play in the world, our participation in this field will be more mechanistic and calculating than the intensity of the work can ultimately tolerate.

If we are fully present, however, and if we do not create a defensive barrier that shields us from being influenced by our experiences—and I do not think such a barrier is really possible—then we will be profoundly affected on a personal level by the people we work with, the conflicts we enter into, and the work we do. For each of us, of course, the impact will be different. For most of us, our work will hopefully improve our own ability to communicate, to empathize with people who may see the world very differently from how we see it, to understand the complexities of public and personal conflicts, and to be creative in the face of seemingly intractable problems. We will ideally grow beyond a tendency to see the conflicts in the world and in our lives in polarized terms. And our ability to appreciate differences and to reach across cultural, age, gender, class, and other divides should thereby be enhanced.

Not all the impacts of conflict intervention are positive or comfortable, however. Perhaps it is age, perhaps it is the perspective that being a parent and having a career give, but my clarity of beliefs and ability to be indignant about social ills are not what they once were. Making a continual effort to understand different sides of an issue or to look for the needs that are impelling distasteful behavior on the part of individuals, organizations, and governments can undercut one's ability to take decisive and unambiguous stands about public issues. I sometimes miss the clarity and indignation about people and issues that I used to have, and every once in a while I look for an area to express this side of my personality.

The world needs advocates, people who are focused on the struggle for social justice, who defend the unempowered, who strive to protect the environment, and who guard against assaults on our freedoms. It needs people who are focused on promoting the interests of a particular group or cause above the goal of resolving conflict or being collaborative. Without the engine such advocates provide for social change, conflict intervention as a field of practice would just be a means of lubricating the interactions of the powerful. Sometimes such single-minded advocates can be a major source of irritation and frustration. But they play a necessary and valuable role. As conflict interveners' ability to embrace the larger picture grows, it is important that their appreciation and respect for such advocates does not diminish. Many of us can look at them and see ourselves at one point in our lives.

As I have written here and elsewhere, conflict allies, including advocates, are an important part of our field. I think many of us struggle with how we can develop our capacity to be effective advocates for ourselves or others while letting ourselves feel empathy for those on a different side of a conflict. Our approach may change over time, and many of us may find that we have become less effective in some conflict intervention roles and activities but more effective in others.

Something is lost and something is gained by any choice we make about how to lead our lives, and our work on conflict is no exception. For me, the overall direction of the change has been positive. My experience as a conflict practitioner has helped me grow as an individual, and it has helped me reconcile my values about human relations and social change. I have felt fortunate to be working in an area that is interesting, challenging, satisfying, and innovative. More important, I have cherished the opportunity to work in a field that contributes to making the world a better place at the same time as it helps individuals with their immediate struggles.

Although many of the roles we play as conflict practitioners require us to act in an impartial way, the field itself is far from being value neutral. Implicit in what we do are very strong beliefs about how to improve the world we live in and about how people ought to relate to each other. These values are the foundation from which we derive our power and energy. A true adherence and commitment to democracy, personal empowerment, and social justice are what allow us to play our roles with consistency, enthusiasm, and strength.

REFERENCES

Allred, K. G. "Anger and Retaliation in Conflict: The Role of Attribution." In M. Deutsch and P. T. Coleman (eds.), *The Handbook of Conflict Resolution: Theory and Practice.* San Francisco: Jossey-Bass, 2000.

Bandler, R., and Grinder, J. *Reframing: Neurolinguistic Programming and the Transformation of Meaning.* Moab, Utah: Real People Press, 1982.

Barris, M. A., and others. *Working with High-Conflict Families of Divorce: A Guide for Professionals.* Northvale, N.J.: Jason Aronson, 2001.

Brewer, M. P., and Pierce, K. P. "Social Identity Complexity and Out-Group Tolerance." *Personality and Social Psychology Bulletin,* 2005, *31*(3), 428–437.

Burton, J., and Dukes, F. *Conflict: Resolution and Prevention.* New York: St. Martin's Press, 1990.

Bush, R.A.B., and Folger, J. P. *The Promise of Mediation: The Transformative Approach to Conflict.* (Rev. ed.) San Francisco: Jossey-Bass, 2005.

Cameron, N. *Collaborative Practice: Deepening the Dialogue.* Vancouver: CLE Society of British Columbia, 2004.

CDR Associates. *The Dispute System Design Manual.* Boulder, Colo.: CDR Associates, 1996.

Coleman, P. T. "Power and Conflict." In M. Deutsch and P. T. Coleman (eds.), *The Handbook of Conflict Resolution: Theory and Practice.* San Francisco: Jossey-Bass, 2000.

Coleman, P. T., Bui-Wrzosinska, L., Vallacher, R., and Nowak, A. "Protracted Conflict as Dynamical Systems." In A. Schneider and C. Honeyman (eds.), *The Negotiator's Fieldbook.* Washington, D.C.: American Bar Association, 2006.

Constantino, C. A., and Merchant, C. S. *Designing Conflict Management Systems: A Guide to Creating Productive and Healthy Organizations.* San Francisco: Jossey-Bass, 1995.

Coser, L. A. *The Functions of Social Conflict.* New York: Free Press, 1956.

Curle, A. *Making Peace.* London: Tavistock, 1971.

Deutsch, M. *The Resolution of Conflict: Constructive and Destructive Processes.* New Haven, Conn.: Yale University Press, 1973.

Deutsch, M., and Coleman, P. T. (eds.). *The Handbook of Conflict Resolution: Theory and Practice.* San Francisco: Jossey-Bass, 2000.

Deutsch, M., Coleman, P. T., and Marcus, E. C. (eds.). *The Handbook of Conflict Resolution: Theory and Practice.* (2nd ed.) San Francisco: Jossey-Bass, 2006.

"Dispute Resolution Overview." eBay Canada. n.d. http://pages.ebay.ca/ services/buyandsell/disputeres.html.

Doyle, M., and Strauss, D. *Making Meetings Work.* Chicago: Playboy Press, 1976.

Dussich, J.P.J., and Schellenberg, J. (eds.). *The Promise of Restorative Justice: New Approaches for Criminal Justice and Beyond.* Boulder, Colo.: Lynne Reiner, 2010.

Etzioni, A. *A Comparative Analysis of Complex Organizations.* New York: Free Press, 1975.

Festinger, L. *A Theory of Cognitive Dissonance.* Stanford, Calif.: Stanford University Press, 1957.

Fisher, R. "Fractionating Conflict." In R. Fisher (ed.), *International Conflict and Behavioral Sciences: The Craigville Papers.* New York: Basic Books, 1964.

Fisher, R., and Ury, W. *Getting to Yes.* Boston: Houghton Mifflin, 1981.

Folberg, J., Milne, A., and Salem, P. (eds.). *Divorce Mediation.* (2nd ed.) New York: Guilford Press, 2004.

Folberg, J., and Taylor, A. *Mediation: A Comprehensive Guide to Resolving Conflicts Without Litigation.* San Francisco: Jossey-Bass, 1984.

Follett, M. P. "Dynamic Administration." In H. C. Metcalf and L. Urwick (eds.), *The Collected Papers of Mary Parker Follett.* New York: Harper & Brothers, 1940.

Freud, S. *Civilization and Its Discontents* (J. Strachey, trans.). New York: W. W. Norton, 2005. (Originally published 1930; originally translated 1961.)

Friedman, G., and Himmelstein, J. *Challenging Conflict: Mediation Through Understanding.* Chicago: American Bar Association, 2009.

Frost, J., and Wilmot, W. *Interpersonal Conflict.* Dubuque, Iowa: Brown, 1978.

Gamson, W. A. *Power and Discontent.* Homewood, Ill.: Dorsey Press, 1968.

Ghais, S. *Extreme Facilitation: Guiding Groups Through Controversy and Complexity.* San Francisco: Jossey-Bass, 2005.

Goldberg, R. M. "How Our Worldviews Shape Our Practice." *Conflict Resolution Quarterly, 26*(4), Summer 2009, 405–431.

Golten, M. M., and Mayer, B. *The Child Protection Mediation Project Manual.* Boulder, Colo.: CDR Associates, 1987.

Grewal, Z. *Death by Culture? How Not to Talk About Islam and Domestic Violence.* Clinton, Mich.: Institute for Social Policy and Understanding, 2009.

Hale, K. "The Language of Cooperation: Negotiation Frames." *Mediation Quarterly,* Winter 1998, *16*(2), 147–162.

Hall, E. T. *The Silent Language.* New York: Fawcett Premier Book, 1959.

Hall, E. T., and Hall, M. R. *Understanding Cultural Differences: Germans, French, and Americans.* Boston: Nicholas Brealey, 1990.

Harper, G. *The Joy of Conflict Resolution: Transforming Victims, Villains and Heroes in the Workplace and at Home.* Gabriola Island, B.C.: New Society, 2004.

Haydon, T. *The Port Huron Statement: The Visionary Call of the 1960s Revolution.* New York: Avalon, 2005.

Haynes, J. *Divorce Mediation: A Practical Guide for Therapists and Counselors.* New York: Springer, 1981.

Haynes, J. *Fundamentals of Family Mediation.* Albany: State University of New York Press, 1994.

Heider, F. *The Psychology of Interpersonal Relations.* Hoboken, N.J.: Wiley, 1958.

Hofstede, G. *Cultures and Organizations: Software of the Mind.* New York: McGraw-Hill, 1991.

Honeyman, C. "Using Ambiguity." In C. Honeyman and A. K. Schneider (eds.), *The Negotiator's Fieldbook: The Desk Reference for the Experienced Negotiator.* Washington, D.C.: ABA Section on Dispute Resolution, 2006.

Innes, J. E., and Booher, D. E. "Consensus Building and Complex Adaptive Systems: A Framework for Evaluating Collaborative Planning." *Journal of the American Planning Association,* Autumn 1999, *65*(4), 412–423.

Jones, T., and Brinkert, R. *Conflict Coaching: Conflict Management Strategy and Skills for the Individual.* Thousand Oaks, Calif.: Sage, 2008.

Jones, W., and Hughes, S. "Complexity, Conflict Resolution, and How the Mind Works." *Conflict Resolution Quarterly,* Summer 2003, *20*(4), 485–484.

Kanter, R. M. *Men and Women of the Corporation.* New York: Basic Books, 1977.

Kathol, J. "Trends in Child Protection Mediation: Results of the Think Tank Survey and Interviews. *Family Court Review,* January 2009, *47*(1), 116–128.

Katsch, E., and Rifkin, J. *Online Dispute Resolution: Resolving Conflicts in Cyberspace.* San Francisco: Jossey-Bass, 2001.

Kimmel, P. "Culture and Conflict." In M. Deutsch, P. T. Coleman, and E. C. Marcus (eds.), *The Handbook of Conflict Resolution: Theory and Practice.* (2nd ed.) San Francisco: Jossey-Bass, 2006.

Kluchohn, F. R., and Strodtbeck, F. L. *Variations in Value Orientations.* New York: HarperCollins, 1961.

Kolb, D. M. *The Mediators.* Cambridge, Mass.: MIT Press, 1983.

Kolb, D. M., and Associates. *When Talk Works: Profiles of Mediators.* San Francisco: Jossey-Bass, 1994.

Kolb, D. M., Williams, J., and Frohlinger, C. *Her Place at the Table: A Woman's Guide to Negotiating Five Key Challenges to Leadership Success.* San Francisco: Jossey-Bass, 2004.

Korobkin, R. "On Bargaining Power." In C. Honeyman and A. K. Schneider (eds.), *The Negotiator's Fieldbook: The Desk Reference for the Experienced Negotiator.* Washington, D.C.: ABA Section on Dispute Resolution, 2006.

Kressel, K., Pruitt, D. G., and Associates (eds.). *Mediation Research: The Process and Effectiveness of Third-Party Intervention.* San Francisco: Jossey-Bass, 1989.

Kriesberg, L. *The Sociology of Social Conflicts.* (2nd ed.) Englewood Cliffs, N.J.: Prentice Hall, 1982.

Lakoff, G., and Johnson, M. *Metaphors We Live By.* (With a new afterward) Chicago: University of Chicago Press, 2003.

Lang, M. D., and Taylor, A. *The Making of a Mediator: Developing Artistry in Practice.* San Francisco: Jossey-Bass, 2000.

Lax, D., and Sebenius, J. *The Manager as Negotiator.* New York: Free Press, 1986.

Lax, D., and Sebenius, J. *3-D Negotiations: Powerful Tools to Change the Game in Your Most Important Deals.* Boston: Harvard Business School Press, 2006.

LeBaron, M. *Bridging Troubled Waters: Conflict Resolution from the Heart.* San Francisco: Jossey-Bass, 2002.

Lederach, J. P. *Preparing for Peace: Conflict Transformation Across Cultures.* Syracuse, N.Y.: Syracuse University Press, 1995.

Lederach, J. P. *Building Peace: Sustainable Reconciliation in Divided Societies.* Washington, D.C.: United States Institute of Peace Press, 1997.

Lederach, J. P. *The Moral Imagination: The Art and Soul of Building Peace.* New York: Oxford University Press, 2005.

Lewin, K. *Field Theory in Social Science; Selected Theoretical Papers* (D. Cartwright, ed.). London: Tavistock, 1952.

Macfarlane, J. *The New Lawyer: How Resolution Is Transforming the Practice of Law.* Vancouver: University of British Columbia Press, 2008.

Macfarlane, J. "Conflict Analysis." In J. Macfarlane (ed.), *Dispute Resolution: Reading and Case Studies.* (3rd ed.) Toronto: Emond-Montgomery, 2010.

Macfarlane, J. *Islamic Divorce in North America: A Sharia Path in a Secular Society.* New York: Oxford University Press, 2012.

Macfarlane, J., and Zweibel, E. "Systemic Change and Private Closure in Human Rights Mediation: An Evaluation of the Mediation Program at the Canadian Human Rights Tribunal." Ottawa: Canadian Human Rights Tribunal, May 2001.

Mansbridge, J. "Commentary on 'From City Hall to the Streets: A Community Plan Meets the Real World' by K. Connolly." In L. Suskind, S. McKearan, and J. Thomas-Larner (eds.), *The Consensus Building Handbook: A Comprehensive Guide to Reaching Agreement.* Thousand Oaks, Calif.: Sage, 1999.

Maslow, A. H. *Motivation and Personality.* New York: Harper & Brothers, 1954.

Maslow, A. H. *The Psychology of Science, A Reconnaissance.* Chapel Hill: Maurice Bassett, 2002. (Originally published 1966.)

Mayer, B. "Conflict Resolution in Child Protection and Adoption." *Mediation Quarterly,* Spring 1985 (7), pp. 69–82.

Mayer, B. "The Dynamics of Power in Mediation and Conflict Resolution." *Mediation Quarterly,* Summer 1987 (16), pp. 75–86.

Mayer, B. *Beyond Neutrality: Confronting the Crisis in Conflict Resolution.* San Francisco: Jossey-Bass, 2004a.

Mayer, B. "Facilitative Mediation." In J. Folberg, A. Milne, and P. Salem (eds.), *Divorce Mediation: Models, Techniques, and Applications.* (2nd ed.) New York: Guilford Press, 2004b.

Mayer, B. "Reflections on the State of Consensus-Based Decision Making in Child Welfare." *Family Court Review,* January 2009a, *47*(1), 10–20.

Mayer, B. *Staying with Conflict: A Strategic Approach to Ongoing Disputes.* San Francisco: Jossey-Bass, 2009b.

Mayer, B., Ghais, S., and McKay, J. A. *Constructive Engagement Resource Guide: Practical Advice for Dialogue Among Facilities, Workers, Communities and Regulators.* Washington, D.C.: United States Environmental Protection Agency, 1999.

McCrory, J. "The Mediation Puzzle." *The Vermont Law Review,* 1981, *6*(1), 85–117.

Mnookin, R. W. "Why Negotiations Fail: An Exploration of Barriers to the Resolution of Conflict." *Ohio State Journal on Dispute Resolution,* 1993, *8*(2), 234–249.

Mnookin, R. W. *Bargaining with the Devil: When to Negotiate, When to Fight.* New York: Simon & Schuster, 2010.

Moore, C. W. *The Mediation Process: Practical Strategies for Resolving Conflict.* (3rd ed.) San Francisco: Jossey-Bass, 2003.

Moore, C. W., and Woodrow, P. J. *Handbook of Global and Multicultural Negotiation.* San Francisco: Jossey-Bass, 2010.

Mosten, F. *The Complete Guide to Mediation: The Cutting-Edge Approach to Family Law Practice.* Chicago: Section of Family Law, American Bar Association, 1997.

"New Cars, a Buyer's Market." *Consumer Reports—Annual Auto Issue,* April 1999, pp. 16–18.

Noble, C. "Conflict Management Through Coaching." Noble Solutions. 2001. www.mediate.com/articles/noble.cfm.

Noble, C. *Conflict Management Coaching: The Cinergy Model.* Toronto: Cinergy Coaching, 2012.

Nowak, M., with Highfield, R. *Super Cooperators: Evolution, Altruism and Human Behavior (or Why We Need Each Other to Succeed).* Edinburgh: Cannongate Books, 2011.

Orr, P. J., Emerson, K., and Keyes, D. L. "Environmental Conflict Resolution Practice and Performance: An Evaluation Framework." *Conflict Resolution Quarterly,* Spring 2008, *25*(3), 283–301.

Pearlstein, A., Robinson, P., and Mayer, B. "DyADS: Encouraging 'Dynamic Adaptive Dispute Systems' in the Organized Workplace." *Harvard Negotiation Law Review,* Spring 2005, *10,* 339–383.

Pearson, J. "Divorce Mediation: Strengths and Weaknesses over Time." In H. Davidson and others (eds.), *Alternative Means of Family Dispute Resolution.* Washington, D.C.: American Bar Association, 1982.

Pedersen, P. "Multicultural Conflict Resolution." In M. Deutsch, P. T. Coleman, and E. C. Marcus (eds.), *The Handbook of Conflict Resolution: Theory and Practice.* (2nd ed.) San Francisco: Jossey-Bass, 2006.

Riskin, L. L. "Understanding Mediators' Orientations, Strategies, and Techniques: A Grid for the Perplexed." *Harvard Negotiation Law Review,* 1996, *1*(7), 7–52.

Riskin, L. L. "Retiring and Replacing the Grid of Mediator Orientations." *Alternatives to the High Costs of Litigation,* April 2003, *21,* 69–76.

Ross, L. "Reactive Devaluation in Negotiation and Conflict Resolution." In K. Arrow and others (eds.), *Barriers to the Negotiated Resolution of Conflict.* New York: Norton, 1995.

Rothman, J. *Resolving Identity-Based Conflict in Nations, Organizations, and Communities.* San Francisco: Jossey-Bass, 1997.

Rubin, J. Z. (ed.). *Dynamics of Third Party Intervention: Kissinger in the Middle East.* New York: Praeger, 1981.

Rubin, J., Pruitt, D., and Kim, S. H. *Social Conflict.* New York: McGraw-Hill, 1994.

Rule, C. *Online Dispute Resolution for Business: For E-Commerce, B2B, Consumer, Employment, Insurance, and Other Commercial Conflicts.* San Francisco: Jossey-Bass, 2002.

Saposnek, D. *Mediating Child Custody Disputes.* (Rev. ed.) San Francisco: Jossey-Bass, 1998.

Schellenburg, J. A. *The Science of Conflict.* New York: Oxford University Press, 1982.

Schelling, T. *The Strategy of Conflict.* Cambridge, Mass.: Harvard University Press, 1960.

Schön, D. *The Reflective Practitioner: How Professionals Think in Action.* New York: Basic Books, 1983.

Schwarz, R. M. *The Skilled Facilitator: A Comprehensive Resource for Consultants, Facilitators, Managers, Trainers, and Coaches.* San Francisco: Jossey-Bass, 2002.

"SDI: Empowering People in Their Relationships." Personal Strengths, USA. n.d. www.personalstrengths.us/index.php/en/sdi/about-sdi-an-overview.

Slaikeu, K. A., and Hasson, R. H. *Controlling the Cost of Conflict: How to Design a System for Your Organization.* San Francisco: Jossey-Bass, 1998.

Stolberg, S. G. "Shy US Intellectual Created Playbook Used in a Revolution." *New York Times,* February 16, 2011.

Stone, D., Patton, B., and Heen, S. *Difficult Conversations: How to Discuss What Matters Most.* New York: Viking, 1999.

Stulberg, J. B. "The Theory and Practice of Mediation: A Reply to Professor Susskind." *Vermont Law Review,* 1981, *6*(1), 85–117.

Susskind, L. "Environmental Mediation and the Accountability Problem." *Vermont Law Review,* 1981, *6*(1), 1–46.

Susskind, L. E., and Cruikshank, J. L. *Breaking Robert's Rules: The New Way to Run Your Meeting, Build Consensus, and Get Results.* New York: Oxford University Press, 2006.

Susskind, L., McKearnan, S., and Thomas-Larner, J. (eds.). *The Consensus Building Handbook: A Comprehensive Guide to Reaching Agreement.* Thousand Oaks, Calif.: Sage, 1999.

Tannen, D. *That's Not What I Meant: How Conversational Style Makes or Breaks Relationships.* New York: Ballantine Books, 1986.

Tannen, D. *You Just Don't Understand: Women and Men in Conversation.* New York: Ballantine Books, 1990.

Tessler, P. H. *Collaborative Law: Achieving Effective Resolution in Divorce Without Litigation.* Chicago: Section of Family Law, American Bar Association, 2001.

Thoennes, N. "What We Know Now: Findings from Dependency Mediation Research." *Family Court Review,* January 2009, *47*(1), 21–37.

Thomas, K. W. "Conflict and Conflict Management." In M. D. Dunnette (ed.), *Handbook of Industrial and Organizational Psychology.* Chicago: Rand McNally, 1983.

Thomas, K. W., and Kilmann, R. H. *Thomas-Kilmann Conflict Mode Instrument.* New York: Xicom, 1974.

Tutu, D. *No Future Without Forgiveness.* New York: Doubleday, 1999.

Umbreit, M. *Victim Meets Offender: The Impact of Restorative Justice and Mediation.* Monsey, N.Y.: Criminal Justice Press, 1994.

Ury, W. L. *The Third Side: Why We Fight and How We Can Stop.* (Rev. ed.) New York: Penguin Group, 2000. (Originally published as *Getting to Peace.*)

Ury, W. L., Brett, J. M., and Goldberg, S. B. *Getting Disputes Resolved: Designing Systems to Cut the Costs of Conflict.* San Francisco: Jossey-Bass, 1988.

Ver Steegh, N., and Dalton, C. "Report from the Wingspread Conference on Domestic Violence and Family Courts." *Family Court Review,* 2008, *46,* 454–475.

Walton, R. W., and McKersie, R. B. *A Behavioral Theory of Negotiation: An Analysis of a Social Interaction System.* New York: McGraw-Hill, 1965.

Webb, S., and Ousky, R. *The Collaborative Way to Divorce: The Revolutionary Method That Results in Less Stress, Lower Costs, and Happier Kids— Without Going to Court.* New York: Penguin Group, 2006.

Wehr, P. *Conflict Regulation.* Boulder, Colo.: Westview Press, 1979.

Welsh, N. A. "Disputants' Decision Control in Court-Connected Mediation: A Hollow Promise Without Procedural Justice." *Journal of Dispute Resolution,* 2002, *1,* 179–192.

Williams, M. *Mediation: Why People Fight and How to Help Them to Stop.* Dublin: Poolbeg Press, 1998.

Winslade, J., and Monk, G. *Narrative Mediation: A New Approach to Conflict Resolution.* San Francisco: Jossey-Bass, 2000.

Winslade, J., and Monk, G. *Practicing Narrative Mediation: Loosening the Grip of Conflict.* San Francisco: Jossey-Bass, 2008.

Zartman, I. W. "Timing and Ripeness." In C. Honeyman and A. K. Schneider (eds.), *The Negotiator's Fieldbook: The Desk Reference for the Experienced Negotiator.* Washington, D.C.: ABA Section on Dispute Resolution, 2006.

ABOUT THE AUTHOR

Bernie Mayer, a professor at the Werner Institute, Creighton University, and a founding partner of CDR Associates, has been working in the conflict field since the late 1970s as a mediator, facilitator, trainer, researcher, program administrator, and consultant. He has worked on many complex environmental conflicts, organizational and labor-management disputes, interpersonal conflicts, planning and development issues, public decision-making processes, and ethnic disputes. He has an extensive background in family and child welfare mediation as well. Bernie is also on the faculty of the Kroc Institute for International Peace Studies at the University of Notre Dame.

Bernie has worked with corporations; labor unions; Native American governments and associations; federal, state, and local agencies; public interest groups; professional associations; schools; child welfare programs; mental health services; and universities. He has consulted on conflict and conflict intervention through-out the United States and Canada and extensively in other inter-national locations as well.

He has been recognized as a leader in applying mediation in new arenas, such as in mental health, child welfare, and disputes between public agencies and involuntary clients. He has also been recognized for his work in bridging the gap between theory and practice in conflict intervention.

Bernie received his PhD from the University of Denver, his MSW from Columbia University, and his BA from Oberlin College. He is also the author of *Beyond Neutrality: Confronting the Crisis in Conflict Resolution* (Jossey-Bass, 2004), which received the 2004 annual book award from the CPR International

Institute for Conflict Prevention and Resolution); *Staying with Conflict: A Strategic Approach to Ongoing Disputes* (Jossey-Bass, 2009), which was awarded CPR's annual book award for 2009; as well as many other writings about conflict. He lives in Kingsville, Ontario, and Boulder, Colorado, with his wife, Julie Macfarlane, and family.

INDEX

Page references followed by *fig* indicate an illustrated figure; followed by *t* indicate a table.